Temple Israel Library
Minneapolis, Minn.

Confess! Confess!

Confess! Confess!

EIGHT YEARS IN
SOVIET PRISONS

by Yehoshua A. Gilboa

Translated from the Hebrew by Dov Ben Aba

LITTLE, BROWN AND COMPANY

Boston   Toronto

Published simultaneously in Canada
by Little, Brown & Company (Canada) Limited

PRINTED IN THE UNITED STATES OF AMERICA

Contents

Confess! Confess!

Prologue

I was born and became a man in the city of Pinsk, in Poland. Shortly before that time Pinsk had been in Russia. For a brief period it had been part of an independent Ukrainian state. During and after World War I, it passed from hand to hand. Various gangs terrorized it. Going still further back it had been in Lithuania. At the beginning of the eighteenth century, Charles XII of Sweden held the city for a full year. Now it belongs to the Soviet Union and is one of the centers of the White Russian Republic.

However, throughout all these periods, until the shocks of World War II, Pinsk remained what it always had been — a *Jewish* city. To this day it is symbolized in my memory by two whistle blasts of the Luria plywood factory on Friday afternoon, the eve of the Jewish Sabbath: one was for closing the stores and the other for lighting the Sabbath candles.

Pinsk was a thousand years old and abounded in legends, tales of miracles, and stories which captivated the imagination. There was an old Jewish cemetery in the center of town. It had not been used for burying the dead for more than a century. Black ravens, like mourners, nested among the thick branches of the trees which sheltered faded tombstones. These tombstones were a sort of genealogical record of the city, with its rabbis and illustrious scholars. And tales were whispered of Christians who would break into the cemetery to desecrate the graves, and steal the tombstones, and who, while climbing the cemetery fence on the way out, would become paralyzed and remain straddling it lifelessly.

Pinsk — Russian, Polish? Seven days a week it vibrated with a Jewish dynamism. The childish imagination was captivated by the eerie tales of the Hassidim. I saw with my own eyes how in the midst of a turbulent city hundreds of young Talmudic students who studied at the Yeshiva, the Talmudic academy, retired from the world in the search for supreme integrity and the elimination of every desire to acquire material goods.

The street we lived on buzzed with legends and tales of miracles. Who knew the secret of their growth? The street itself was nearly always broken, full of bald spots, and strewn with dislodged cobblestones. People used to say that the streets had remained that way since the days of the demonstrations against the Czar's regime, when Jewish revolutionaries would pull out stones and hurl them at the police.

I was born after the reign of the last Czar. But even during the period of Polish rule, I saw all around me the seeds from which legends grow. About a hundred yards from our house, our street was intersected by another street which Jewish representatives on the municipal council had succeeded in naming after a writer, Y. L. Peretz. A bit of struggle flared up over the Jewish name of the street. At night Gentiles would smear tar over the signs bearing Peretz's name and early in the morning Jewish men and women would scrape off the tar and restore Peretz to his respected place. This war of the street signs lasted many days and nights.

The atmosphere in our town became increasingly more oppressive. Jews were attacked on the street, openly. Tension mounted. The image of my father in those days still shimmers in my memory. One Passover evening when he was conducting the Seder ceremony recalling the Exodus from Egypt, Mother (always more restrained and cautious) said to Father, "Itsik, perhaps this time we'll open the back door [from the kitchen to the yard] when the 'Pour out Thy wrath' prayer is recited and not the front door?" To which Father replied, "Rachael, how can I ask the Prophet Elijah to come in through the back door?"[1]

A similar dialogue was repeated on Friday evening, the eve of the Sabbath. There is a beautiful legend about the angels who accompany Jews home from the synagogue on Sabbath eve. The legend is interwoven in the benediction and prayer: "Peace be with you, Ministering Angels, Angels of the Most High." I especially cherish this legend because of a bit of advice Mother gave Father one evening before he entered the house on the way back from the synagogue. She suggested that he close the shutters (ours closed from the outside) during such times because it was better "not to draw too much attention." But to this, too, Father replied: "How can I let the angels wait outside?"

Father and Mother, on the day when your souls ascended to heaven from the pit of slaughter, what honor did the Ministering Angels, the Angels of the Most High, render you?

[1] In Jewish tradition, it is believed that the Prophet Elijah enters each Jew's home at the recitation of this prayer and takes a sip of wine from a special cup.

I Tarried at Uncle Elisha's

Until 1937, I lived in Pinsk, and from there I went to Warsaw to serve on the executive council of the Zionist youth organization ha-Noar ha-Tsiyoni. In the last month before the outbreak of World War II, in August, 1939, I was directing a leaders' training camp which the movement maintained in Troki, near Vilna.

In the camp's last days, war was already in the air. The day after it closed, at the end of August, the authorities began requisitioning horses and wagons and cattle and grain from the farmers, followed by the classic symptoms of panic — hasty purchases, soaring prices, and hoarding.

With other members of my movement I hurried to Warsaw, fearing that the roads would become impassable and I would be cut off from my headquarters. I arrived on the evening of August 31. The following day German airplanes were already circling over the city and you could hear the shrieks of air-raid sirens and the blasts of exploding bombs.

The German invasion of Poland marked the outbreak of

World War II. Several days later, Britain and France declared war on Germany. Warsaw, which had already lost much blood in the first days of the conflict, smiled briefly, and crowds cheered in front of the British and French embassies.

But with each passing day, perhaps each passing hour, it was clear that Poland's conquest was a matter of time.

On the seventh of September a radio broadcast summoned Warsaw's men to dig trenches and erect earthworks for the city's defense. At midnight I went to an assembly point on the outskirts of the city and worked five hours. At dawn I returned to my movement's headquarters and found a note on the door informing me that the others had left for the east. It turned out that during the night the radio had ordered all men of military age to go to the eastern part of the country. Later, rumor had it that these and other contradictory instructions had been broadcast by Nazi agents in order to spread panic and increase the confusion.

I packed a few things and also headed eastward. The roads were choked with refugees. A whole nation was in flight: in wagons and automobiles, on horses and bicycles, and mostly, on foot. German airplanes roaring overhead were bombing the roads. People sought refuge in the fields and woods; families were being separated; husbands and wives and mothers and children were losing each other. The air was full of screams.

Little by little, the road became covered with bundles, bags, and valises. It is easier going empty-handed. But what would they buy food with? Money no longer had any value. The road was strewn with cars, abandoned for lack of fuel. "Where should I go? Where?" People had stopped by the roadside. Many began returning to Warsaw. "I want to die in my own bed." For the first time in my life, I had pity on the Polish policemen. They now looked so pathetic, lost in the crowds of refugees, covered with dust, unshaven, tired, indifferent, with eyes full of despair, they represented the debased pride of Polish statehood. And, of course, there were also the Jews.

I was on the way to Pinsk. Someone like me, with a family and a home in the eastern regions, was considered lucky. My only thought was to reach home.

After some friends and I had crossed the Bug river, we encountered a train which still ran for a short distance. We leaped aboard and covered a large area in a short time. Suddenly the train was bombed and we jumped off. My friend Shalom and I lay in a ditch near the track while German bombers zoomed over our heads. It was then that the idea occurred to me for the first time to leave an "announcement" just in case . . . I was already closer to my parent's home than to Warsaw. I told my friend that were I to die here, he was to inform my family. He replied that he was not a safe candidate for such a mission because one bomb here would kill us both.

I arrived in Pinsk the second day of Rosh ha-Shana (the Jewish New Year), the opening Kol Nidrey prayer was chanted under red flags, for the Red army had crossed the Polish-Soviet frontier on September 17. The petitions to Our Father in Heaven in the synagogues were mixed with the sounds from loud speakers in the streets praising Our Father in the Kremlin.

In our town, rooted in tradition and Hassidism and dedicated to Zionism and the Land of Israel, many questions were being asked. The air was full of expressions of mixed feelings, but joy, or at least a feeling of relief, predominated. I am not talking of those whose satisfaction was occasioned by political motives — people who regarded this event as their greatest hour. I refer to the ordinary people, simple everyday Jews, who were swept away by the stream of hopes and enthusiasm. I was not among those who went out to welcome the Red army at the entrance to the city, but I saw the circles crowding around the soldiers. The Jews asked many questions and their faces were radiant with pleasure.

There can be no mistake that first of all they were happy at the alternative which saved them from the Germans. There was no third way out. Poland was finished. And the fact that the Jews immediately found a common language, pure and simple, with the new soldiers played an important part in shaping their reaction. Most of the older generation in Pinsk spoke Russian fluently. But Russian was not necessary to communicate with the ordinary Russian soldier. Many of them spoke Yiddish. Another fact made a tremendous impression and stirred the hearts of the people — our fellow Jews were not only simple soldiers but also officers. Jews who perhaps would never even have dared look at Polish junior officers were talking freely to Russian top brass, Jews and non-Jews, as if they were one of us.

It was their behavior which aroused amazement. They did not at all act like "soldiers." What courtesy, what manners! An old man tried to push his way into one circle and even before a way was made for him, the officer urged him on, "Come closer, Grandpa, closer. What do you want to know?"

I remember a God-fearing Jew spoke to me with Hassidic wonder of the songs of the Red army soldiers. "I tell you, they have the fervor of the Baal Shem-Tov's[1] disciples." And then he compared the marches of the Polish army, which always savored of illicit sex, to their songs — their soft, cultured, extremely soulful tunes.

The high point in this upsurge of emotion was the glittering prospect of seeing relatives from the other side of the former border, from whom they had been separated for twenty years.

But the ones captivated the most by the "Comrades" were Jewish refugees who had already tasted Nazi occupation. I remember well the words of a pupil of mine in our movement after he crossed the new Soviet-German frontier; the streets, he said, were singing and the sidewalks were giving forth music.

The rejoicing quickly vanished. It was not long before the other side of the "liberation" became apparent. First of all, there was the concrete hunger for every kind of commodity which the

[1] The founder of the Hassidic movement.

new proprietors displayed. The practice of immediately buying up whatever was available constituted a factual denial of their verbal abundance expressed in the words, "We have everything where we come from." The idyllic relations faded away. More and more Blue-Caps — the men of the NKVD — appeared in increasing numbers and a local prison which the Reds had immediately taken over again became full to overflowing. The authorities began regulating the "unsettled" life of the city. "Commissars" were appointed to supervise various institutions. "Committees" were set up. "Reorganizations" were carried out. "Hints" were dropped that public bodies should disband. Libraries were sifted and confiscated. New instructions and regulations were frequent. A muteness settled over the city. Dejection grew. Zionists were given a clear indication of what lay in store for them by the reorganization of Hebrew and religious schools "in accordance with new principles."

Father had relatives not far from Pinsk, in the vicinity of Minsk, on the other side of the frontier which had just been blotted out. His mother had died there several years before. I had never known my grandmother; her son (my father) had not seen her, could not see her the last twenty years of her life. He was aflame to see what remained of his family. We recalled that every year before the High Holidays, Father used to send a Jewish calendar printed in Hebrew characters there as if it were to a remote land of mystery. Is that what the future held in store for us?

Meanwhile, in the beginning of October a rumor began circulating that the city of Vilna, which had also been occupied by the Red army, would soon be handed over to the Lithuanians. This was a gesture of the mighty to a tiny country and its people, who throughout the period of independent Poland had claimed that they had been robbed of their historical capital. The "Comrades" were correcting the evil and restoring Vilna to its original owner.

The Zionists, perhaps no less than the Lithuanians, regarded Vilna as a gift from heaven. We indulged in fantasies. This time-honored center of Jewish tradition would provide a refuge from both dividers of the Polish loot. Even pessimists among us did not conceive of a storm engulfing the entire world. We told each other that from Vilna there would somehow be a way to reach the Land of Israel. (Emissaries of the Zionist youth movement had previously felt out the situation in the Soviet-Rumanian region — formerly Polish-Rumanian — and discovered that it was stringently guarded by the Soviets.) If we could not organize mass emigration to Palestine from there, we could at least live as Jews and foster Zionist and Hebrew cultural activities until the storm would blow over, we believed.

At first instinctively and spontaneously, later in an organized fashion, large groups of Jews streamed to Vilna. Everyone had the same idea — to reach the city by train unimpeded as long as it belonged to "us," the Soviets, and remain there after their departure. So the trains to Vilna were jammed.

The Soviet authorities really left the city, but not entirely empty-handed. They took along some confiscated equipment and property to cover the cost of the journey. They dismantled the Elektrit radio set plant and transported it to a Soviet area. They also took along some human cargo, hundreds of civic leaders, high Polish government officials, writers, and scientists, including famous Jewish personalities.

In the middle of October I was standing in a Vilna street to watch a parade of the Lithuanian troops entering the city. After having become acquainted with the true strength of the Polish army and having behind us encounters with the Red army and the German hordes, there was something operatic in the pretentious demonstration of the midget state. The marchers consisted of nattily dressed units carrying shiny weapons, military policemen, and a company with dogs.

The joy of the Lithuanians at having their city restored to them could apparently not be complete without shedding a little Jewish blood. During the early days of their rule, a small pogrom broke out. Jews were attacked and fired upon, windows smashed, and Jewish property plundered. There was a widespread opinion that this was an act of anti-Semitic provocation committed by the Poles, angry at having lost Vilna. Jewish personalities warned the authorities of the results of the rioting and demanded that it be curbed and the participants punished. Local Jewish leaders met with representatives of refugee groups to discuss the organization of defense groups. I took part in this meeting, the very convocation of which made a strong impression on me.

The city quickly calmed down. The number of Jewish refugees mounted daily. Vilna became a center for all the Zionist youth movements of former Poland. On the executive council of the ha-Noar ha-Tsiyoni, I was in charge of maintaining communications with members still living in areas which had been Poland.

I spent a great deal of time in border towns. The winter of 1939–1940 was extremely severe; the Baltic Sea was covered with ice. Many of the people crossing the border would reach Lithuanian territory with frozen limbs and required urgent medical treatment. Some of them were literally carried by their comrades after they had stopped in the snow completely exhausted. The manifestations of brotherhood and comradeship on the borders and in the trackless wastes lent us courage.

The name of one border town, Ejszyszki (Eisiskes), was engraved in my memory and on my heart because of the devotion of its Jews and their concern for refugees. They would receive the new arrivals — by way of the cemetery, which was located almost on the frontier — and give them shelter and assistance and a refreshing feeling of being among their own. Often the Lithuanian police attempted to round up the "illegals"; the Jews of the town, together with the members sent there from Vilna, would form a cordon around the group of refugees (or around the vehicle which was supposed to take them to Vilna) and beat off the policemen.

The groups in Vilna associated with pioneer movements increased. Activities became stabilized. However, a feeling of dissatisfaction mounted. The thought that we were living off someone else began to gnaw at our spirits, even though we tried to find cultural occupations within the groups as well as productive employment. But the principal source of our dejection was the realization that Vilna would not become the point of departure for a mass emigration to Palestine. We seemed to be in a bottleneck.

Emissaries from Vilna came back to relate encouraging stories of attempts to keep the movement alive in Soviet territory and of the courage of our members keeping their group going in German-occupied areas. In one place they buried the flags of their branch deep in the ground, and somewhere else they hid the archives. Our people filched books from libraries in order to save them from destruction or confiscation. In German-occupied territory, contacts between Warsaw groups and those in other cities were extended. But our representatives also brought back nightmarish reports of German activities. We also learned that in the Soviet areas many Zionists and others had been arrested and sent away.

One day I suggested to our head office that they allow me to leave Vilna for Soviet-occupied Poland. I thought it was not fair to send just emissaries from the rank and file; and since I was in charge of contacts with former Poland, I felt it was my moral duty to cross the borders myself. At night, I woke several members of our group, including my brother Leibke, to say goodbye.

One of our border-crossing organizers was Lilka. She had experience and luck. Her family lived in Vilna but she carried out missions to both the Soviet and German zones, where she established ties with loyal members and with the relatives of comrades of ours who were already in Vilna. After crossing four "green" frontiers, she returned to Lithuanian territory on a frosty night with frozen feet and brought back a packet of letters and information. Now Lilka wanted to join me, but we did not want to grant our approval; we didn't have the heart.

Another of our emissaries was Hayyim, about whom it was said that he went out to steal across frontiers as if he were going to the movies.

When Hayyim started out with me, he was already a veteran of sixteen hikes, from all of which he had returned safely and in good spirits. Only from the mission with me — his seventeenth — did he not return. Together we journeyed great distances and our fates became interwoven.

In the Lithuanian-Soviet border region there were two Jewish towns about three miles apart — Old Swieciany and New Swieciany. One day one Swieciany became Lithuanian and the other Soviet, and it was up to Hayyim and me to cross this border. On the Lithuanian side, we waited several days for a dark night. We managed to secure a guide who was supposed to receive payment in a Jewish house after bringing a note from us which we had prepared in advance, confirming he had taken us across.

The snow crunched under our feet. Now and then shots sheared the air. Our footsteps may have echoed and made enough noise to alert the border guards, or else the soldiers were simply firing to deter people. There were stretches of terrain where we had to crawl on the snow. At whom were the dogs barking so loudly? Were they routine barks or had they sniffed human footsteps? We were nearly on the border when the firing became more intense and some flares were shot up into the sky. We were already quite certain that Soviet patrols were on our trail.

Our guide was scared. He refused to go on. But neither did he want to lose the money promised to him, and he demanded that we give him the prepared note we had, the confirmation. We were afraid of becoming involved in this place — alone in the vast night — with this stranger.

Lengthy bickering would have endangered us still more since the slightest sound would have given us away. The man had not done his job but, still, we gave him what he asked for and, having no choice, continued on alone, guided by Hayyim's sense of smell for frontiers, which proved to be reliable.

Early in the morning, we were already on the other side of the border in an attic of an address which we had memorized. We were received warmly, but our hosts begged us to leave quickly. In recent weeks, they explained, much had changed where they lived and surveillance of people dwelling in border regions was increasing.

Among the places we came to was Pinsk. Here I had to be more careful than in other places; many people knew me and there was a rumor circulating in town that I was active in Vilna and "on the border." The possibility of being handed over to the authorities by an informer always had to be taken into consideration. As my train drew closer to Pinsk, stopping at stations on the way, I wrapped part of my face in a scarf and supported it in my hands, as if I had a violent toothache. However, my facial disguise was of no avail when A.H.N., an old Zionist, boarded the train. He was surprised at meeting me and asked numerous questions. I answered quickly and warned him not to breathe word of our encounter to anyone. At the train station, I hired a sleigh and rode off to my parents' home.

The joy of our reunion was mingled with fear. Father and Mother wept and did not know what to do first. They took me into their bedroom. Father had acquired some experience in the underground and hung blankets over the window curtains to prevent someone from the outside looking in. He told me of suspicious inquiries made about me. He was asked where I was and what I was doing. He, of course, had no idea. In this room Father arranged for me to meet several members of the movement. They were all of one mind — I had to get out of there quickly. Father also advised me to do this, in a choked voice, and asked the few friends who came to see me to keep the fact of my visit a complete secret.

By midnight I was already out of the house. I did not allow Father to accompany me to the station. At the door, I bade farewell to Father and Mother and my married sister. This was goodbye forever.

For about seven weeks, I wandered with Hayyim through various towns and forests in the Soviet zone. We met comrades of ours organizing holiday celebrations, passing out mimeographed programs for discussions, and meeting to read a Hebrew book together and sing a Palestinian song. Sometimes they succeeded in picking up Hebrew broadcasts from Jerusalem on their radio sets. One of the major activities consisted of "burying" Hebrew and Zionist literature as well as passing around such books from one house to another for individuals or groups to read.

Our boys and girls wrapped the insignia of our movement — a lily inside a Shield of David — in cloth, transforming them into buttons for their shirts to serve as a living reminder. At the same time they were busy hiding flags and other everyday appurtenances of our organizational life. News of Palestine which we brought to our members was like a refreshing breath of air for them.

The time came for Hayyim and me to return to Vilna. It was becoming increasingly more difficult to get around. New documents were required and it became necessary to register frequently. The frontier guards were increased and persons harboring illegal border-crossers were threatened with severe penalties and ordered to hand them over to the authorities. The longer we attempted to seek out a safe way to return to Vilna, the more pessimistic we became. But every additional day in the border regions exposed us more and more to arrest. Writing to our headquarters in Vilna, we told them in a prearranged code that we were on our way to Aunt Leah (a Vilna friend of ours), but if we failed to arrive, it would mean that we had tarried at Uncle Elisha's (this was Elisha Rodin, Hebrew poet in the Soviet Union who suffered a great deal because of his love for Hebrew and Palestine).

One dark night we placed ourselves in the hands of two guides whose price for leading us across the border was excessively high. Furthermore, we had no way of assuring ourselves that they would not betray us. Usually when native guides had to be hired they were not paid until they brought back a note confirming that they had brought their charges to safety. But we had no such arrangement. Our two guides led us for hours along twisting paths through barren country. Suddenly they began quarreling over the direction. At first, we considered this a minor mishap. However, instead of coming to an agreement, they began shouting more vociferously. If we had not been nearly certain that the whole quarrel was staged, we would have regarded it as quite amusing!

Our guides did not stop arguing even when several shots pierced the air. On the contrary, the dispute waxed more furiously. We no longer had any doubts; we had been sold.

We were surrounded by soldiers with bayoneted rifles. An order was given, "Hands up!" The soldiers searched us superficially for weapons. For appearance's sake our guides also lifted their arms and they, too, were frisked. However, no more play-acting could convince us that we had not been betrayed. Their quarrel had been designed in order to give our exact location away. The soldiers angrily shouted, "Where were you going, heroes?" Shortly afterward, we were already locked up in a cell of the frontier guards' station from which we managed to see our guides being released.

The moment we were caught we sought an opportunity to get rid of all the documents we were carrying. We had previously agreed that in the event of capture, we were both to say that we were refugees from the German zone where we had been students at the University of Warsaw. We were on the way to relatives in Vilna.

Hayyim originally came from Bialystok in the Soviet-occupied zone. However, he was carrying the documents of another member of our group who had come from Czestochowa in the German zone. I had my real papers on me until our arrest. At the first chance, I slipped them into the snow and trampled on them with my heavy boots, thrusting them deep into the white mantle. I was determined not to make any mention of Pinsk to any policeman or investigator.

There were several reasons for our decisions. The excuse of being refugees from the Germans fleeing from Nazi brutality appeared a reasonable one to us. An investigation about me in Pinsk would have revealed my activities on the border and my mission from Vilna into Soviet territory. And finally, I wished to avert punishment from my family and my parents. It is an accepted Soviet practice to visit the iniquity of fathers upon their sons, and those of sons upon their fathers. I was certain that my parents might be arrested or exiled because of me.

Asked about papers, I told them that I had lost mine in my flight from Warsaw. However, I kept my real name — Yehoshua Globerman. I only gave them another place of residence and changed my father's name, calling him Yaacov Shlomo instead of Itsik. I did this out of fear that too many untrue details might confuse me sometimes.

In this fashion, I cut myself off from my family for the sake of its peace and safety. Much later, I saw Father's tear-stained letters. In one of them, he compared his lot to that of Jacob who had lost his son Joseph. I indulged in the hope that I could save my parents from prison or exile with my stratagem. Who can foresee the serpentine path of fate? Perhaps if I had not saved them from imprisonment and exile, they would have remained alive.

This was April 15, 1940. From this time on, I was a Soviet prisoner until the end of 1947 — with an intermezzo of about a year.

I had tarried at Uncle Elisha's.

First Permanent Residence in the NKVD's Domain

Hayyim and I were transferred from the border guards' station to a dark, moldy basement cell in the police station of the nearby town. It was so overcrowded that the prisoners could not help rubbing against each other all the time. Nevertheless, they continued putting in more prisoners, most of whom were captured on the border. In time, I learned that the capacity of a prison cell is limitless. Somehow we fitted into this human mosaic in which one person whispered Hebrew prayers and another crossed himself, one man cursed and someone else wept, where one man recited biblical texts while his neighbor read a sexy story. In one spot we ate and not far from it we urinated. These were quarters for prisoners in transit and the few days we remained here were an introduction to the long journey into the night.

When they took us out of the detention cellar and brought us to the station in a wagon under heavy guard, we saw that a number of local Jews were waiting for us in the street. They knew of our arrest and understood that soon we would be transferred to more important prisons. Consequently, they kept their distance and waited for us to be taken out so they could at least hand us some food. They were afraid to utter a sound, but our hearts heard their blessing and their concern.

My first permanent residence in a real prison was in the town of Vileika. Until that time I had only heard the name in connection with an insane asylum. It was there that I first became acquainted with the institution and practices with which I later was expected to feel at home. This was neither local militia nor border station, this was the domain of the NKVD.

Upon arrival we were subjected to a thorough examination. They rigidly inspected whatever we wore and carried, meticulously searched our clothing, felt all the seams, undoing them here and there, and rummaged in our shoes, carefully tapping the soles and expertly scrutinizing the places where they were sewed together. After that, you were made to stand in front of your hosts naked while they looked into your ears and mouth, inspected your armpits, peered between your fingers and toes, and told you to bend over to enable them to examine closely the intimate parts of your anatomy. All pencil stubs and pieces of paper as well as every pointed article were taken away. In this lodging house the authorities were also responsible for your personal safety. To eliminate any technical possibility of suicide, you were also deprived of thread, strings, shoelaces, belts (women had to give up their hair ribbons), and even metal buttons.

Until you found some way to keep your pants from dropping, you had to keep pulling them up and hoping for a miracle. I later came to understand that this is one way of softening up the prisoner who must eventually plead guilty between these walls. This is the beginning of making a man lose his human image when he becomes a caricature in his own eyes.

There was a good deal of paperwork attached to this. Whatever had been taken from you was listed and described and various questionnaires had to be filled out. After that, you were given a bath, physical examination, and haircut. Then they took you to your cell.

During this "cult of the personality" processing, I was separated from Hayyim and thrust into a cell without him. I at once learned that this was a solemn hour, for all the cell's inmates were engaged in the collective enterprise of searching for lice. Upon seeing this, I could only wonder at my bath of a short while ago. The prisoners came over to have a look at me; one by one. The cell chief designated by the authorities showed me to the place coming to me by virtue of the unwritten, universally accepted law of the prisoners' world — near the parasha, pretentiously called slop pail, not far from the door. This traditional vessel from the time of the Czars was not overthrown by the Revolution. Its stench filled the whole cell. Those using it step on you despite their caution and bestow upon you acoustic as well as olfactory stimuli. But among convicts the principle of seniority has a quasi-professional sanctity — whoever comes in last takes up lodging near the slop pail.

I put down my belongings and looked around. I was dejected because of my separation from Hayyim. I was told there was no hope of ever seeing him again. Persons held for the same offense are never kept in the same cell, to prevent them from talking to each other and coordinating their behavior and their stories. While I was reflecting on my isolation the door suddenly opened and a new inmate was flung into the cell. It was Hayyim. My mood swung upward. Let him be near the slop pail as long as we were together again.

Even in the dull routine of a prison cell, two are better than one. We all slept on the floor. It seems that the beds had been removed from the entire prison now that it had to hold three and four times its capacity. So the two of us were able to use one coat for a mattress and another as a blanket. We shared our food, clothing, and small personal articles; and most importantly, our opinions and ideology.

Hayyim was not only a loyal member of our movement and a good friend; by virtue of his skillful hands, he quickly became a power in the cell. It was not long before he succeeded in fashioning chessmen and dominoes out of bread crumbs, needles out of fish bones, and a knife out of a buckle which had escaped detection. We sacrificed a shirt in order to use the thread for making shoelaces and belts (the remnants were cut up into small pieces to serve as toilet paper to supplement the pages of old books given to us; we were allowed no newspapers for this purpose, in order to insure our complete isolation). The prestige of Hayyim rose when someone resorted to anti-Semitic expressions. My friend lifted the slop pail and warned the offender that the next time he would pour it over his head.

Gradually we moved farther away from the slop pail. Isolated individuals were summoned from the cell never to return and new inmates were constantly joining us. This meant that our rights continued to increase. In time we actually reached the place of honor. We no longer felt twinges of conscience when a white-haired newcomer (sometimes a Ph.D.) appeared and moved into the spot beside the slop pail as custom required. Twice a day the bucket was emptied. No one, not even old men, was relieved of this duty, which each one carried out in turn. It did not take long for us, Polish aristocrats and intelligentsia who were most of the cell's inmates, to learn the rules and ethics of convicts.

The cell and its inmates were our whole world. The Vileika institution was conducted as a "domestic prison," which meant that it was intended for offenders against state security. The cells were completely isolated from one another. Only rarely could you find out who was in the next or some other cell. When someone was summoned for questioning, the guard did not call out his name but only the initial. We would sometimes joke about this. The guard would ask, "Any 'S' in here?" and we would chorus, "Slop pail."

While escorting a prisoner for questioning or to the doctor, the guard would whistle or clap his hands to avoid meeting another inmate on the way. When necessary, the guard would order his charge to face the wall without moving until the coast was clear. The windows were not only barred but were covered on the outside with slanting awnings to restrict to a minimum whatever was visible outside. The prisoners called these *namordniki*, "muzzles." Special security and isolation measures were taken whenever groups of prisoners were taken out into the yard for their daily walk or to the toilet.

Nevertheless, we were still able to piece together some information out of all kinds of signs. Our senses became more acute and we could guess how many persons there were in the neighboring cells from the number of splashes of the ladle when soup was being dished out for lunch or from the steps in the corridor when the inmates of another cell passed ours.

Several weeks after my arrival I was taken to participate in two important ceremonies which are generally conducted the first day in prison: fingerprinting and photographing in profile and full-face. Vileika had fallen behind because of the pressure of work. The persons to be photographed were brought in groups. They included many refugees who had refused Soviet passports, fearing they would lose their Polish nationality. A number is hung on the person photographed. It is strange but I have been photographed in about ten different prisons and I can recall none of the numbers except the one at Vileika: it was 1002.

At about this time, both Hayyim and I were summoned separately for preliminary questioning. This did not last long. Apparently the interrogators did not have the time for us. They had too much to do. In five or six sessions, they "finished" with each of us.

The rules for a prisoner undergoing questioning constitute a special code of law. The interrogator explained them to me right away. Seated on a chair in the corner I must always look directly in front and hold my hands on my knees. However, the important thing is to answer "honestly." The questions and answers are re-corded and later combined in a file bearing the words *Khranit vyechno*, "Hold forever."

Naturally, frank, truthful answers were only for my own good.

"Do you know what Gorki wrote?"

I was familiar with some of his works, *Mother*, and *My Universities*. But my interrogator meant something more lofty; he had in mind the phrase, either rightfully or otherwise attributed to the proletarian writer, which all the interrogators solemnly repeated: "An enemy who surrenders is to be pitied; a rebellious one is to be destroyed."

My questioning went fast. No confession had to be forced out of me, since I had been captured on the border. If I wanted to think over my reply, I would take advantage of my broken Russian and ask to have the question repeated, as if I had not understood it. This would give me a little more time for thought. Sometimes the interrogator would attempt to vary the questions a little: "Do you know what kind of regime you wanted to run away from?"

"It's not too clear to me. It did not interest me. I ran away from the Nazis and my sole wish was to find relatives."

"Such a naive baby," he responded and dropped political problems.

He finally came to the point. He requested a detailed history of my life and a complete description of the crime. Our pretending to be refugee students was accepted and recorded in the protocol although my interrogator was a little skeptical about my being a student. This I understood from one interchange.

"Do you drink vodka?" he asked.

"No," I replied.

"Do you go to prostitutes?"

At first I wanted to object to these questions; they seemed to have nothing to do with the interrogation, but once again I answered weakly, "No."

To this he retorted, "Some lousy student you are!"

My interrogator also had difficulty with my name and newly adopted patronymic in Russian. Yehoshua son of Yaacov Shlomo is pronounced Yegoshua Yakub Shlomovich in Russian. The Yaacov Shelomo confused him. "What, you had two fathers?"

I became confused when addressing my interrogator. In keeping with Soviet usage, I once addressed him as "Comrade Interrogator."

He was irate, "What sort of comrade of yours am I?"

I called him, "Mister (gospodin) Interrogator," and he flew into a rage — "We have no masters."

"Then how should I address you?" I asked.

"Call me blackguard. As far as you and the likes of you are concerned, I'm a blackguard."

Later, I learned that a prisoner uses the term "Citizen" in addressing a free man.

That was the first time I had been called an "enemy of the people." From now on, I waited in my cell either to stand trial or be sent off somewhere. Perhaps I might even be released. Who knows? Meanwhile, how could I kill time? There were numerous occupations. First of all, there were regulations to obey — cleaning up the cell, taking the slop pail out, and daily roll call. An important job was passing out bread. All the portions were laid out on the table. One of the prisoners then turned his back on the table and faced the wall. The cell chief would point to one portion after another and ask, "Whose?" and the man facing the wall would call out a name. Tension ran high during this period.

Meals were eaten slowly and methodically. The prisoners told riddles and jokes and recited literary creations. We did tricks with numbers and interpreted dreams. We took daily "walks" inside the cell (six paces in one direction and six back in a cleared area). Whenever a new inmate arrived we all crowded around to hear news of the outside. We played games to test our intelligence and did exercises to sharpen our wits. Some time was devoted to mending our possessions.

The list includes the hour of solemn cleansing which I have already mentioned — the daily examination of our clothing. Not everyone knew how to do this properly and effectively, seam by seam. It was both tragic and comical to see a deputy with a lawyer on one side and a professor on the other, discussing politics or mythology, crushing lice with their nails. People who had suffered considerable anguish because they could not use the slop pail slowly peeled off one layer after another until they got rid of every feeling of shame. The viciousness in man became more apparent in the relations of the cell's inmates to one another. Hayyim and I sought interesting persons in the cell and managed to find men of great learning. We learned Russian from them and increased our knowledge of the sciences and literature. I well remember how shocked I was when I saw how these noble and learned people employed all kinds of stratagems to secure another crumb or a spoonful of soup at the expense of a fellow prisoner. Some even fell lower and risked outright thieving.

The despair and suffering in the cell increased steadily. June came and the heat and congestion became unbearable. There were seventy inmates in a cell designed to hold ten. Sweaty, sticky bodies swarming with lice became weaker and thinner from day to day. We were hungry but all we asked for was to open the window or the door to the corridor for a while. It was the same in all the cells and one day the cry for air was taken up and spread throughout the prison building. The feeling of suffocation consumed us, causing dizziness, fainting, and insanity. Even if you did not have to go, you took advantage of the two group trips to the toilet just for the sake of being able to breathe a little more air.

Meanwhile, a system of barter developed in the cell. Some

were content with fifty grams less bread which they exchanged for half a matchbox of powdered sugar. There were many transactions of this sort. The commonest was the bartering of tobacco. Confirmed smokers unable to procure tobacco suffered from a severe case of nerves and would exchange their minimum survival rations for a pinch of the dried plant.

However, the most fascinating transactions were those conducted on a grand scale. As time wore on, part of a forest, an estate, a lot, a house or apartment and other kinds of real estate were offered in exchange for several slices of bread. All this property was either in the German zone or had been expropriated by the Soviets. Similar offers were made bartering partnerships in stores, factories, and flour mills. At first, everyone believed that the war would not last long. The Soviet Union would also have to restore Poland's territorial status and the prices of land and real estate were relatively high. But gradually the prices dropped to almost nothing so that there was no one who would exchange a bit of tobacco in this world for a hereafter.

Together with us in the cell were many whose questioning had ended and who were just waiting for a trial. Was this naiveté or plain "western decadence"? None of us ever faced a judge. Every day prisoners were summoned from the cell and informed of their sentences handed down in absentia by nameless judges. Some days the sentences were read out wholesale, one right after the other. They had probably arrived in the same dispatch either from Moscow or Minsk, the capital of the Byelorussian Soviet Republic. A number of prisoners were sent off to prison camps where they finally learned of the sentences they had to serve.

My turn to hear my sentence also came. I had been sentenced by the Os-So (Osoboye Sovietcheniye; literally, "Special Consultation") to five years' imprisonment in a concentration camp called Work and Correctional Camp (for the correction of one's attitudes, of course). Hayyim was called out separately and really got a "bargain" — just three years' imprisonment. The organization known as Os-So remained shrouded in mystery. Among the numerous rumors which circulated about it was one which identified it with the mysterious Troika or Trinity in charge of combating domestic enemies.

In the final summing-up it may be said that the interrogator did not entirely make up a story when he once told me, "Our penal system is an educational one," and that I, too, would probably be sent for "reeducation." Once when he was in a good mood, he said to me, "There, people work at their trade," and by honest work I, too, could do penance for my crime. But who knew where "there" was located?

Whither, Whither, Whither Have You Gone So Far Away?

There is a refrain in a Russian popular song which goes "Boundless is my native land." I had my first taste of these distances in the locked and barred cars which took me and hundreds of others from Vileika to the Far North. Among these shipments of human beings I received my initial instruction in the country's geography.

In addition to marches, I became acquainted over a period of years with various methods of transporting prisoners. One of these had a glorious tradition made famous by the name of the Czarist minister of the interior in 1906; his name was Stolypin. A Stolypin train consists of cars attached to an ordinary train and, except for bars and several other accessories, it looks like all the other coaches from the outside.

However, it was too much of a luxury to employ Stolypin coaches for transporting masses of prisoners. We were pushed into cattle cars equipped for their new purposes with a few simple architectural innovations. These consisted of several tiers of shelf-like boards to serve as beds, a not too inconspicuous corner for use as a toilet with a drain pipe going outside — and of prime importance, barred windows and locks with good strong bolts.

The train was also made up of cars for the armed escort and dogs, weapons, storage, and reserve equipment. Throughout the journey, whether in motion or stationary, the train was guarded by troops either standing on the buffers or on specially constructed platforms between the cars. The guards made use of communications equipment and projectors. At every junction the entire train was shunted off to a siding for feeding, roll call, change of guard, and safety check. At such times, soldiers came into the cars peering intently at everyone and everything and feeling the floorboards while others were examining the roofs and drumming with their boots over the heads of the passengers.

Our food consisted for the most part of dry rations, that is, rusks and dried or salted fish, and a little sugar. Warm food was a rarity on a journey of this sort. This enhanced the importance of the kipyatok — boiling water available free of charge to travelers at nearly all Russian railway stations. However, we only received our kipyatok at junctions when the guards and service personnel had time to bring it from the kipyatilka, where it was boiled, and distribute it among the prisoners. The dry, salty food not only did not satisfy us but also made us very thirsty. It was from these prisoners that I learned the current expression "a fish loves to swim," meaning that eating fish increases the need for drinking. At this time, we begged for water without aphorisms.

In the city of Polotsk, we were taken off the train and housed in the local jail. It was here that I met Hayyim again. We were once more in the same cell.

We stayed here one week. Here, too, Hayyim displayed his manual skill. Out of bread he fashioned the image of a prisoner lifting a sledgehammer above his head as if he were pounding rocks with his legs shackled to a wheelbarrow. Was this some sort of intuitive perception of the days to come? Meanwhile, it was a pleasant-looking object standing on a table in the center of the cell. Once the director of the prison himself came into the cell, accompanied as usual by an escort of guards and inspectors. Noticing the provocative piece of art at once, he inquired who made it. No one answered. However, when he threatened to impose a severe punishment on everyone in the cell, Hayyim stepped forward. A flitting smile crossed the director's face. Putting the chained bread prisoner into his pocket he said that this time he would forgive us.

Hardly had the party left the cell when Hayyim began preparing doughy bread for another exhibit. Several hours later, a new charming figure graced the table. It was a man sitting at a slop pail. This object was found in Hayyim's bundle during the search preceding our next entrainment and was confiscated. It probably ended up in the house of one of the senior jailers as a piece of decorative art.

In Polotsk Hayyim and I took turns for two nights at staying awake while the other slept. We were the only Jews in the cell and there was an anti-Semitic Pole in with us who suddenly lost all control of himself and began threatening that he would strangle us in our sleep; the whole war, he cried, had broken out only on account of the Jews. During the day we would shut him up, but in the night we decided to stay on the lookout.

The journey went on. The train grew longer. Now we "zapadniki" (westerners) were already mingling with former Soviet citizens. While marching the lines lengthened and the guards screamed, "Don't spread out."

The third prison I came to know — after Vileika and Polotsk — was the one in Marc Chagall's birthplace of Vitebsk.

Through the namordniki hanging over the barred windows it was difficult to discern whether the houses in the city were really endowed with the legendary picturesqueness in the paintings of the great artist. Perhaps some Jew shrouded in a spell was still hovering over the mysterious roofs? . . . Meanwhile one senior

jailer was busily running around, issuing orders to his sub-
ordinates, bounding from one place to another and returning
to us as if smelling something, seeking something, until he once
actually brushed past a group of Polish Jews standing together in
the mass of prisoners and uttered "Goot Shabbes," slipped away
and disappeared. He must have been unable to stifle the desire to
somehow express before us the minuscule vestige of Judaism still
throbbing inside him — and more than that he could not, he did
not dare.

It was in Vitebsk that we had an illuminating run-in with one
of the prison supervisors. According to regulations, twenty minutes was the time allotted to each prisoner for a walk in the yard.
This was stated clearly on a sheet of regulations hanging on the
cell wall. Actually, during these walks all we did was take monotonous steps in a circle, single file. All we could see was the path
we walked on and the prison walls. However, these were precious
moments, enabling us to get some air into our lungs and give our
minds a change of scenery.

But at Vitebsk they would take us outside for two or three
turns not lasting more than five minutes and order us to return to
the cell. Apparently the exercise yard was not large enough for
the mounting stream of prisoners and our time had been cut down
to give each cell a chance to use it (a cell like ours had so many
people in it that they had to be taken out in four or five groups).
When we attempted to object and make demands, citing the law,
an ironical smile formed in the corners of the mouth of the supervisor who had been rushed in to our cell. "As far as you're concerned, *I* am your law." And he was right. The law and our air
for breathing were in his hands.

We quickly bade Chagall's hometown goodbye. And now,
where? This was our constant occupation — trying to guess the
direction the train was taking. Russians and "westerners" who had
been in Russia prior to the Revolution strained their eyes to detect a clue. Slowly, concrete signs and intuition combined to

point out our destination. We were headed for the polar bears. I could not even conjecture what was in store for me. I would sell half of my daily bread ration for a place beside the window through which I could look out of the fast-moving train at the silhouettes of human beings, blurred faces, huts, flocks, and fields. Curiosity about the unknown passing before my vision made fear of the unknown of the next day recede.

After several weeks in the prisoner train (someone called it "Cook's Wagons-Lit"), our organized tour reached the city of Kotlas.

I do not know how it looks, how large it is, and what shape it has. However, Kotlas is in the Archangel oblast of the Komi Autonomous Soviet Socialist Republic, which except for an insignificant number of natives — the Komi people — was inhabited only by prisoners and their guards. Kotlas is the gateway to a primeval land which the Creator handed over to the NKVD and said, "Go and rule it!" A gateway, very wide when you enter it but extremely narrow when you seek to leave.

Who said that the world is round? This seemed to be the world's very edge. After several days of all kinds of "sanitary processing," repeated registration and roll calls, and medical examinations, we were brought to the bank of a mighty river at night; it was the Northern Dvina, which flows into the White Sea. At this point, near Kotlas, the Vychegda river flows into the Northern Dvina. Here barges were waiting for us, closed barges specially prepared for transporting prisoners across rivers. Specially prepared simply meant that they were loaded with men instead of sacks, timber, or cattle.

Nevertheless, we had only a single desire that night — to board the barge. It was cold and we had no shelter in the pouring rain. The thunder was punctuated by cursing voices, and lightning blended with the light of lanterns. By the time the loading was complete, we were wet through and through and our clothes and bundles were soaked with water.

The happy hour came. We were already inside. We were pressed against each other and jammed into a single mass of human beings who could only lie down together on the same side and only all together turn over on the other side at a given signal. Wherever we stepped on this wonderful vessel we trod on emaciated, dirty, withered bodies with contorted faces. The congestion on the barge was so suffocating that we could only see those persons nearest us. Strangely enough, I met someone from my hometown there and had to make him understand at once not to recognize me and to keep in mind that I was not from Pinsk. We exchanged several words. He knew that I had been in Vilna. I briefly told him what had happened to me and we agreed that we would pretend to be chance acquaintances.

You could see the flow of this great river only if you went up on deck to move your bowels. However, even there, you could not devote your time and attention to watching the scenery. The physiological need was the most horrible of nightmares. You were surrounded by numerous guards shouting and urging you to hurry for fear you might wait for an opportune moment to leap into the water. And as a matter of fact, some did try it and were shot. All this time, the line of those who had to go grew constantly longer at the bottom of the ladder leading up to the deck, so that sometimes you had to wait for hours. The solution selected by some was never to leave the line for a moment. As soon as they had finished on deck, they came down and stood at the end once more. In this way, they went up again and again, having to go by the time their turn came.

As soon as we came up on deck we noticed right away that our barge was not the only one. A whole flotilla covered the Northern Dvina. The barges were tied to each other with ropes and pulled by a tugboat.

While we floated on the river this question never left our minds: Where were we going? The world still regards Siberia as a place of horror, as a place beyond human ken. The word arouses historical and political associations of revolutionaries, fighters, and rebels. Russian revolutionaries used to sing, "We shall not fear Siberia — for Siberia is also Russian soil." As it happened this Siberia was much more pleasant than the country which was about to receive us.

The time came to disembark. We were taken off the barges at Aykino. We were in Syever, the North, in the midst of a wilderness of eternal forests. This was the *Far North*. But not far enough; from here we were taken to a railroad and loaded on flatcars. There were guardhouses along the chain of flatcars, equipped with light and heavy weapons. It turned out that trains ran for some distance on a rail line constructed by previous prisoners. It didn't matter. There was still a long road ahead and "Boundless is my native land." I, too, would be a pioneer in conquering the North.

During the day it was not yet too cold, but at night we shivered on the flatcars or in trucks. There were no settled areas anywhere. Only burning fires in the dense forests around us reminded us of human habitation. Tongues of flame cleaving the darkness combined in my imagination with ancient creatures doing wild dances on untrodden roads.

Where were we going? What country was this? Only one thing was clear; we were in a land of watchtowers. Wherever we looked our eyes met watchtowers, or — as the Poles called them — "Storks."

The road came to an end, literally. The railroad and highway terminated. Several hours later, we already knew we would extend them. We were to continue building the highway and laying the tracks for the railroad on and on.

We were ordered off the trucks and told to continue on foot on rough paths. It was pitch dark and a strong wind was blowing. There were no stars out. Nature was spinning a great intrigue. Was this, too, part of the NKVD's secrets? No, we had simply reached our destination at the change of seasons. Ill-tempered au-

tumn had come to the North. An angry rain was beating down
and we told ourselves that it was good that we had arrived, as the
commander of our guard announced when he ordered us to halt.

Soaked, shivering with cold, hungry, worn out, we lifted our
eyes to look around us. But where was this place, the "place" an
officer had pointed out as ours? There was nothing around us but
space. But we quickly found where our "place" was. On a tall,
thick tree, an old pine similar to many others, a piece of plywood
had been nailed. There were two words printed on it: POINT 501.
This meant that we were five hundred one kilometers from Kotlas. This and nothing else was the whole place.

There was not much time to look around. Several men in civilian clothes came toward us. It turned out that one of them was
the head of our camp site. He was a free man. The others were
prisoners with special privileges. We were ordered to line up and
begin building. They brought us shovels, saws, axes, and ham-
mers. First of all we cut down and split several trees and built a
fire. Then we began digging in the ground, cutting out clods of
moss, uprooting saplings, gathering twigs, and chopping off
branches to build living quarters for ourselves.

Later on, the standard of our houses improved, but our first
homes were mud huts, ziemlyanki. Like primitive creatures of the
wild, we were concerned with keeping the rain out. At the entrance to our mud hut we lit a fire. Sometimes the smoke nearly
stifled us. But who was to decide what was worse, smoke or cold?

One of my neighbors in the first ziemlyanka was Hayyim —
we had met once more. Another one was a man who was half
cantor and half amateur singer. While we were still traveling,
either in freight cars or on platforms, he would regale us with
renditions of the prayer Hashkivenu, the sentimental Yiddish bal-
lad "A Yiddishe Mameh," and operatic selections. When we were
settled in the ziemlyanka and had managed somewhat to warm
our bodies pressed one against the other, the tension which had
accumulated in all of us was suddenly dispelled by a popular mel-

ody from the opera, "Kuda, Kuda vi udalilis" — "Whither, whither have you gone so far away?"

Men and Horses

Our mud huts were nearly finished. But the next day it was made clear to us that we were not on a Boy Scout hike with exercises in camping out. We had not been brought here for the purpose of constructing dwelling places for ourselves but to become part of the great Socialist upbuilding. This primeval land, which became entirely mantled in snow within a few days, conceals fabulous natural resources. They must be delivered to the happy people to make their life and future gayer and brighter. But first of all, they must reach these treasures; and we were to be the trail blazers.

We had been selected to work on two jobs, the railroad and the forest. At first we saw neither roadbed nor rails. For months we merely excavated and transferred earth from one place to another according to a blueprint. Performing plastic surgery on the earth, we either lifted or lowered it. I handled thousands of cubic yards of the soil of this distant strange land, raising, lowering, loading, and unloading it. I had a part in its new topographic shape. I helped to flatten hills and make new slopes. With my own hands, I straightened out thousands of square yards of land.

My first principle means of transport was a wheelbarrow (a sort of stretcher came second). Remember the mysterious institution Os-So which sentenced people in absentia without a trial? In the North we transformed the abbreviation Os-So into a comic play on words. The wheelbarrow was called an "Osso car." To the question what an "Osso car" was, the answer would be "Dvye ruchki, odno kolesso," meaning "Two handles, one wheel," *kolesso* ("wheel") rhyming with *osso*.

Several months later, we had recourse to more efficient technology. Blasts of dynamite sent lumps of earth flying and part of the transporting was done by horses and wagons. This made work a little easier, but, on the other hand, the tempo was increased for fear the horses would, God forbid, stand idle, or for the purpose of coordinating the work of man and horse. To this very day, the shouts of the foremen and the overseers of labor brigades to the brigade heads, "Give us men, the horses are idle," or "Give us horses, the men are idle," resound in my ears.

Our other job was the forest. I had been born and raised in a forest region. However, I had rarely seen such trees. We shattered the repose of these centenarian aristocrats and disturbed their traditional growth cycle. Until our arrival in their midst, they had never looked upon the face of man. Their crowns concealed the heavens, which seemed afraid of being responsible for what was going on here on earth. Sometimes we hewed a path to the trees through snow deeper than a man's height. We had to advance step by step, shovel in hand, clearing a path before us by cutting the snow into blocks, which we piled on either side. Mighty trees were toppled together with young pine and birch saplings.

Proud nature surrendered to the saws and axes in the hands of human slaves. On the spot we would saw the trees in pieces, trim off superfluous branches, and clear the trunks of knotholes. Then we would load the thick, long timbers on our backs and either haul them to the railway or to a place where they were kept for local construction in the camp. In time, horses and sleighs were employed to drag out the logs on paths we had cleared for them. We also had to remove roots growing deep in the earth.

Working in the forest is associated in my memory with a prisoner friend of mine who had made a living in Poland dealing in woods and lumber. The camp director quickly learned that among us there was a Jewish tree expert. This man had cut down many forests in his life. He could tell the age and quality of a tree by sight, and in the twinkling of an eye, he was able to give a nearly accurate estimate of the number of cubic meters of timber it would provide. The camp's director wished to make use of this man's professional skill. Although this would have alleviated his backbreaking toil, the lumberman made an effort to have himself transferred from the forest to the railroad. His contact with forests had always been for business or commercial reasons. Nevertheless, he felt somewhat lyrical about them. He could not bear the destruction of a forest here where not only what had to be cut down was felled but future generations were also destroyed. His professional pride rebelled against this "disgraceful exploitation," against harm done to the forest's soul.

"This they call lumbering," he would contend heatedly; "this is murder." His face would radiate compassion, as if he were speaking of spilling innocent blood. I must admit, looking at him as I did at all the others, in our habits and clothing as we stumbled under heavy loads, frozen by the cold and our stomachs pinched with hunger, I felt that what my friend was saying about "barbarism against nature" sounded strange and somewhat irritating. However, I respected a person who was still able to wax poetic in this primeval forest and feel close to it.

But in the forest I felt still greater respect and admiration for those emaciated, starved Jews who enlisted the trees in a secret pact with the Almighty and took advantage of the hours of slavery beside thick trunks to be alone with their Creator and whisper a prayer to Him. None were permitted prayer shawls, phylacteries, or prayer books and it was difficult to murmur a petition to God in the muddy hut. Constantly subjected to incessant urging, scoldings, and the scrutiny of murderous eyes, where could they slip in a drop of holiness in this avalanche of defilement, stench, obscene language, tainted food, and evil? But in the forest, the wall between a Jew and his Creator vanished and he could worship while sawing and cutting trees and dragging and loading logs. It seemed to me that such a prayer would climb up the tree, take hold of the branches, and actually reach heaven through the crown.

I shall never forget the Jew (how I admired and envied him!) who for several days was my sawing partner and who always maneuvered himself into facing east in the morning in the direction of the rising sun. This was simply a preliminary jockeying for position so he could be facing east for the Amida prayer in compliance with orthodox law. Afterward, he would not move his feet but only shift his body in a combined sawing and praying motion and fervently recite, "Hear our voice, Lord our God; spare us and have pity on us; accept our prayer in mercy and favor." He said "*our* voice," "spare *us*," "*our* prayer," all in the plural according to the text of the prayer. But at the time it seemed to me that he was using the plural because he was also speaking for me.

An echo of our North reached my friends. I have a New Year's card which Hayyim and I sent to Vilna on December 1, 1940. It was written on a piece of paper we had found and sent in an envelope we had fashioned out of another piece. Hayyim had written it because we had to be careful about associating in the camp and signed it with his assumed name, Rosenbaum. It was addressed to our friend Leah Epstein ("Aunt Leah").

"As for me, I'm alive, healthy, working, and happy with my fate. I am in the Far North. The frost is very severe. Zundel [1] is here with me. He is alive and healthy. He will also write you soon . . . If possible send some money and a package."

The return address gave no indication that we were in a prison camp. It simply gave a post office box number in a postal region of the Komi ASSR. The note communicated everything that was important, "alive, healthy, working, and happy with my fate."

[1] A name I sometimes assumed.

Globerman's Debt to the State

Whatever I did, I tried above all to keep out of the way of the officials. If we slowed down, they would inundate us with vile abuse. The mildest of these were "carrion," "bitch," "malingerer," and "parasite." The foreman or overseer would look at me as I stood with trembling knees, heavy feet, and an aching body from which every bit of vitality had been sucked, and measuring with his eyes the hole I had managed to dig or the tree I had felled, would ask, "So, Hat, you decided to be a nobleman here, too, and sabotage our great work of construction?" (They called me Hat because of my headgear; they found it difficult to remember or pronounce the name Globerman. Actually, it was not really a hat but a winter cap called "ski-cap" with earflaps and a visor which was common in Poland before the war.)

During all this time, it was difficult to preserve in my heart the principles I had been brought up on in my youth movement about the sanctity of labor and its redeeming qualities. Against the background of my enslaving and degrading surroundings, memories of these principles echoed like taunts.

But the most cynical mockery came in the evening after our return to camp from the forest or the railroad. Right after we had gulped down the soup, the "educator" would come into the hut. He was called educator to bear out that "our penal system is not vindictive but educational." The educator's task was to give us pep talks to complete the quotas, work harder for the good of the country, and do penance for our sins. It was not enough that our square and cubic meters of work determined the size of our bread ration, impelling us to greater effort for the sake of one or two hundred grams. It also seemed necessary to try to transform sinners and jailbirds into partners in the grand pretentions of the fatherland, partners of a mighty people sweeping along in an access of love toward the brilliance of Communism.

Hungry, dead tired, and wrapped in stinking rags, we had to participate in meetings conducted inside the camp and listen to harangues designed to lift our morale.

The educator came to our hut nearly every evening to summarize loudly the achievements and shortcomings of each inmate — who had done his duty to his country, exceeding his quota, and who, perish the thought, had lagged behind, living on charity, because even a punishment ration of three hundred grams of bread a day, which made you shudder, is a handout to a loafer. The educator read from a table in his hand, "This one one hundred percent," and this one hundred twenty, and that one eighty or ninety. "You have to get on the ball a little," he would tell the latter. Frequently he would come to Globerman and read off bitterly, "In all, fifty or *sixty* percent. Then he would announce, "Globerman still owes a debt to the state." Despite my dejection, I could scarcely contain my laughter. I would whisper to my companions, "We're not so badly off after all. I have business relations with the Soviet power. Now I am in debt to it and tomorrow it will be in debt to me as is customary between partners in business. No, my stock is not entirely worthless — I still have status."

One hundred and twenty percent of the quota, one hundred, eighty, sixty. Perhaps that is how the wretched have always been making the world progress? Since the creation of the world is it not the slaves who have been building civilization?

The civilization builders of the Far North were awakened before dawn. Officially reveille was at five, but in practice it was earlier. The strokes of a hammer on an iron bar rent the stillness of the night and spread terrifying sounds to all corners of the camp. Reveille! Like ghosts shrouded in rags, the camp's denizens staggered to the kitchen for their morning soup. The tumult in the camp mixed with the howling of the watchdogs. The watchtowers exchanged blinker signals. Shouts of hurry came from all directions. In a few minutes, it would be time for each prisoner to go to work with his labor brigade.

The camp was in a turmoil. Men were falling in. There were curses, reprimands, and shouts to hurry. The boilers of hell began heating up. Near the gate there was continual counting. Various numbers were written down on plywood tablets. Each labor brigade received its armed escort.

The same procedure was followed every day. As a group left the gate, the rifleman escorting it would call out a familiar refrain, "A step either to the right or the left is like running away. I shall fire without warning." After we had been there a while, we no longer let the soldier finish his announcement. When he began with "A step either to the right . . ." we completed the rest in chorus. It was a game with us — like school pupils who already know their teacher and everything he can possibly say. The soldier, on his part, generally did not complain of our joking. We even bore him no ill; there was certainly nothing to envy him for. Although his food and clothing were far better and he did not have to do backbreaking work, there are greater pleasures than being attached to a group of prisoners in the northern forests for twelve hours a day.

When we reached the work site, either in the forest or near the rail line, the soldier accompanying our group would mark off the boundary beyond which we dared not go. This boundary would immediately be obliterated by rain, snow, or a storm. How could a boundary be recognized in this wilderness other than by a tree or a topographical feature? If someone wandered too far afield and went beyond the boundary by mistake, the quiet and usually restrained soldier would fly off the handle and shout curses and beat the man with his fists and rifle butt. He was very much afraid of his account; he had to return the same quantity of living merchandise to the camp at the day's end.

Today, friends of mine like to joke at my lack of a sense of direction. But my ability to find my way on roads and in streets was not always so bad. I would venture a guess that I lost my sense of direction because of the escorts. For seven years, I did not have to — I was even forbidden to — seek a road for myself or look around. I was always taken and led and all I had to do was follow whoever walked in the lead or to move forward without looking to either side. This is exactly the opposite of what happened to the partisans and people fleeing from the Germans, for example. Their sense of direction became keener. In a few moments they could find their way on unbeaten paths in the depths of a forest.

We liked to tell the joke about a man who was arrested in his hometown and marched away under an armed escort walking behind him with a bayoneted rifle. The prisoner was well known in town and was greatly ashamed at being seen by the passersby. When some acquaintances asked him in amazement, "Where are you going?" he replied, "Hunting."

To the question, "Where's your gun?" he answered, "The man behind me is carrying it."

I repeat this joke because I am grateful for all those among us who kept their sense of humor. I do not really know if laughter is a weapon against dictators, as is commonly believed. However, in my own life, I am certain it served as a strong armor against the vicissitudes of time.

A Land Wrapped in Shrouds

The work was backbreaking. We were tormented by hunger. Dirt consumed us. But there is a scale of preferences in distress. To me it seems that first place in our feeling of anguish went to the cold. A bit of warmth, a moment of thawing out, became an ideal superseding all other desires and taking precedence over longing for one's family, the horrors of lice, and a tortured stomach. In physics at school I had learned that heat causes bodies to expand and cold to contract. This applies not only to inanimate bodies but to living beings as well. It also works this way in the mental sphere. The world of feeling and desires also withers. It seems as if all the desires become concentrated in an exhalation of breath on blue hands.

There were numerous victims of frostbite around me with frozen fingers, noses, and feet. I was not spared either. During the period of my imprisonment in the North, I did not remain all the time at Kilometer 501, where temperatures of 40° (F.) below zero were common. When the mercury dropped to 58° below, there were no horses to do the work, but we still used to go out to build and lay the tracks for the railroad. I also went to a still colder region, the tundra, where frost is eternal.

As chance would have it, the trip from Syev-zhel-dor-lag[1] to Pechorlag[2] afforded me a moving Jewish experience. And fate also wanted me to have this experience while I was watching one of the most "grandiose performances" of the Urkachi.[3]

On the way from one camp to another, we stopped at a distributing station. It was a large "station" divided into separate fenced-off pens between which all contact, not to mention movement, was forbidden. Now and then, a pen emptied — the inmates were taken out to resume their journey — and it filled with new men who had just been cast out of the barges, or railroad cars. It was quite a bustling station.

One day a shipment of prisoners from the Baltic countries, which had been annexed by the Soviet Union in 1940 (just as were Bessarabia and northern Bucovina), arrived and was housed next to my pen. Despite the prohibition, we pressed close to the fence to see what we could find out. Together with us, the Urkachi also stared at the newcomers. Their eyes bulged out of their sockets. Most of the men brought from the Baltic countries still smelled of home and acted as if they were still there. We kept our belongings only in sacks, while they still carried valises of various shapes and colors with shiny locks and zippers. They were neatly dressed and conducted themselves courteously. Many noble, intellectual faces regarded us, although weakness had already left its mark on them. The Urkachi were unable to overcome their astonishment and went into action at once, at first modestly. They started off by offering to barter small articles through the fence, for example, sugar and tobacco for stockings and handkerchiefs.

---

[1] Syeverni zhelezno dorozhni lager: Northern Railroad Camp.
[2] Camps in the Pechora river basin.
[3] Professional criminals who wielded considerable power in the camps, which they terrorized. A special chapter, "Review in Two Acts," has been devoted to their practices and behavior.

Generally, however, the Baltic merchandise would come through the fence, but the Urkachi compensation would somehow be delayed; or bundles full of straw instead of tobacco would be passed to the "Baltic zone" — the Urkachi were experts at restoring old, empty packaging by filling it with ordinary refuse. However, all these subterfuges were not enough to satisfy the desires which had been provoked by the fine clothes; "Where we come from people don't go to the theater like they're dressed for coming to a prisoners' camp," was a common reaction. And quick as a shot they began to clamber over the barbed wire fences and vault into the tantalizing "western zone" for purposes of "cleaning out" the inmates, robbery, and terror while we zapadniki stood close to the fence in order to breathe in something of that other world from which we were already so remote.

At about this time I happened to meet Menahem Begin (who subsequently led an anti-British underground movement in Palestine, headed the nationalist Herut party, and served in the Israeli government as minister without portfolio) among the prisoners brought from Latvia. Several minutes before, I had heard him praised by non-Jews for his noble comportment in a prison cell and in the prisoners' society (that's how it was: at the time that was our principal criterion for measuring a man's worth). I had not known him personally before then, but we exchanged several cordial sentences through the fence, through cracks.

From Begin I learned for the first time of the painful fact that the Revisionist leader Ze'ev Jabotinsky had died several months before. Beside me there stood an eighteen-year-old boy who had belonged to the Beitar — Revisionist youth — organization in a small town. Even here he had "kept his place" all the time and had not dared come too close to Begin. But I cannot forget how, at hearing of the death of Jabotinsky, he choked with tears. And when I passed on the news to an old Jew with whom I had become acquainted at the way-station camp, he went off into a corner and recited Kaddish — the prayer for the dead.

These were drops of purity in the defilement of the distributing station in the Far North.

A brief lesson in geography: the Pechora river is about 1,110 miles long. It originates in the northern Ural mountains and flows into the Barents Sea which is part of the Arctic Ocean.

We were inside the Arctic Circle, not far from the Vorkuta camps which became known to the world after Stalin's death in the summer of 1953 by virtue of a prisoners' mutiny. I must admit that when I heard about this uprising, with action committees, flags, dead and wounded, and negotiations between the prisoners and the authorities, I felt an intimate relationship with them, as if this was news from my native land. However, at that time, in 1941 when I lived in that region, we were impressed mostly by the rumors that at Vorkuta the prisoners were given a hundred grams of vodka daily in addition to their regular rations, for the purpose of withstanding the cold. We could well imagine the severity of the frost there if vodka was included in the menu.

But we had our own troubles. We would pray for the temperature to drop to −76° (F.). According to regulations, we did not have to work when it was that cold. Such days were deducted from the work schedule. However, we only had such luck very rarely. The mercury was possessed of a diabolic patriotism. It would often stop at −74° or −75°. If, thanks to the Creator of frost, it did drop to −76°, it would go up a few degrees and they would hurry to organize work parties, even if half a day had already been lost.

If you had a slice of bread in your pocket, it turned to stone and you couldn't bite into it until you held it over a fire to thaw out. If we stopped moving we could become blocks of stone. Here, in the "Land of the White Death" — which we named a "Land Wrapped in Shrouds" — I encountered what is defined as "geological ice." When we had to dig a ditch, we scraped the surface with sledgehammers and mastered it by millimeters.

In these regions, I sometimes beheld fascinating sights. One of them was the northern lights about which I understand little. I learned that they are the glow of upper atmosphere strata. It seemed to me as if the heavens were indulging in nocturnal carnival games and were scattering colored lights all around them. A wonderful glow filled the entire horizon of the Land Wrapped in Shrouds.

Another sight was the white nights. Quite simply, these were days without nights. It was light all the time, twenty-four hours a day. However, before you have begun to enjoy this natural miracle, you begin to feel its practical side on your skin. At such periods we lost all conception of time. We had no watches and sunrise and sunset marked the beginning and the end of a day for us. But now we went to bed in the daytime and awakened in the daytime. We went to work in the daytime and could not figure out how much more time before we went back to our hut.

I must admit, it was not until I was released from the North that I began to grasp the full splendor of the arctic natural phenomena which I had viewed on a tour for which there had been no charge. There we had other, more prosaic dreams than to admire the scenery.

Government clothes had to protect us from geological cold, eternal frost, blizzards, and rain storms. Our personal clothing gradually wore out. In the beginning we expended a great deal of effort in dragging our bundles with us either out of a naïve reckoning that we would have something to wear when we went home, as merchandise to barter for additional rations, or out of a sentimental attachment to home, to the past. But these clothes were not suitable for the northern polar winter, and the bundles were a burden on our journeys. Weeks of sleeping in clothes completely disfigured them, and our conspicuousness attracted the attention of hoodlums, so that gradually much was either sold or stolen. We did our utmost to take care of our woolen sweaters and socks, but their end came soon, too. It was not long before we were just like everyone else there. We were at the mercy of the storeroom.

The central feature of a prisoner's clothing was cotton batting. We were wrapped up in it like delicate precious objects. Our trousers, a sort of vest, and a short overcoat were all made of thin cloth padded with a layer of cotton batting. The cloth would quickly tear and the cotton batting would inquisitively peek out at the Lord's strange world. If the spark from a cigarette or fire fell on such a garment, it immediately burst into flame. In our attempts to put out the fire we would pull at the cotton and our clothes would begin looking like some monstrous being with fluffy tufts peering out of the eye sockets. Later on, at night in the camp sewing room, the holes would be covered with a series of patches, one over the other, in all sorts of geometric forms and in all colors and hues.

Ruffians and privileged characters in the camp received felt boots for their feet. We others were given a more original substitute for felt boots also made of cloth and cotton batting with soles fashioned from pieces of old tires. In a few days, these shoes would lose their shape and fall off the feet so that they had to be tied on with string and ropes. But, worst of all, they could not withstand wetness even for a few hours. On the contrary, snow and water were absorbed by the cotton. The prisoners called these shoes Che-Te-Ze (the initials of the name Chelyabinski Traktorni Zavod — a famous tractor plant in Chelyabinsk), because the soles were made of waste from the tractors' tires.

In time, the dukes from Poland and other western areas looked like scarecrows for frightening starlings and keeping crows away.

In a special account book all the rags we received were listed and we were financially and even criminally responsible for them. Woe be unto us if something was lost or stolen. Amusing names were used for various articles of clothing; for example, the cotton batting vest was called a "body-warmer" and, more lyrically, a "soul-warmer."

But these were empty words. They did not warm the body, and certainly not the soul. The cold killed. The frost increased the fear of hard labor.

It is no wonder that the nicest dream one had in such a place was to secure some kind of service job inside a building. The westerners had no prospects of working in the kitchen, bakery, bathhouse, workshops, or offices. However, one of us was accorded the special privilege of taking care of the hut and another, of drying the prisoners' clothing at night so they would be ready when the men rose before dawn. The drying room reeked with a suffocating stench. Human sweat and bodily secretions mixed with moisture gave off a horrible odor. But it was warm there.

It's no use talking about the envy of the lucky man who was appointed the director's personal servant in his home. So be it, at least let a friend of yours achieve such happiness; some of his good fortune may drop into your lap, too. He eats there and no longer needs the official soup ration and meager portion of bread.

And so we come to the story of food in the northern camps.

A Man Is Not a Pig

A time came when this whole misfortune of being deprived of freedom, of living behind barbed wire fences in a remote alien land, assumed an abstract, neutral appearance and one felt only the minor irritations of the horror. The great tragedy was splintered into small dramas. Outstanding among these minor irritations were matters pertaining to eating. You forgot your sentence and stopped keeping accounts when it would end; but you were sunk in deep despair if you lost the wooden spoon tied with a rope to your waist or shoe.

We would go to the kitchen for our soup tingling with anticipation. All concern for our fate was thrust out of our consciousness and but a single thought dominated our mind. Would fortune smile upon you and the cook handing out the soup stir the
pot well before pouring your half a liter[1] into your can? There
were a few lucky ones who exultantly proclaimed that they received soup so thick that you could stand the spoon up in it. Some
were even luckier because their portion consisted of soup so thick
that it was almost mush. You could hear tales of wonderful experiences about this.

On the other hand, there were cases of a man's whole world
collapsing about him. You are in line approaching the distribution
window. The soup barrel is nearly empty and way down at the
bottom the soup is naturally thicker. Pieces of fish are floating
around in it and the turnips and potatoes are visible above the
surface of the liquid. The blessing of heaven is to be yours. And
just then, blast it all, several additional pails of soup are brought
from the stove and poured into the barrel and the soup is once
more liquid just when your turn comes. You witness the tragedy
with your own eyes and your heart contracts and fills with grief.
You mutely curse your rotten luck and still try to save the day. In
a plaintive voice of entreaty you appeal to the cook dishing out
the soup, "Give me a little from the bottom, why do you take
only from the top? At least, stir it." But no stirring will change
your luck and get you some of the thick mush.

Five years of imprisonment — what are these compared to
the moments of excitement and trepidation you feel each morning
when bread rations are handed out? Tense with anticipation, you
pray for the heel of the loaf and not the center portion. Even if
they are the same six hundred grams, there is a fatal distinction
between a center slice and a piece from the end of the loaf, which
has more crust. The rations are so microscopic and moist and the

[1] A little more than half a pint.

dough so watery that the extent of the crust has an inestimable value.

Every day there were problems with weighting. You already hold the treasure in your hand. We used the diminutive of endearment to designate our bread; "breadlet" we called it. You heft the piece in the palm of your hand. Sometimes you take advantage of your right and go to have it weighed again. It comes out exact. Not a gram is missing and you are bitterly disappointed. The ration is so tiny and hunger so demanding that you have been having optical illusions.

When the bread was being cut and weighed, it was not always possible to slice the portions exactly correct as required. Consequently, many portions had additional pieces on them. These extra pieces were attached to the ration with a splinter to keep them from falling off and to make sure they were where they belonged. Damn it, it always seems that the extra piece fell off your portion. It sometimes actually happened that the splinter was stuck in the bread but the extra piece had fallen off. They would look for it in the box, in the basket, or in the blanket — depending on how it had been brought. If there was no splinter at all, you would scrutinize the ration from all sides, seeking the hole from which a splinter could have fallen out; perhaps after all this was not the whole portion.

I think the constant sensation of hunger was the main factor in the process of our deterioration to the level of animals, against which a heritage of culture and manners was ineffective. It was in Kotlas, the gateway to the northern camps, that I first saw men with diplomas taking a ration of mush in hats, caps, handkerchiefs, and even cupped hands because they had no dish and would not give up the cooked grits.

This bestial struggle for an extra morsel of food created a new world with values, longings, and fantasies of its own. First of all, while still in prison, we attempted to deceive the stomach by crumbling the bread until it was almost like flour and mixing it with salt and large quantities of water. This delicacy was called "bread sauce." The salty water took on something of the color and taste of bread. You drank it and the bread pap remained. You poured more water on it until the final drop of bread flavor was squeezed out of it. If you ate this bread sauce for dessert after you had filled up on bread water, as it were, it had no taste at all, but you created an illusion for yourself by stretching several hundred grams. However, the optical and time illusion quickly exploded. On the contrary, the salt water only stimulated the appetite and sometimes caused swelling in the body.

I used to do the same to the dried, salted fish. I would soak it in water overnight or for several hours, not, God forbid, to remove the saltiness but, on the contrary, in order not to lose any of its substances and make use of every drop of oil on the bones, fins, and scales. This liquid could be used for making bread sauce and then you really had a delicacy fit for a king.

Another of these illusory maneuvers was to burn bread crusts for the purpose of putting them into boiling water. Allowed to steep, this brew resembled tea in color and some say it even had an aroma.

I felt hungry all the time in the northern camps. During my early days at Kilometer 501, my friend Joseph would sometimes bring me an additional jar of pap. He did well in a trade very much in demand in the first days of the camp's existence; he became a sign painter. Signs had to be posted on all kinds of structures that were going up — the kitchen, office, dispensary, bread-cutting hut, installation for boiling water, and so forth. Joseph had announced that he was an expert in drawing letters. Thanks to his signs, which graced the kitchen and pantry, he received extra food rations. But how long could he drag out his sign painting?

I was overwhelmed by nightmares of hunger. My intestines shrank. Nevertheless, I could not help wondering where all the food I sometimes ate at one sitting went to. Occasionally I would have a stroke of luck. A well-fed cook would come to my hut, or I would hang around the kitchen like a dog near a butcher shop, with my side arm — the drinking can — at the ready. If I was asked to help cut wood or wash the huge pots after a day's work in the forest or on the railroad, I would leap at the chance. Then the question would arise, where did the four or five liters[2] of thick soup I received for my work go to all at once?

The same miracle would happen, but less often, with bread. How did you stuff in three to four kilograms[3] at one sitting without feeling it? Or those rare monthly, bimonthly, or quarterly sugar rations which, for some strange reason, were distributed at night. You received three or four hundred grams of powdered sugar and by the time dawn came, you had finished it, without bread or water, unless you had an account to settle and bartered it at once for bread or soup with one of the privileged inmates.

To tell the truth, it was not only hunger which moved you to eat whatever you received immediately. You were also afraid to leave part of it because it might be stolen. Put it into your stomach and you free yourself of the necessity to mount guard over it; it's the safest storage place.

And what didn't we eat? I shall not go into detail. I shall only repeat a Russian saying current in the camps, "Man is not a pig, he devours everything." We had dreams about every imaginable kind of delicacy. Dreams. Nearly every one of us became dietetics experts. Today I have no idea how many calories I need every day and what nutritional elements the food I eat contains. But then I became a full-fledged professor, an authority on calories and vitamins. I knew all about calcium, carbohydrates, starches, fats, and iron, which foods contain what is good for the eyes or the bones, spine, and kidneys. This familiarity stemmed not only from the instinct of self-preservation but also from the

[2] 1 liter = 1.057 qt.
[3] One kilogram = 2.2 lbs.

fact that officially the camp menu was based on the amount of calories and other elements necessary for survival.

For survival, pure and simple. The Russians actually told you, "We do not live here, we survive."

After several years, I learned that many Russians know how to distinguish clearly between food for calories and food for taste. But at that time we had little interest in taste and kept accounts of our calories. Some even drew up balance sheets of calories and movements — a sort of income and expense tally. They knew how many calories were required for a certain physical effort and attempted to economize on expenses (movements) according to the income (calories). A solution was never found to the controversial question: Which was preferable, economizing on energy with less bread and soup, or squandering energy and more bread and soup?

The feeding system in the camp was based on various caldrons chiefly corresponding to your productivity, to the quotas you filled, within the framework of your physical classification. Your quotas determined the size of your bread ration and the kind of caldron from which you were fed. It sometimes happened that the worst caldron was superior to the best one. Generally, however, there were considerable differences among them for the prisoners. When you broke records, you could enjoy the Stakhanovite kettle which also contained something baked and a special sauce. However, that did not answer the question of the cost in energy you had to pay for the calories in these foods.

An army moves on its stomach. The army of prisoners I was in reduced all its desires to its stomach. When new inmates arrived from other camps, the first question they were asked was, "How is the food there, in the place you come from?" I used to let my imagination run wild. I would imagine myself being set free and making sure that I always had a store of foodstuffs with me, bags of bread, jars of oil, and a sack of potatoes and onions. I was a speculator hoarding goods in flights of fancy.

I must admit that I was not free of this nightmare for many years after I had been released and had left Russia, after years of plenty. There were times in Russia when I not only did not lack calories but also had a varied diet. But I had conceived such a respect for bread that I always ate it carefully to keep crumbs from falling off and when a piece did fall, I would pick it up and put it into my mouth.

And to this day I am allergic to leaving any food or throwing away leftovers, and especially to wasting bread in any form whatsoever.

Wounds and Bruises and Festering Sores

I once described my daily life in the northern camp to a group of friends and someone asked a naive, amusing question, "What did you used to do in the evening?" The problems of an affluent society seeking ways of killing time and "Where are we going tonight?" did not trouble us. Not only did you return from the forest or the rail line dead tired but the evenings were completely filled up with various occupations.

First of all, of course, we were getting something to eat and seeking desperately for an extra morsel.

In Hebrew there is a disparaging expression, "worth a garlic skin." It has a Yiddish equivalent, "It's worth an onion." But in the camps such locutions are not worth anything; and, on the other hand, a clove of garlic or a leaf of onion skin were substantial acquisitions for us. In order to secure these items, you had to employ guile, resourcefulness, diplomacy, pull, perspicacity, and sharp wits, not to mention the need for luck.

A second occupation consisted of sewing or taking articles to the sewing room and drying your clothing yourself or taking it to the drying room in order to be ready for the following day's work.

Among all these, you come to the bathhouse, one of the North's greatest nightmares. When, on your return to camp, you passed in through the gate and were informed that there was a "bath," you felt as if you had been told Job's news. To make sure no one evaded the bath, the group would generally not be fed until its return from washing. The bathhouse was a torture chamber. The taps seldom worked. There was never enough hot water. There was constant fighting over possession of the wooden bucket. You often stood soaped in the thin, stinking soap without being able to rinse it off. Often the bathhouse was not heated and you shivered. It was there that you underwent the charming "sanitary processing." Scores of men were shaved in the groin and under the armpits with the same razor.

After all these attractions, you had to go out from the main hall and wait naked in the corridor for quite a while until the window of the disinfecting room opened and the clothing you had handed in previously was returned. This disinfecting room bore the descriptive designation of voshoboika (lice-killer). You could hardly recognize your garments, firstly, because of the steam issuing from them, and secondly, for the reason that each bundle was just like the other — the same cotton batting and the same rags. Here, too, I cannot help mentioning the wonderful sense of humor of men living in a hell on earth. The man in charge of the voshoboika would lift up each bundle and inquire whose it was and each time someone would reply, "The director's." They all belong to the director. You received them all from the government. They all look exactly alike. They are all the director's."

Going to the dispensary was one of those occupations having predestined significance. You went there with aches and pains, burns and wounds, dizziness and fever, diarrhea and vomiting, but you also went there with a spark of hope for a miracle. Perhaps you would be granted one day off from work.

The master of the dispensary was not a physician but a "medical assistant." This man's medical knowledge was doubtful and his authority limited. He could only release from work if the patient had a certain temperature and the number of releases he could issue was apparently subject to a quota. If to that are added the favors to be done in exchange for a bribe or for fear of bullies, it is obvious that prospects of anyone from the rank and file of prisoners receiving a work release, even though he might be writhing in agony, were very slim. Some of us would pray for a slight illness in order to be accorded the happiness of remaining in the hut for a day or two. If this hope materialized for someone and he had the necessary temperature, we would congratulate him and wish him health. However, usually you would return from the dispensary disappointed, with some kind of standard pill.

In desperation some men tried to realize their desire for a day in the hut by manipulating the thermometer (we had one official rest day once every few weeks which they filled with all kinds of "activities"). However, an act of this sort nearly always resulted in curses and even blows, and disappointment was not late in coming. Someone attempted to rub the thermometer a little but he was detected and his temperature taken again, revealing the ruse. There were men who were taken in by the rumor that several drops of kerosene in water would perform the miracle. Some began rubbing garlic under the armpits. Whether or not it really helped or was useless, the smell gave them away in advance and their malingering tricks were severely punished.

Extreme acts of desperation were expressed in attempts to maim oneself. This was the most dangerous form of deception not only because of the risk of remaining a cripple but also because of the seriousness of the offense of inflicting bodily harm on oneself which was liable to bring in its train additional imprisonment.

It was not so easy to get to the dispensary. Sometimes you stood in line for hours in the cold outside the door, freezing, shivering, and shifting from one foot to the other. For there were many who came to seek assistance and try their luck. Sometimes the line would not grow shorter at all and you would stand in one place without moving ahead. One after the other, bullies of one kind or another would come and go inside without waiting. Sometimes they too would come for treatment but usually they just wanted a little alcohol, or if there wasn't any, a few drops of valerian as a substitute. And you just try making a remark; you would never look for justice here again. Once, one of us westerners told such a ruffian that there was a line, and it was the latter who spoke in the name of justice, or, I would say, broad, human, historical justice, "We have already stood in lines enough; now, you stand for a while."

I and many like me stopped depending on the dispensary after a while. We reached the state where the dispensary lost all authority for us. We were classified in categories which Socialist reconstruction no longer took into consideration.

This you must know. All the time the prisoner is in the camp, he is classified, numbered, and given a designation. He forms disciplined lines for health, work category, to fill his drinking can, and also for political and police purposes, depending on the offense and the section which determine what his rights and restrictions are. I began my career in the North at "heavy hard labor," quickly passed to "medium hard labor," and then proceeded to "light hard labor." In all these categories, the variations are still small and you go out to "production," which means you work outside the camp and not on service jobs inside. Later I was assigned to "weak units" numbers one, two, and three. Shortly after that, I was transferred to a sort of small hospital, then to a "recovery center," and finally back to the top again quickly to descend the whole gamut once more.

Hygiene had long since become a nonsensical joke to us.

Through all sorts of devious subterfuges, someone managed to keep a toothbrush, but how long would this queer person hold out with his brushing? Sheets and pillowcases were inanities of the pampered. For weeks you did not undress or change a shirt. For days you did not rinse your rusty mess gear. You only wiped them after the meal with a piece of bread, chiefly for the purpose of salvaging something edible, and licked your spoon before sticking it into your boot or pocket. Ten mouths inhaled and sucked your cigarette butt. The lice swarmed over the body and in the clothing in battalions and heaps, and you would fling handfuls on the ground into the snow. We even stopped scratching.

And now, for our relations with medicine. We were witnesses of a typical phenomenon. The husky, muscular, and corpulent men were struck down by diseases, infirmity, and death more often than the naturally weak and thin ones. The self-indulgent ones, I would say, withstood hunger better than the rugged types whose bodies demanded more and collapsed more quickly in times of want. In any case, the number of deaths increased.

Those among us who knew Russian recalled a sarcastic revolutionary slogan from before the Revolution: "The Czar has issued a manifesto [in Russian, *manifest*]: For the dead — freedom; for the living — arrest."

I do not know which was more horrible — the fact of death or the behavior of those remaining alive who used to play a trick on the authorities and receive the bread rations apportioned the day before to a prisoner who had died during the night. It is a question also, which was more dreadful — the actual dead who had reached their last stop, or the potential dead wandering about like ghosts. The prisoners invented a terrible name for them: Dokhodyagi — "Those about to approach it." Many have gone to their eternal rest in unmarked graves under the snow of the Far North. Only in our hearts would we accord them the last rites. But the officials and camp ruffians were unimpressed. "We have enough earth for all of them," they would say.

We were ravaged by two principal diseases: dysentery and scurvy. Both result from a deficiency of food elements. Not only did we suffer from constant undernourishment, but for many months we had no fresh vegetables. Everything came out of cans, including potatoes and onions. The first symptoms of scurvy were spongy gums and falling teeth. In its more severe stages, when alimentary dystrophy (what a vocabulary I acquired at the University of the North) appeared, the body swelled and became covered with sores running with blood and pus so that the men could not bend and had to move their bowels in a nearly standing position.

As far as I can remember, I only declined to the state of a Dokhodyaga physically. For it is also a mental condition of indifference and insensibility and of helpless resignation.

The first malady I tasted was "chicken blindness." I recall it well. Together with several others, I was being taken to work at cutting hay in a very damp place. We were brought there on foot. We had to cross the river, either in boats or on foot, half naked. We were eaten up by mosquitoes, against which they gave us nets. It was difficult to breathe under the nets and they were not entirely effective. The mosquitoes would slip inside and remain there, unable to leave. One day while being escorted back to camp from the field, I discovered that I could not see my way (there were soon many others in the same predicament), and a friend helped me. This was the modest beginning, the next stages of which are competently described by the prophet Isaiah, "From the sole of the foot even unto the head there is no soundness in it, but wounds, and bruises, and festering sores; they have not been pressed, neither bound up, neither mollified with oil."

In this condition I appeared before a medical board. Three physicians, all prisoners, came to us from a camp serving as an administrative center. Despite the fact that they themselves had been sentenced to ten years' imprisonment, they had wide powers. But that is not what I remember about them. I shall not forget the glow of their faces. They were enough to rehabilitate a man. They were the personification of humaneness and compassion. Their white gowns remained pure. Their wearers had not betrayed the image of man and their professional mission. For the first time I was not being examined just to fill out another form. For the first time I felt kindly eyes and not the look of a robot.

All this could have been a little pleasant if I had not overheard them sadly whispering my sentence to each other, "Finished and only a question of time." The days that followed, even though they stretched out more than the allotted time, nearly confirmed the medical forecast proclaimed by the mode of our existence. Some fellow prisoners no longer hesitated to devise means of laying their hands on my bread ration of the morrow or the day after, which I would no longer need.

Even before the arrival of the medical board, an all-out war against scurvy was inaugurated in the camp. The fight was intensified on the board's appearance. How did they combat the disease? We had to stand in line to a special station (in order not to put an excessive load on the dispensary) for a spoonful of cod-liver oil and a clove of garlic. After that, they began giving us special scurvy rations consisting of fresh vegetables, including raw potatoes, cut into tiny pieces or mashed. Finally, the battle assumed a mass, wholesale aspect on a grand scale; pine needles were boiled in huge cans. This, by the way, was the special task of the "weak units." They had to pluck thin pine branches and strip and cook the needles. Drinking this beverage was recommended wholeheartedly by various slogans. This was supposed to have saved us. The brew was as bitter as gall but we drank it greedily. Someone remarked, "The problem of drink has been solved; soon we shall begin eating pinecones and the food problem will also be solved." We grasped at a slim belief that the pine drink really had secret medicinal properties and gulped it down, moved by the poetic words hung across the camp on a huge banner and painted on the huts, "Pey khvoi, nye zaboleyesh tsingoi [Drink pine needles and you will not come down with scurvy]."

I do not know whether or not this potion helped me a great deal. But what does it matter by what means or wonders death was cheated? Anyway, it was a collective miracle. Just as the number of victims grew, so did the number of those escaping their doom increase.

And I am sorry for them, for the wretches who turned into jackals besetting a person about to become a corpse. They already made plans how to put one over on the authorities in order to get an additional miserable ration of bread — and my fate played a trick on all medicine. I swear, it's not my fault for having disappointed them! . . .

Straw of the Mind

We were neither dead nor alive but merely existing, for man is an adaptive creature. I think the commonest expression heard in the camps was "You'll get used to it." Purists and sticklers among the privileged inmates and old-timers would add, by way of explanation, "If you don't get used to it, you'll croak." Apparently, I made the first alternative. It was only at the outset that I thought every day would be my last and that if I remained alive, I would certainly go out of my mind. Slowly, you "get along" with the new life and become reconciled to it. You adapt yourself and come to feel at home in this existence with its fears and nightmares, its futility and senselessness.

Now and then some secret mechanism deep in the soul would produce a kind of self-encouragement, "Just hold on." Various rumors reflecting the operation of this secret mechanism would make the rounds and go from mouth to ear. I found out that in all the camps prisoners are nourished by doses of similar rumors of improvements, easier conditions, and amnesties just over the horizon.

Our rumor mill worked at top speed. This was furthered by the fact that we were outsiders and war refugees. There was fertile soil for rumors of intervention, demands from abroad, negotiations, and similar prospects. Thus, someone "heard" that Molotov, as commissar for foreign affairs, was having some "unpleasantness" because of us and that Churchill himself was interested, that Roosevelt had made inquiries, and that the Polish government in exile in London was not giving anyone any rest — in short, the whole world was in a turmoil because of us.

The rumors would become more stubborn before dates and holidays suitable for generous gestures. So it came about that we expected great news just prior to the anniversary of the October Revolution, on the eve of the First of May and the birthday of Stalin the merciful and the compassionate, on Lenin Day, at the approach of Constitution (Stalin's) Day, Red Army Day, and New Year's. At such times, you always heard that "something is cooking" in Moscow and that in camp the first signs of it had already been discerned. Perhaps there would not be wholesale release but our files might be reexamined. Many saw their sentences being reduced. "Listen, Russia cannot afford to tell the whole world to go whistle. Listen, lists are already being compiled in the documents office. Listen to this, means of transportation are already being considered. Certainly, they will not tell you anything until the last moment. They keep everything a secret but preparations cannot be concealed."

One day a rumor became widespread that the "foreigners" were being sent away, deported pure and simple. Reactions were, "Let them deport us — we'll take off our hats and say thank you." "We'll kiss their hands," the Poles would add with their inborn politeness. Another time, a rumor appeared that we would only be transferred to camps in the South. This, too, was regarded as salvation. *South* was an enchanting dream in the frozen North.

And if not complete release, deportation, or transfer to the warm, dreamy South, there was a rumor of changing our sentences to what was called "free dismissal." You would again become a "citizen" and could move about within a considerable radius and live as you wished. They had already begun to check lists of those who were leaving; they had already begun "preliminary registration" (what beautiful, intelligent-sounding words rang out in the savage northern wastes).

Rumors came and went but the camp remained. Disappointment would sweep away the lift in our moods and bury the sweet illusions. And precisely on the eve of holidays, there would be rigorous searches instead of releases and improvements. The practice in Soviet prisons and camps was to carry out a closer scrutiny for forbidden articles before holidays. ("We have a cannon hidden in our behinds," we would tell the searchers.) In the camps such searches aroused smiles of amazement. They gave us tools like axes, sledgehammers, and saws, but in the huts, penknives were confiscated. Roll call was also ridiculous. Each one had already repeated the refrain of his data numberless times — his given name, surname, patronym, number of the section under which he was sent up, and sentence. Apparently searches and roll calls were an important ceremonial in the daily life of the NKVD's empire.

Slowly the feeling of being privileged which we "refugees" and "aliens" had had vanished. We also ceased waiting for miracles or mercy. The heavens were high and Moscow was very far away.

Some of the knowing ones among us believed that the various attractive rumors had been circulated on purpose from time to time by our "bosses" on the assumption (a correct one) that bad morale and complete dejection also interfere with production plans. The officials were also interested in calming the men as a prophylactic measure against resentment and possible mutiny.

However, I tend to the view that these rumors were essentially the result of wishful thinking, born of the instinct of self-preservation. For not only did we grasp at the straw of the body but also at the straw of the mind to save our lives.

Just as we did not know how these rumors came into being so we did not know how they disappeared. It was difficult to play around with illusions for any length of time. Reality all around us violently contradicted them. What was there to say? The words of an official who would spur us on with pathetic speeches rang truer: "Throw all thoughts of the past away. You're going to live here until your dying day, so why don't you pool all your strength together, as a team, to make life in this place beautiful."

The shattered illusions gave rise to an opposite conviction, pointed up by the Russian saying, "Moscow does not believe in tears."

Human Landscapes on the Move

I regarded the camps as a kaleidoscope of mankind whose human landscapes were always on the move and quickly changing. I knew thousands of them. I myself was shifted around many times from place to place and the same happened to thousands of others. The world of prisoners is in constant motion, like barter merchandise.

It is a fact that construction methods, production, and economical considerations determined the distribution of all this manpower. These masses of men can be credited with mastering remote regions, establishing gigantic enterprises, and building railroads, power stations, and canals.

As I heard from Russian epigraph writers,

Belomor Kanal kopal, kopal,
Da domoi nye popal.

Which means, *Belomor Canal*,[1] *I dug, I dug,*
But home I did not return.

There is no problem here of mobilization, persuasion, propaganda, and volunteering. Who would travel to a northern wilderness of his own free will? For the reeducation techniques of the NKVD it is only a question of transportation. That is not so difficult since the travelers are not choosy. Another problem is that of providing guards. But that is why there are permanent NKVD military units.

Some people say that the transfers are simply a part of the punishment calculated to feed you an additional dose of suffering. I cannot determine the truth of this version. I feel sure that, among other things, the journeys had a simple function, that of preventing a sort of settling down of the prisoners, to keep them from feeling too much at home in a certain locality and eliminate the possibility of close ties with officials, guards, and free hired laborers employed in services and as white-collar workers. Such ties could lead to a breach in the prisoner's isolation and sometimes cause him to think about and even make plans for escaping. Ties between prisoners, ties which might grow closer in the course of living together, were frowned upon since they might be a source of trouble and association for all sorts of purposes. Consequently, the transfers were like shuffling the cards every once in a while for the purpose of unexpectedly and at one fell swoop breaking up associations and friendships.

The prisoners were used to it. Confirmed criminal offenders who spent all their lives — with the exception of short "vacation" intervals — in camps completely lost all their ties with their real native country. For example, when a man of this sort came to

---

[1] The Belomor Canal, which had been named for Stalin, linked the White Sea with the Baltic. It was a huge project completed by vast numbers of prisoners.

us we would ask him where he was from. It would never occur to him to say Kiev or Minsk or whatever his hometown would be. He would answer, Kalima (a famous camp in the Far East), Karaganda (a camp in Central Asia), Murmansk, or Archangel. His native land was the place where he stayed the longest in his prison career. However it may be, this state of affairs caused a varied parade of human landscapes to cross my path.

Who were the camps' inmates? Early in my life as a prisoner, my contacts were limited to people from regions I was familiar with. Over a million and a half persons were arrested or expelled in western Byelorussia and the Ukraine (parts of former Poland) from the date of the Soviet occupation (September, 1939) until the German invasion of the USSR (June, 1941). These were joined by prisoners from Bessarabia, Bucovina, and the Baltic countries annexed by the Soviet Union. It was only natural that a sort of common fate should bind me to these "foreign" masses of humanity, especially to the large numbers of Jews among them.

Gradually, however, I was engulfed by Great Russia around me. I actually felt as if all of the mighty Soviet Union was with me, every class and nationality, every occupation, every social level, and all punishable ages (apparently from thirteen and above) of both sexes. Everyone was represented here — city and village, the worker-farmer-intellectual triangle, permanent citizens and visitors from abroad, privileged characters and ordinary Russians, officers and soldiers, top-ranking officials and simple workers. It was a wonderful fusion, an ideal equality of opportunity. It is possible to fill many pages with jokes and sayings at the expense of this comprehensiveness, all having the same point — all of us are either actual or potential jailbirds.

I met the victims of various purges. They were brought here in waves for arrest and trial. Most of them came under a very broad section of the law, dealing with counterrevolutionary activities. This section has many subsections. The worst are dealing with treason and armed rebellion (or attempted rebellion). There is also a section entitled "Trotskyite and counterrevolutionary activity." However, Section 58's most popular subsections are 10 and 11, dealing with anti-Soviet propaganda (10: alone; 11: together with others). The Russians simply call these subsections "chatter," for usually all this agitation consists of is an unpremeditated conversation, a slip of the tongue, or a chance remark.

As far as we westerners were concerned these were the vast horde of political prisoners. However, the Soviet authorities do not recognize this terminology. They call them enemies of the people, counterrevolutionaries. I was told that until the middle thirties these people had some privileges, constituting a special class in the camps. However, during the wild rampage of the Stalinist terror, they lost the last of their preferred status. On the contrary, the authorities treated them as the lowest of criminals. Counterrevolutionaries also included people incarcerated under no specific section of the law but defined as disloyal elements, dangerous social elements, or harmful social elements. Many of them were labeled "P. Sh.," meaning that they were suspected of espionage. There were people here from the times of Yezhov and Yagoda and even earlier purges. You could find prisoners sentenced to five and ten years who were here long after their period of "reeducation" had expired. The people serving terms in excess of their sentences were mostly from the ranks of the counterrevolutionaries. When the time for their release came, they would be called in to listen to an announcement that their imprisonment had been extended "until further notice."

There were people charged with every conceivable sort of offense. The long list included gangsters, saboteurs, arsonists, smugglers, murderers, rapists, terrorists, thieves, embezzlers, former prosperous farmers, peasants opposed to collectivization, pickpockets, burglars, abortionists (violating a 1935 prohibition), persons who had come in contact with foreigners, members of religious sects, mystics, Subbotniki (Sabbatarians), priests, deserters, spies, foreign agents, givers and receivers of bribes, self-mutilators, procurers, nationalists, inciters to rebellion, and agitators for the secession of constituent USSR republics. There were also people sent up by some administrative decree punishing them for absenteeism, negligence at work, and making inferior products. You could find persons charged with squandering public property, stealing from the government's treasury, failure to hand over internal enemies, and illegal border crossings. You met pure-blooded Russians and the members of various minority groups. There was one man there called "Raskolnikov" and another, "Al Capone."

I am purposely listing them all mixed up since I cannot enumerate them all with all their differences, for that is how they really looked to me. All of them were in one huge mill grinding young and old, intellectual and illiterate, ruffian and weakling. It seems to me that if every year I used my annual vacation for traveling, I would never until my last day make the acquaintance of the human mosaic which the NKVD "tourist agency" showed me in concentrated form. They took me to a rogues' gallery and presented living criminals to me in an ethnographic and sociological museum.

I learned a great deal through observation, listening, and close contact. For example, the sentences showed obvious relative clemency for thieves and burglars operating against private citizens. Sentences for stealing large sums were, as it is called there, very "childish." On the other hand, a relatively small theft of government property was severely punished.

There was one matter I thought about a great deal. Be it as it may, there were very many political prisoners here, opponents of the regime and its enemies. One could say that these were people rooted in the past, held down by an obsolete tradition, who had never reconciled themselves to the fact that they had been deprived of honor or possessions. They were individuals clinging to certain social and religious ideas. But why were there so many criminal offenders, corrupt petty thieves like the ones caught misappropriating apples in collective farms here? Wasn't I also one of those who believed that crime only resulted from a cruel regime of exploitation, want, and robbery? I shall not discuss the types and various kinds of my social acquaintances in the camps any further. I shall only write about two categories. The first are the confirmed criminals and nearly perpetual inmates of the camps. I shall touch of them later on in describing my next arrests. But now I should like to tell about the Communists who attracted my special attention and constituted a group apart. My encounters with these were very instructive.

Before a Broken Trough

Former Communists felt more than others the need to pour their hearts out to someone. They were sunk in deep dejection. Sometimes they would be overcome by a desire to talk and their words would come in a swelling torrent.

Apparently I had a name for a good listener. To tell the truth, I liked such stories and swallowed them with hungry curiosity. That was perhaps the background for the close friendships I formed with a number of former Communists, even though each of us reached the camp from different worlds. Furthermore, paradoxically, they gave me some encouragement because they were the only ones among those whose fate I shared who envied me a little. I suffered like them. I was as hungry and emaciated as they, but my mental, spiritual world had not crashed. Theirs had collapsed like a house of cards. Their suffering was hugely magnified. Their whole aim in life had been swept away. They considered themselves cheated, shamed. No hostile regime could have left them as morally naked and exposed as the regime which was their ideal and for which they had been ready to give their lives. They were confronted by an empty trough, not knowing how to begin again.

I made my first acquaintance with a Jewish Communist from Poland while working in the forest. We were a team uprooting and splitting trees some distance from the others. He had confidence in me, which loosened his tongue. Except for me, there was no one else in this place, outside the birds, who could have overheard him. I must admit that first of all I was enthralled by his talent for telling a story and his ability to spice his stirring tales with self-deprecatory anecdotes.

In our first conversations he already found a humorous way of his own of drawing a parallel between us. Once when he was still in Poland and deeply involved in the activities of a secret Communist cell, a young couple from a Zionist youth movement came to ask him to contribute to a fund for planting trees in Palestine. His reply to them was, "Really, why do you have to work so hard to plant trees in such a barren land? Who knows how much it costs to plant a tree in such desolation? In Russia, you can find as many forests as you want, enough for your children and grandchildren. Go and enjoy them." And after a brief pause, he went on, "And here we are, the two of us, standing in these forests and enjoying them, enjoying them immensely."

How did he get here? He came from a Polish city occupied by the Germans. He fled from there to the "liberated" part of Poland. He had never wanted any credit for his work in the Polish Communist underground, persecuted by the authorities, and for the years he had spent in a Polish prison as a result of his activity. However, when he reached the Russian-occupied zone and came to a western Byelorussian city, the Comrades tendered him a warm welcome. He was at once given a position worthy of his past and his abilities.

But his honeymoon with the liberators and redeemers was short-lived. It was not long before he began to sense a cooling off, a drawing away from him, and discomfort. The explosion was not late in coming. It began with "transfers," demotions, and discharges and ended up with "invitations" to come see the head of a certain department. It turned out that these were preliminaries to investigation and arrest.

All his trouble stemmed from the fact that he had been released from the Polish prison in spite of everything after having served his sentence. Something smells here; they were suspicious. What does it mean? These Fascists take Communists and set them free just like that? There must be a very obscure chapter, apparently some ineradicable stain, in his biography. He must have promised them something. He probably joined them, signed up, made revelations, began working for them, serving them, burying former comrades of his, informing on them. In short, he had become an agent of theirs. Actually nothing could be proved. His former party comrades had nothing against him. That, however, only heightened the suspicion that he was a talented, well-trained agent good at dissembling. Of course, he had held his own during the investigations and succeeded to such an extent that he had convinced the interrogator to delete some of the original charges against him. However, this success in no way affected the outcome. The nameless (and notorious as well) institution pronounced him "unreliable," and he was relegated to the great melting pot.

"Is all this really new to you?" I asked. "Didn't you know that hundreds and thousands were arrested in Russia in the thirties? That many were exiled and vanished? Didn't the great trials which set the world agog touch you at all before this? Everyone knew that unbridled terror had reigned against tens of thousands in addition to the great trials."

Despite the incoherent manner in which he spoke, his answers were organized and systematic. You could see that he knew how to carry on a discussion. There was something of the lecturer even in his heart-to-heart, friendly, almost intimate conversation.

"It would be a flight into falsehood," he began formulating his reply, "to claim, as many Communists have done, that I did not know anything, or rather, to say that such a possibility never occurred to me. I was never taken in by the oversimplified explanations that all accounts of a Red terror were a lot of hogwash and were not more than atrocity propaganda invented by enemies of the Soviet Union. I did, however, assume that the reports exaggerated a great deal, but I was certain that there was a grain of truth in them. And, to tell you the truth, I don't mind admitting openly that that was what hurt most; not that I did not deny these accounts either to myself or to others but just because I did, I lent a certain credence to them without my being in the least shocked. On the contrary, it all seemed perfectly natural to me. A certain kind of terminology was, as far as I was concerned, a wall of reinforced concrete against which heretical doubts crashed even before becoming fully formed — 'Capitalist encirclement, historical truth versus subjective justice, the necessity of self-defense, vigilance against imperialistic wolves constantly weaving intrigues,' and finally — 'It is better for hundreds of innocent persons to be in prison than for a single guilty individual to escape the protectors of the Communist system.' Yes, I was immune to shocks and I learned well the popular proverb which we all knew by heart and which seemed so indisputably right, 'Splinters must fall where trees are being chopped down.' There was no avoiding this inexorable law so long as Communism had not achieved its final, worldwide victory."

"Until you yourself became one of those splinters!" I interrupted.

He was not embarrassed. Here, in the Far North, he had long ago stopped seeking refuge in speculative logic and simply replied, "Maybe. Perhaps I really do see myself now as a fallen splinter. I possess the insight resulting from personal experience. But there is more to it than that. To tell the truth, my complete collapse did not come about at my arrest or while I was being interrogated or my sentence was being handed down but when I became aware of this reality.

"If the regime is suspicious of everyone who is part of it and associated with it, it is obvious that it has no trust whatsoever in its superior qualities. What sort of a regime is it in which an entire nation can go to prison? Everything is so topsy-turvy, mixed up, strange. Tomorrow or the day after, I'm liable to meet my interrogators or judges in this place. Who else represents historic truth here? Perhaps only the Man with the Moustache [this was one of common names for Stalin]. So that's how it is; two hundred million people are neither reliable nor safe and only a single individual is to be trusted? It's like an iceberg. Nothing is stable."

We had several conversations like this one. Actually, they can hardly be defined as conversations. They were more like monologues of his interrupted by my heckling — monologues affording psychological release.

And He That Increaseth Knowledge
Increaseth Sorrow

I made the acquaintance of another one after our "housewarming," when we moved from a mud hut to our first wooden shack. We became neighbors on an upper shelf. Incidentally, the shelf was made of rough logs we had cut down in the forest, from which we had stripped the branches; but it was a great step to a better life.

This neighbor of mine had been a Talmudic scholar. He had long ago studied in an orthodox Jewish religious school and had subsequently abandoned his faith. I do not know whether or not he made much use of the sacred studies he was steeped in during the period of his activity in the Polish Communist underground. However, in his conversations with me, he generously displayed his knowledge. He often used to quote the verse from Ecclesias-

tes, "And he that increaseth knowledge increaseth sorrow," adding the interpretation of a famous rabbi, "But it was worth it."

"That was perhaps the only worthwhile compensation for the
suffering of myself and others — we gained knowledge," he
told me.

His life story had many points in common with that of my
previous friend. He came to the Communist underground by way
of an international society for helping revolutionaries. Its avowed
sincere aims were to make legal and material aid available to persons persecuted for revolutionary ideals. The society's members,
mostly young intellectuals, collected money, sent packages to
prisons, and contacted lawyers not especially out of political identification but chiefly because they sympathized with people fighting for an ideal and because of their belief in mankind. But his
society was a hothouse for filling Communist ranks and completing its cells. The party had its eye on it and operated inside it.

He admitted to me that the underground itself attracted him to
Communism as much as the ideology. It held out a special charm
for a man of good family, something of the fascination of a journey to an unknown land, a mixture of vision and adventure, sacrifice and danger, a combination of life as it was and as it would be.
A leap out of the commonplace and release from routine beck-
oned to him. It was also running away from the home which had
oppressed him with all the good in it. He had sought a refuge
from the boredom of plenty and the emptiness of satiety.

However, in time the underground did its work. He encountered people for whom clandestine activity in the party was
neither wine nor the frills of a dessert but rather a slice of coarse
black bread. When such persons sought refuge in the underground, they looked for escape from the wretchedness of everyday life to a world of the future in which everything would be
good.

Let us take a shortcut in the story of my friend and neighbor.
He finally ended up in the place he knew he might reach any

day — Polish prison. There his insight was forged and he spun dreams centered around the destruction of all prisons. He would colorfully describe his fancies behind the bars of Fascist prisons. Perhaps they should not be demolished. Some thought and means ought to be devoted to building them over and transforming the gloomy structures into clubhouses, theaters, and museums. Achitecturally that would not be so easy. All signs of horror and melancholy would have to be obliterated and every memory of bars and bolts, heavy locks, and iron doors would have to be smashed. The torture chambers would have to be completely rebuilt and redone in gay colors. But it would be done. He was confident that a day would come and a mighty blast would shake these walls. Then he would be carried out on the shoulders of his comrades. He was particularly sure of that because of the pride he took in the pathetic speech he had delivered with head erect at his trial. "Now you sit in judgment on me," he flung at the tribunal, "but the day is not far when the people will sit in judgment on you." However, now his romantic words had changed to a minor key. In this place one could not rail and shout. Nothing could make these walls and barbed wire fences shake. They were like the last stop for dreams and fantasies. Henceforth, there would be no more dreaming.

Once more he gave utterance to a romantic tone. "I'm not lamenting my shattered life now, but the dreams of which I have been robbed. Who will restore them to me?"

I Came, I Saw — And I Was Conquered

N. told me a breathtaking story. He was not one of those to whom the Soviet Union had come in 1939 with the "liberation" of the western Byelorussia and Ukraine. He had gone to the USSR from Poland of his own accord, together with his wife, in the early thirties. This happened after he had already served one prison sentence, had been released, and had once more immersed himself with a passion in the activities of an underground cell. One fine day he discovered that he was being followed. He was certain they were planning to arrest him again. He gave his shadowers the slip and lay low for several weeks. His comrades brought his wife to his hideout. Then it was decided to take him across the redeeming border. They only had to wait for a suitable night, a friendly, starless, dark night for an underground worker. Such a night came. It was a wonderful night. One of those about which people say, "Not even a dog should be driven out on a night like this." And if a dog barks, his howling is drowned out by the shriek of the wind, and the pouring rain wipes out your footprints, and your shoes make no sound in the mud. On a night like this, N. headed eastward, his heart beating with hope and anticipation.

The night of redemption it was. He crossed the border and fell into the arms of a patrol, the Comrades who were already waiting for him. All the nightmares were now behind him. He and his wife were jubilant. Their feelings corresponded so much to the huge illuminated motto on the Soviet side of the border town, "A cordial welcome to the persecuted toilers of the west."

In a large Byelorussian city he received a job and an apartment and was content with his modest lot. However, as time went on he discovered that his enthusiasm was waning and being replaced by small doubts. Something he himself could not quite define began gnawing at his fervor.

This man also spoke of a dream that vanished. Naked reality beat against his fantasies and hardly left enough of them to save his life. First of all, he found the propagandistic bragging unbearable. He could not stand the self-praise of the Socialist state and its government for every elementary act they were obligated to do and for every service they had to provide for the citizen. It was

understandable that abroad, in the capitalist world, it was necessary to intensify such propaganda and describe incessantly the
good life and happiness in the fatherland of Communism. Here,
however, if there are happiness and a good life, they should be
apparent, they should be felt. Why should they be a constant subject for conversation? Why must the happy be persuaded so
much of their happiness? Why should so many millions be spent
on matters which should be obvious for everyone to see? And
above all, what was there really to boast of? "We built so many
hospitals and schools." Or, "We constructed cities and roads."
Why not — since the government controlled the entire budget?
The government is the employer. It pays the worker. It is the
cashier. It receives the tax moneys. It manages the entire econ-
omy, and there is no activity outside that conducted by the state.
What sort of benefit is it conferring on the citizen by providing
him with all these services?

The shrill boasting of the achievements of the Communist regime was accompanied by distorted pictures of life abroad which
also offended his sense of the truth. As a matter of fact, he had
seen much poverty and distress in Poland, he went on to tell me.
His work for the party had been chiefly among wretched land-
less farmers and exploited or unemployed workers. However, he
could not stomach generalizations of the sort which claimed that
masses of people were dying of hunger in the streets. Were they
talking to ignoramuses and primitive tribes? He was also bothered by the worship of Stalin and the idolatry surrounding the
man. Is this how intelligent Communists, the avant-garde of mankind, expressed their admiration and respect for their leader?

Another discovery which depressed him was caused by the
misery and want he saw around him while certain groups were
living well and even in luxury. People living from hand to mouth
existed beside drunkards and gluttons. There were long lines for
staples and a curious institution for privileged individuals called

"zakriti larok" (closed shop, that is, closed to outsiders) or "spets torg" (special market). This could not be it! This was cheating, especially the workers in the West dreaming of equality.

He was swept away on a cascade of words which breached the barrier of self-imposed silence to which we were accustomed. "People suffered and were frightened. Nevertheless, they could not keep quiet. They complained and were indignant. I, who had transformed the distress of workers and peasants in Poland into a lever of the Revolution, how was I now to react to the bitterness and complaints of workers and peasants against Socialism fulfilled? I knew that the wisest course for me was to keep my mouth shut. But I also carried on debates with myself. It was not easy to digest my resentment. Somehow, defense mechanisms against threatening doubts came into being inside me. This bitterness, I made an attempt to explain to myself, is perhaps tied to human frailties and is a remnant of bourgeois psychology. Far-reaching changes have not yet been effected. They have not yet managed to plow a deep furrow; and the possessive instinct is still operating among the masses."

However, his doubts increased. At first they were tiny persistent drops corroding the iron of his consciousness. These soon became great blows as people began disappearing. Acquaintances and friends simply vanished.

"Even when confronted by this terrible fact," he continued, "I still tried to argue with myself, as if I were protecting myself from an imminent landslide. I mean a moral, spiritual landslide, the collapse of my world of ideas.

"I could still not imagine in my wildest fancy that the evil would also reach me. Then people of whom I could never believe that they had been traitors, that they had betrayed their country, were arrested. A fog took possession of my mind and clouds began billowing in all directions. Who knows? Hadn't there been instances in our party circles in Poland when good loyal Communists had been seduced from the straight and narrow path and had become informers and traitors? Perhaps in the same way those or some of those arrested had been seduced, missed a step, tripped, and turned agents and saboteurs? Maybe, as time goes on, it will become clear that a mistake was made and they will be sent home? Meanwhile, the Revolution must not be jeopardized."

N. went on with his account. "Friends of mine actually waited for their arrest. They prepared some belongings in a bundle, ready to leave at a moment's notice." As a matter of fact, whenever steps were heard in the front hall, the hearts of N. and his wife began pounding. Perhaps their time had come? However, they banished these illusions and clung to the remnants of their faith with all their remaining mental powers.

One day N. and his wife went to see a movie recommended by those in authority. I have forgotten its name, but I recall what it was about just as he related it to me. Workers from abroad come to the Soviet Union. They display enthusiastic patriotism and manage to become production workers. They are trusted in the factories which they subsequently sabotage. An investigation reveals that they had been originally sent to the USSR as agents of the capitalist secret police.

Skepticism had been raising havoc in the minds of N. and his wife. Nevertheless, they were furious at those "dogs" and filled with admiration for "our security forces" which knew how to protect the country from such dangerous elements and ferret them out and destroy them.

The artistic reality of the movie was paralleled by the gray truth all around. Arrests increased and became more frequent. The wives of men who had been taken away and disappeared were summoned somewhere to sign statements that their husbands were foreign agents, saboteurs, spies, intelligence operatives, and Trotskyites. Some women became hysterical, and others answered firmly and restrainedly, "That's impossible." Then, the interrogator would calmly ask, "How do you know, comrade, that your husband did not keep secrets from you?"

"What do you mean?" the unfortunate woman would argue, "He's my husband and we have lived together in complete harmony for many years." To this there would come a question with a crushing innuendo, "So you have no confidence in the NKVD, comrade?"

In spite of everything, N. did not yet capitulate completely. Explaining his reactions to all that went on around him, he did not resort to the popular proverb of the trees and the splinters, but employed something more original. "I told myself, here is a field. Most of the weeds are just in the place where vegetation is thickest and more work has to be done to pull them out. These are the signs of blessed growth. Yes, that is how we grasped at every possible straw, like a drowning man, until the last one also gave. People closest to me, intimate friends, disappeared. As far as these are concerned, I said to myself, you can kill me but I will not believe that they also succeeded in playing a double game to me. However, I no longer had much time to torment myself with riddles. One night, they knocked at our door, too. A demand to identify myself, a search, and a warrant for my arrest put an end to all my doubts. On a friendly night, friendly to a revolutionary, I crossed the border into the Soviet Union. How many nights since then have I been tormented in interrogation cellars — nights friendly to a revolutionary."

It was not N.'s life story which made the strongest impression on me but the way he told it. He called it a confession. An unforced confession after a series of "confessions" in the course of being questioned. Sometimes he asked me to forgive his sentimentality. And at times, it did sound very strange coming from a revolutionary man of iron who had experienced much suffering and persecution. How does a man become so soft? He himself explained it. "I have to talk now just like a person has to breathe. I'll suffocate if I don't get everything off my chest, if I don't talk either to you or anyone else. 'You can laugh at the world,'" he used a Jewish saying. "You will get out of here sometime and look back at this period as an interlude. It's not so terrible. But I have to begin everything from scratch. I literally have to learn how to walk, to take steps, like an infant. Where shall I get the strength? Even if my 'sojourn' here ever ends, I have morally lost my entire hold on life. I have nothing to stand on. For, I came, I saw, and I was conquered. I was conquered — I only use this expression for the sake of the saying's phraseology. It would be more correct to say that I have fallen into a pit and not only my body but my spirit has been crushed."

Just One Wish: To Be Buried Among Jews

S. could not forget the good old days when he was moved from one Polish prison to another. He had nothing to eat in those days, but he did have *faith*.

His wife had also been a Comrade and was in prison, too, in another cell. If the days they were together during their twelve years of marriage were to be added up, they would scarcely total two years. They were held in the grip of a vicious circle, for there was no coordination between their periods of imprisonment and freedom. S. told me, "We rarely saw each other but we were living together in our dreams. Nothing deterred us, neither want nor danger. Together we breathed the hatred for those who deprived us of our liberty and knew that their end was imminent. We knew it would take time but we were still young; the years we had lost would be restored to us, for they were not really lost. We scorned people poor in spirit and ideas and regarded ourselves as being worthy of the envy of the provincial-minded. Meanwhile, our hair turned gray, our faces became more wrinkled, and our teeth began falling out. But we told the world to go whistle."

S. went on, "It is only here that I am tired and confused. I would like to sink into a dream once more. But all our dreams have been confiscated just as our belts and shoelaces. Am I entirely disappointed? Worse than that. I do not even have the strength for a complete, ripe disappointment. I am mixed up, stupefied. I feel like a woman whose man has disappeared. Maybe he is still alive somewhere? Maybe he'll come back yet? But, no, the idea will never return. Nevertheless, I do not have the courage to say goodbye forever to it. I feel suspended between heaven and earth; I have been cut off from one spiritual base and I cannot anchor myself to another one.

"Perhaps I am indulging in self-pity?" S. continued. "That may be. Because I have already lost count which arrest of mine this is; and nevertheless, it's my first one. An entirely new count begins. There in Poland, in all sorts of prisons, I wove beautiful dreams, and here I live with no flag whatsoever to stir my heart. Not only do I not have my old dreams of the future any more, the visions of the certain destruction of the exploiting capitalist system, but I no longer have the sweet delusions of martyrdom and self-sacrifice. There are no heroes in the camps and dismal cellars of the NKVD. Here no one has any identity. Your fighting is over and you leave no memory for history. You are offered on no altars. At best, you vanish.

"What hurts me most," he pursued, "is not that I have become a cipher as far as my existence is concerned, but that I have become nothing ideologically and spiritually. I no longer have any ideas and ideals. I say to myself, you won't fool me any more with words or slogans. Just as they say in Polish, 'The whole world is a brothel and people are whores.' No, I don't give a hoot for the world any more. My heart has become impervious to any sort of holiness. But for some reason or other I have, or to be more exact, I have acquired here, a single wish which surprises me very much." He began speaking hesitantly as if he were ashamed of what he was about to divulge and of the very sentimental tone of his words. "The devil knows how this sole wish ever occurred to me but I at least want to be buried among Jews and I would like to have a gravestone on which would be engraved my name and that of my father, whose son caused him so much anguish. And I want it to bear the date of my death. I have never thought of such matters before. Even when during my underground activities I was exposed to dangers and had mentally reconciled myself to the possibility of dying. Such fairy tales did not interest me in the least. I remember several Jewish suicides in my hometown. They were buried near the cemetary fence as if to say, a person capable of such a deed does not deserve to lie among respectable dead. They were people who did not have the strength to face the struggle for existence and had taken their own lives; then the gravediggers came and increased their punishment after death. I used to laugh at such a punishment, and I imagined that if those suicides would have been able to come back to life for a moment, they too would burst out in hysterical laughter. All his life such a person lived in a hovel and rotted in wretched poverty, darkness, hunger, and filth. And that was not even a punishment imposed by man; it was fated by nature. But after death, the choice of an eternal resting place for him is determined by a single last act. Believe me, let's say I care more about my place for one theater performance than I do about where I'm going to lie after I die. It makes a big difference where the worms gnaw at you? But now, for some reason or other, it appears to me that it really does make a great difference."

S. fasted on the Day of Atonement. He told me it was the first time since he had been confirmed. I asked him, "Have you gotten religion?"

"Not especially," he seemed to be trying to justify himself. "It's much simpler. I can go hungry when the NKVD wants me to so why can't I go hungry when I want to? It's my way of protesting; or else it's a demonstration of a personal ambition. Maybe it comes from vague longing. I myself don't know for what."

The Dreams of Those Transforming the World

In the camps I made the acquaintance of former Communists who told funny stories about their past. Either the incidents had really happened as they described them, or else they changed events into anecdotes after they had occurred.

One of them, of a pious Hassidic family, would occasionally barge into his father's synagogue, take possession of the pulpit, slap his palm on the stand to quiet everybody and transform the platform from which the Scriptures were read into a stage for preaching revolution. One Sabbath he shouted, "What is it we demand? All we are asking for is work and bread!" The bearded father grabbed a corner of the young man's coat, "My son, you were never anxious to work; and as for bread, come home. We have fine white bread and fish and all kinds of pastries."

I also managed to meet former Communists who did not give in. Manipulating all sorts of excuses, they did not let ideological despair take possession of them. Using a highly intellectual tone, some of them resorted to dialectical points while the less sophisticated would say, "You're right. I cannot explain all that. But should the baby be poured out together with the dirty water?"

These stubborn ones used to argue more acrimoniously with their own comrades than with someone like me. One of them, a former Communist, was jeered at by his friends who would say about him, "He still has a red heart."

They told me a piquant story about the man with the "red heart." He came from a family of class-conscious proletarians and inherited his "red heart." His father had a revolutionary past. The son, who already was well aware of the techniques employed by the NKVD, used to tell how the Czarist police operated. Once, at the beginning of the century, his father took a train to attend the convention of a Socialist party and was arrested on the way to Warsaw. He was detained for three days, the duration of the convention, and released. By comparison with the war against "Enemies of the People," the Czarist regime was childish.

I avidly listened to former Communists, whose fate I was now sharing, telling romantic stories full of heroism and wonderful tales of idealism. I also learned details of revolutionary techniques which sounded like detective stories and tales of adventure.

I heard stories of stormy demonstrations during the funeral of a man murdered by the police when his bloody shirt was borne aloft like a banner. They told me how pieces of red cloth had been hung on telephone and telegraph poles and could only be taken down by special police cars or by firemen. There were accounts of "reacquisitioning" for the purpose of financing revolutionary activities and of outright robbery in the guise of working for the Revolution. My fellow prisoners described illegal printing presses, doctored papers, forged documents, the smuggling and dissemination of literature from the USSR, special groups, and cells. I was told about strikes, proclamations (this imposing word was used to describe leaflets), forbidden meetings, Mayovkas (open-air meetings in May, but not necessarily in that month), boyuvkas (combat units), and clashes.

There were many tales of agents provocateurs in party cells who displayed unusual zeal in order to win the confidence of the members and rise in the hierarchy for purposes of subversion. They told me many stories of successful agents as well as of others who were done away with.

I also learned a great deal about internal relations in the Polish Communist party, of intrigue, the stifling of criticism, muzzling the expression of opinions, and betrayal in the underground cells even before they assumed power.

But above all, arrests — everyone was occupied with stories of arrests. The stories told of party members being apprehended and imprisoned, of escapes and releases, were legion. And they related accounts of a kind-hearted father and a compassionate mother and brothers and sisters using their influence, but in vain. To entreaties and exhortations, "Perhaps you've had enough?" they would reply, "No, I'm sticking until the end. There is no retreat from the only way." And so they returned to prison and to interrogations and torture.

The interrogations were conducted by special branches of the Polish security, police notorious for their cruelty. One of their favorite techniques was breaking fingers in a door. There was organized obstruction to the interrogators with refusals to answer them or recognize them. And there were trials transformed into dramatic spectacles at which the accused or his attorney made impassioned speeches.

I was told of courageous struggles inside the prisons, first of all for the purpose of securing the special status of a political prisoner, and then for the right of taking walks in a group and not alone. Finally, they had to fight for anything they wanted from the prison authorities, especially for the privilege of receiving mail and books.

I heard accounts of clandestine ties with members on the outside and of a secret organization of political prisoners inside the prison. There were also hunger strikes and demonstrations and escapes and breaks. My fellow prisoners told of singing the "Internationale" behind bars and of raising flags on the walls. There were times of mass jeering and mass cheering. Sometimes, members on the outside would send doves bearing little red flags to perch on the bars in order to encourage the inmates and infuriate the prison authorities.

Most of all I marveled at the self-teaching of these revolutionaries. On their own, many of them studied philosophy, politics, sociology, economics, and world literature either in groups or by avidly reading books in the brief hours when they were not at work or engaged in revolutionary activity. This self-teaching was intensified in prison. Debates and discussions were held and groups were organized for studying languages, and natural and social sciences under the guidance of experts who happened to be in the same cell. Many began an unofficial academic career and produced their first literary creations inside prison walls.

A man who had been a frequent inmate of Polish prisons told me in a Soviet prison camp, "Simple peasants and workmen would fall into the hands of the police together with members of the Central Committee. They were idealists with a highly developed political awareness either wholeheartedly devoted to the party or sympathizing with its aims. Some of them, however, were complete illiterates. These were taught how to read and write in prison. The prison courses were divided into various grades ranging from elementary reading groups to actual classes for advanced studies in which the lectures were given by educated prisoners. What didn't we teach and what didn't we study? Our courses varied from basic subjects to the organized life of the bee based on Maeterlinck's work and from a folk tune to Marx's *Capital* (which was considered an 'undesirable' book but was not forbidden). It was sometimes really difficult to reconcile the blackboards, chalk, maps, and writing materials with a prison regime. But we never ceased demanding additional privileges."

"And what is most important," another prisoner, a former Communist, told me, "there, in a Polish prison, you felt that the great Soviet power and its mighty peoples were behind you. And now — now, I tell you, I myself am ashamed of the change in me. I don't think anything any more. On the other hand, the attitude of the petite bourgeoisie which I made such fun of, the provincialism which I held in contempt and the poverty of whose world I pitied so much are also attracting me. If there is anything I still think of all the time it is neither of the world nor of any idea but of a small room, peace, a corner of my own, pictures hanging on the wall, framed family portraits, windows with curtains on them, an animal's hide spread out beside the bed, slippers, a small bookcase, and perhaps of a wife and child, too. I would hold the child in my lap and spoil it. We would prate together. The woman would prepare breakfast. The child would go to school and later we would boast in front of visitors, 'What marks.' In short, the time-honored pattern which strangled me is now my ideal world, my dream."

That was the great dream of a person planning to rebuild the world, to live like everybody else. Always, after a conversation of this sort, the "terrible revolutionary" would hum popular songs. They were never vengeful songs of anger summoning the populace to rise but sentimental melodies, lilting rhymes expressing a private sorrow. For example, he was fond of a Jewish song with a heart-rending tune, "Play fiddle, play, songs of hope and happiness."

Despite differences in language and motif, a professional criminal, one of those scorning or staring in amazement at the ideological prisoners, would follow the Jewish melody with a sort of echoing chant by an unknown composer. It was a slow monotonous melody of nomads tugging at one's heartstrings and losing itself in the vast limitless expanses of the forests. "In the wilderness on the shores of Lake Baikal where gold is mined in the hills, a nomad sings a sad song. . . . He crosses Lake Baikal and his mother comes to greet him — Hello, mother, are my father and brother still alive? — Your father, my son, has long been in his grave, and your brother has long been clanging chains in Siberia."

Southward, Southward!

I have already mentioned the rumor mill which produced hopes from which illusions giving rise to new disappointments emerged. The German invasion of the USSR brought fresh prosperity to the rumor mill. From the end of June, 1941, waves of rumors swept over the camp. When I look back at them, it seems to me that at the beginning, they had no roots in fact but were all simply the result of sound logic. It was inconceivable that under the new circumstances, when the Soviet state considered it necessary to mobilize every bit of patriotism and effort for the war against the mighty external foe, it would squander energy on keeping millions in prison. It stands to reason that instead of wasting trained, armed manpower on guarding us, it would do well to add it and us to the manpower on the fighting front or occupied in producing goods for immediate use in fighting the invader.

This principal logic gave rise to secondary considerations, just as logical. Foremost of these was the Allies. Now the western democracies would stand in one anti-Hilter front together with Russia, and camps of this sort belonging to the new "member" of the alliance, with their millions of prisoners including so many "foreigners," would just not be nice for the Allies. Someone had already "heard" that Britain and the United States had even demanded that the Russians release the "foreigners" or had delicately alluded to the matter.

In the variegated prisoners' society, there were elements for whom this combination of logic and hope worked in reverse. Either out of excessive realism or wishful thinking, there were some who foresaw changes and a new life for themselves in the wake of the defeats and setbacks which the rapidly advancing Germans would certainly inflict on the Russians. However, I should like to stress right away that even where I was, such elements were an infinitesimal minority. Despite the normal tension which exists everywhere in the world between prisoners and the authorities, gloating here was rare and restrained. The patriotism of the political prisoners and "counterrevolutionaries," the vast majority of whom had sincerely and enthusiastically loved their country before their incarceration, had not been beaten in the prisons and camps into moral treason. As for the professional criminals, they harbored the seasonal enmity of their trade for policemen, detectives, and judges, but it was not enough to overshadow their love for Mother Russia. Some time later, I heard that those who were released and mobilized for front-line service or whose sentence had been exchanged for combat duty displayed exemplary courage and were in many units the best and bravest soldiers.

To exclude the possibility of a mistake, among *Jews*, whether westerners or old Soviet citizens, with whom I spent my time in camps, I detected no traces at all of vengeful glee, although we did not yet know what the Germans had done to the Jews in Poland and in the rest of the conquered countries, and we certainly had no inkling of what they were still plotting to do.

Coming back to the rumors. This time we did not have to wait long for many of them to come true. In the latter part of August, 1941, we learned of an agreement between the Polish government in exile in London — the government of General Sikorski — and the Soviet authorities providing for the organization of Polish military units in the USSR for fighting the common German enemy and the liberation of Poland. We were told that in this connection it had been agreed to release Polish subjects imprisoned in Russian camps. This was the so-called "Sikorski Amnesty" which applied to those persons who were Polish nationals until September 17, 1939, the day the Red army entered the territory of former Poland.

There was no longer any question of whether it was true or untrue. The camp authorities spread the rumor almost openly. Everyone was only apprehensively asking, when? Suppose something goes wrong? Would they change their minds? How would the provisions of the agreement be carried out in actual practice? Did it also absolutely apply to Polish Jews? Did it also clearly mean people from areas defined by the Soviet authorities as western Byelorussia and the Ukraine?

The gist of all the tormenting doubts was, "Do the amnesty terms apply to us?"

For me, the nerve-racking suspense lasted about two months and I nearly despaired of the prospect of deriving any benefit from being a Pole. In alphabetical order, my family name was among the first. As far as my sentence was concerned (five years), I was an intermediate offender, if not less. My appearance in the NKVD's domain was from the very outset as a citizen of Warsaw, that is, a pure Pole, and not of Pinsk, which had been annexed to Soviet Byelorussia. So why did the amnesty seem to exclude me? August had passed and September was over and no one had sent for me. A notion preyed on my mind that perhaps *they* had found out my real identity. A dark prediction began to eclipse the final shreds of hope. "This is the end of you. As far as you are concerned, the official's prophesy 'You're going to be buried here' will come true."

Meanwhile, news of the amnesty had peeled off additional layers from the minds of the camp's inmates. The men were waiting for personal notification and still going around hungry, frozen, and ragged. But they had already begun to build their lives anew. They were once more arranging deals, forming partnerships, making agreements, and setting dates for appointments. The true Poles were especially interesting. Degraded and oppressed as they had been for months on end without any certainty of imminent freedom, there were already swaggering Poles treating Jews with insolence. Some of them still looked emaciated and unshaven, as if on the verge of death; but they were already twisting the ends of the moustaches upward in the style of Polish nobles and behaving arrogantly toward the "kikes" from their homeland and even browbeating them. Hadn't they really forgotten anything and learned anything in this northern slave university?

But who was I to be concerned about the evil nature of Poles about to be released? Wasn't I remaining here anyway? Often I would ask friends and acquaintances included in the Sikorski agreement to think of me sometime. I even had them learn certain addresses in order to let someone know what had befallen me. I was already seeing myself in the gloom of "normal" times stretching on interminably and pondering upon my new situation without the company of westerners around me to remind me of another life.

But man should never despair. Despite everything, my hour came in October. I was notified that I would be released according to the terms of the Soviet-Polish agreement.

It was natural for me to acquire new friends. Wherever I came, I would ferret out Zionists, especially members of youth movements. If I "suspected" a man of being such a person, I could naturally not ask him outright in order to confirm my suspicion. A surefire method was to hum a Palestinian tune which the other man could hear. The melody of "Perhaps these events had never occurred" (V'ulai . . .) by the poetess Rachel was unusually successful in such cases. After humming it, I would watch the person closely to see whether or not something had stirred within him and the gap between our hearts had been bridged.

My heart tells me to mention several more new friends, older than I. One of them was a walking Jewish calendar. He did not allow the Jewish time reckoning to escape our attention. In our special state where we were cut off and isolated, it was a difficult, complicated task, but we attached special importance and sanctity to it. And not only did this friend of ours calculate the traditional holidays and festivals for us, but he also remembered and reminded us of special dates like the anniversaries of the deaths of Herzl and Bialik, to keep our spiritual threads from being rent. He was also the authority for determining the dates of the anniversaries of the deaths of close relatives when someone wished to conduct a service of ten men and recite the Kaddish — the prayer for the dead.

Another friend was a living repudiation of the environment, for a while. One could not help marveling at the way he set aside times for prayer. Like the rest of us, he also went out to work in the forests and on the railroad on the Jewish Sabbath. However, in some way, his clothing differed from the garments he wore during the week. It was the Sabbath best of a Jewish prisoner. "Why do you try so hard to look a little like a Sabbath observer?" he was asked. "For myself," he would answer. It was really possible to derive some warmth in the frosty wilderness of the North from his pure heart. And no less than his pure heart did his clean language arouse my admiration, for not a speck of vulgarity had cloven to it. What wonderful immunity this was against the impact of the ubiquitous environment which drop by drop injected its "culture" and customs into you.

By the time my release was due, I had no close friends in the camp. I was among the last to be amnestied and so I left for the great strange world immensely stirred but also possessed by a feeling of loneliness.

Peculiar thoughts came to you traveling on a normal railroad the tracks of which you helped lay just a year before. This is the line you helped extend in the opposite direction.[1] Slaves really brought life to these northern wastes. This life was fertilized by death; how many human corpses carpeted the roadbeds and railroad ties of the Komi republic! But — I speculated — who knows what is going to be here in another ten years, in another generation? On the way back from the North, trains were already speeding on the rails, semaphores were signaling, smokestacks were spouting swirling clouds, and the lights of human habitation were glittering where just a year before there had only been virgin forests. It would be interesting to live several more generations and see what history would be focused on, progress or its cost.

But all these thoughts were eclipsed by a single overweening desire, to get out of here quickly, very quickly. Not even for home, or Poland, or Palestine, but just to leave this land wrapped in the shrouds of death. My first wish was to go south. The second one was to join the Polish army. All we wanted was to be part of the Polish units being formed on Soviet soil in order to fight Germans and to take hold of something "extraterritorial." It would remind us of our native land and serve as the hint of a prospect of taking leave of the Soviet Union. Last but not least, it would shelter us from the material worries with which we would have to concern ourselves as free men in an alien land completely penniless. And if, as we had heard, the Polish army was located in the southern part of the country, then of course, our route was southward.

[1] This is the railroad about which the Bolshaya Sovietskaya Entsiklopedia writes, "It connects the Pechora arctic region with various parts of the USSR. It was constructed chiefly during the War under difficult natural conditions of tundra and taiga and numerous rivers which had to be spanned by great bridges." True, but not the whole truth.

Three Black Marks in My Biography

From the northern tundra and taiga with their eternal forests and perpetual ice we traveled to a land bathed in sunshine, to Tashkent, the City of Bread, the capital of Soviet Uzbekistan. It was a long journey in packed trains past noisy stations. Everywhere there were evacuees; tens of thousands of them. I had been weaned from such human landscapes and I said to myself, "Look, there are children in the world." The time was October, 1941, about four months after the German invasion of the USSR. There were masses of wounded soldiers and civilians everywhere. Empty sleeves and crutches of men in uniform had already become signs of the times.

It was a long journey. Russia has enormous space. This time, however, the words of the song "Boundless is my Native Land" had another ring to them. The Russians are used to such distances. You could hear them saying about a certain place, "It's quite near, a trip of no more than three days." Spending three or four days on a train, if not for the fact of having been uprooted and evacuated, aroused no special excitement. They took along food and a tea kettle. At nearly every station, they swarmed off to obtain boiling water and purchase a little more food. Vendors were to be found everywhere, but their prices were rising all the time. Some travelers would secure food only by bartering away articles lacking in the region. I had no reason for getting off the train at the various stations. I had very little money and what did I have to barter?

Hundreds, even thousands of former prisoners crowded the cars. Few of them bought tickets. I did not want any more trouble with the law over a trifle. This cautiousness compelled me to save more on food and now and then I would offer my services as a porter in a number of stations. Many of the released prisoners made some money this way.

I wondered about the attitude of the refugees and evacuees to former prisoners. We were now citizens like them. Still, I hardly noticed any of them asking us "Where are you coming from?" or "Where are you headed?" Generally they tried to keep away from us and have nothing to do with us. The faces of some of the people indicated that they felt sympathy for us, but they were extremely careful about uttering an extra word in such a public place as a train. We had no alternative but to become accustomed to this continuing isolation although we were free.

I moved ever southward by rail, highway, and water, stopping at a town called Buzuluk, near Kuibyshev, where there was a newly organized Polish unit. However, it already had its full complement, and so I continued on my way looking for other units.

I reached Tashkent. There were thousands of so-called "Poles" here. What should I do now? For the present, a night's lodging was to be had in a park near the railroad station. At nightfall, tramps and people looking like us were kept out of the station itself. We spent our time between the station and the office representing the Polish government in exile. At the office, we secured a

little food and listened to rumors. We had few prospects of settling in this large city and making a decent living in it. The flood
of refugees coming here was constantly swelling. It would be
necessary to go still farther south. Meanwhile, representatives of
the local factories came among the refugees and former prisoners
looking for skilled workers. There was a great demand for book-
keepers, machine shop workers, and electricians. However, my
only useful "trade" was carrying baggage. Be it as it may, one had
to live. In Tashkent there was a great deal of work for a porter
between the park and the station.

It was in Tashkent that I made my first acquaintance with
lines, "free" lines. Certainly, these were wartime lines for commodities of which there was a shortage. However, I soon learned
that waiting in line is a well-entrenched institution of the Soviet
scene. I shall only repeat a single joke because of its "literary"
standard and because I actually enjoyed it when it was told to me.
The joke is based on the famous fable of the Russian Krilov
which the narrator told me exactly as it had been written. He
only changed the last stanza. It seemed that for the sake of per-
suading a crow to open its mouth and drop a piece of cheese it
was holding in it, a sly fox flattered it extravagantly, praising its
beauty and its bill, neck, feathers, and eyes. Krilov's version has
the crow opening its bill to sing and losing the cheese to the fox.
The Soviet punch line was as follows, "Taking the piece of cheese
out of her mouth the crow tucked it under her wing and smil-
ingly said to the fox, 'My friend, these are not Krilov's times. If
you want cheese, stand in line.' "

I was not inspired by freedom in Tashkent and tried my luck
in other parts of Soviet Central Asia. Wherever I went I found
Jewish refugees and naturally associated with them. I would
venture to say that it was a sort of meeting with Russian Jewry,
which until that time had been an unknown tribe for me. I felt
that despite suppression brought on by the war and by being uprooted from their homes, Russian Jews were experiencing a cer-

tain spiritual awakening, a certain anticipation of a change in connection with their expression of Judaism. Their sentiments were predicated on the simple assumption that Enemy Number One of the Soviet Union is Enemy Number One of the Jewish people. At the same time, they clearly realized that the common fate of the Allies and the Soviet government's wish to rally the world's public opinion to the war effort removed the barriers between Russian Jewry and various Jewish communities throughout the world. The appeal of the Jewish Anti-Fascist Committee in Moscow to world Jewry began with the words "Fellow Jews," and this phrase alone was enough to announce a turning point after twenty years of denying world Jewish unity.

There were other manifestations of ties between the representatives of Russian Jewry and the Jewish people of the rest of the world, and their emergence warmed the hearts of the Russian Jews and inflamed their imaginations. In their minds many were already seeing the government permitting things which until then had been "taboo," absolutely forbidden. And the Nazi outrages intensified their feeling of sharing a common fate and common agony with Jews wherever they happened to be. To all this was added the fertile influence of encounters between Russian Jews — after many years of being cut off — and Jews from the republics and regions annexed to the Soviet Union or with Jews from Poland who had fled to the USSR as war refugees. These were meetings with Jewish communities rooted in tradition and national culture, dynamic, active communities, and such a confrontation once more revived in the hearts of Russian Jews the latent yearning for a more abundant, richer, and more dynamic Jewish life.

From my meetings with the Russian Jews during that period, I remember a number of episodes which I would like to relate because they are either characteristic or piquant.

It was market day in one of the cities of Central Asia. I happened to become involved in a conversation with a Russian Jew who had fled here from the horrors of Nazi occupation. He spoke a rich folksy Yiddish interspersed with Hebrew expressions, and spouted biblical quotations right and left. I asked him in amazement, "Where did you get this proficiency in Hebrew lore?" Twisting his lips in a strange smile, he replied by asking a question, "Who do you think I am?" A moment later he added, "I was once head of a Talmudic seminary at Bobruisk." To my inquiry what he was doing at the time, he replied that until the evacuation he had been serving as an NKVD interrogator at Zhitomir in the Ukraine.

I often thought about the fate of the head of a Talmudic seminary who had become an NKVD agent, and to a certain extent his fate appeared to me not only that of an individual.

I recall one of my acquaintances — a party card-carrying Russian Jew. Neither his conduct nor his appearance indicated that he was Jewish. He actually made an effort to demonstrate his indifference to his origins; but this time, he was unable to restrain himself and gave expression to his innermost feelings. During a rare moment of self-revelation, he brought up something of his mental struggle. His wife was on the verge of having her first child, and he said to me, "I wish she would give birth to a girl." There was something extraordinary in the special emphasis of a prospective father before the birth of his first child. Realizing my amazement, he explained, "You understand, if I have a son, I'll be faced with the question whether or not to have him circumcised. If I have a daughter, I'll be free of these inner conflicts and twinges of conscience. Actually, there's no law here forbidding the circumcision of sons. But you must understand that as a party member, I must be more conscious of my duties."

I enjoyed the new acquaintances. But I also had to eat and live under a roof. Everywhere, I encountered difficulty in finding work and lodging, and of course I had trouble in registering. I went from one institution to another and from factory to factory. Wherever I looked for work, I was required to fulfill just one small formality — jot down my *autobiography*. Here I already had two black marks against my name. I could not appear as a proletarian whose father had also been a member of the working class and I was unable to conceal my period of imprisonment. I had actually served part of my sentence and had done a little penance for my sin. Finally, I had been amnestied. However, the black mark remained.

I got fed up with wandering about "free" in the inviting land of sunshine, constantly looking for a place to spend the night, living from the unsteady income earned as a porter and from the handouts of the Polish office and dragging myself to delousing stations. For fear of a typhus epidemic resulting from the influx of refugees, the authorities began demanding a delousing certificate. Such certificates could be bought, but where was I to get money for them? Incidentally, a new experience for me at these stations was the fact that many of the workers in the men's section were women.

Under the circumstances, the advice of the Soviet authorities to go to Nukus, capital of the Kara-Kalpak Autonomous Soviet Republic in the Uzbek Republic, sounded attractive. We were told that this republic was at the end of the world in an out-of-the-way place where no one paid any attention to biographical black marks. There were many jobs to be had and a special demand for "educated" people. The question was how to get there. We slowly sailed down the Amu Darya, arriving in Nukus a few days later.

The country, mostly desert, consists of one hundred and sixty thousand square kilometers with a population of about half a million. Summers are very hot and winters quite cold. Kara-Kalpakia is supposed to have rich mineral sources. Its principal agricultural products are cotton, rice, and subtropical fruits, all raised by irrigation. Sheepherding is important, especially for raising caracul.

What we had been told turned out to be true. In a few days I succeeded in securing a position as a jack-of-all-trades at the local hospital. I served as guard, wagon driver, assistant administrator, porter, purchasing agent, and yardman — a little of everything and actually nothing at all.

But in Nukus I ate my first square meal. I had enough to eat for weeks. The hospital staff was good to me. I was becoming myself again. My salary was very small but I hardly spent anything for food, the principal expense item in the budget of an individual or a family. I received a place to live — the corner of a storeroom for myself and my belongings; sometimes I stayed with new friends I had made. I could already begin to worry a little about a pair of stockings, shoes, and even trousers, and a shirt.

It was not long before I went to the tolchok — market — to purchase some secondhand articles. It was Sunday and I experienced a rather bitter, albeit amusing, incident. In the market there were some refugee Jews, mostly from the Ukraine and White Russia, who were walking around trying to sell secondhand goods. One of them had a shirt which seemed to be what I wanted; it was made of plain, strong cloth in a color which does not soil easily. I haggled a great deal. I walked off, returned, and felt of it again, but the vendor and I could not get together on the price. This happened a number of times. Suddenly I heard the husband say to his wife in Yiddish spiced with Hebrew words, "The uncircumcised one wants to pinch something and not buy. Keep an eye on his hands." The blood rose to my face. All my anger and bitterness surged to break out, but I did not know how to react. I would tell them who "the uncircumcised one" who wanted to "pinch" their rags was — let them choke on them — but I restrained myself. Actually, what did I want of them? Perhaps I should make them a simple explanation and show them their ridiculous mistake? No, not that either! Let them go to hell with their wonderful sharp eyes. Suppressed pride did not allow me to present myself to them. But for many hours I could not get over it. Here, at Nukus, I tasted a tear of freedom for the first time: here, this is your face, the face of a brodyaga (vagabond), of a criminal. How did they used to put it up there in the North?

Just for a face like that alone you should get ten years. I continued to struggle with myself: should I or shouldn't I go up to those Jews and tell them? But I did not return to them — and that was my revenge: they lost a buyer for the secondhand gymnastyorka (shirt).

When I recall my prisons and camps, I am entitled to refer to them, a la Gorki, as "my universities."

But not only the prison camps taught me a great deal; I also learned much about life and about Russia during my brief periods of freedom. One of my teachers in the art of living was my immediate superior at Nukus. He was a sensitive, intelligent man with a "job" card — a popular designation for a membership card in the Soviet Communist party. He made a rule of inviting me to help out when animals had to be slaughtered even though it was not part of my duties and did not take place during working hours. The first time he asked me, I hesitated. What could I do to help since I knew nothing whatsoever about such things. He laughed at my naiveté and said, "What do you care? You'll hold the animal's tail." When I came, I found a large group of respectable "helpers" like me and quickly found out why so many were anxious to help out and watch the ceremony. When I stopped being an innocent lamb, I joined the others in leaving the ritual with "souvenirs" of meat and fat.

My boss could not stand my being so undiscerning. For example, whenever some high officials would come to visit the hospital, he would say to me, "Go get it." Wide-eyed, I would ask, "Get what?" And he would observe, "With you I won't go far. We need something wet and you're standing like a dummy." I soon learned that as soon as a commission appeared or someone came on business to discuss supplies or construction, I had to hie myself posthaste to the nearest store for a bottle or two of vodka.

I began to learn a great deal about the people here. Various officials became frequent visitors to the storerooms I guarded. They would come and take whatever they wanted. They would answer my look of amazement with a smile as if to say, "What are you surprised at, dummy?" Some would fill their pockets and even their boots with oats which we kept for the work animals, in order to stuff their own geese. I slowly grew accustomed to this life and became part of it.

Nukus's greatest fault was its distance from large centers and from main highways. I made all sorts of plans for contacting friends and even wrote several letters. However, by virtue of its geographical position and my own lack of orientation, Nukus was a remote island as far as my friends and I were concerned. At the Polish office there they would attempt to calm my fears, "They know about you. They haven't forgotten you and your time will come, too."

And sure enough, one day we Poles were notified that we were to leave for a Polish army camp somewhere in the vicinity of Bukhara. We were told to settle our affairs and hold ourselves in readiness for sailing back. I had no affairs to settle. My fellow workers at the hospital came to say goodbye and brought me some food for the journey. Together with all the others in the Polish shipment, I boarded the vessel.

But some vicious, clowning demon must have had it in for me. Just when we were already on the river and when I believed that my hour of redemption was near, the Amu Darya, the river in Central Asia with the most water, froze over. The ice floes shut us in and prevented our further journey. I clearly remember that morning of gloomy prophesies. Catholics and Jews staked out places of worship on deck and prayed for deliverance. Meanwhile, the boat was brought to shore with considerable difficulty. After we disembarked, we were distributed among various collective farms where we were to spend the winter until the ice would melt.

I was sent to a miserable collective farm where there were not more than a dozen people who could read or write. Technological progress was represented by the donkey, camel, and wagon. The natural vegetation of this sandy waste was saksaul, tangled root-like bushes very good for heating purposes. Dried dung and bundles of dried cotton stalks were also used for building fires. The people lived in kibitkas, circular mud huts which kept out neither dampness nor cold. They generally had no windows and only an aperture in the roof allowed some light to penetrate. However, it seemed to me that the inhabitants of this collective farm were always "happy." They seemed to have plenty of time. They could squat or sit cross-legged for hours contentedly sipping tea out of bowls. Sitting on my haunches like them for half an hour made me dizzy.

I worked in the fields and my wages consisted in workdays, in keeping with the practice followed in collective farms. I was paid in commodities — small quantities of flour, groats, and vegetables. What could I do with them? Several families and I, a bachelor, would pool our food resources and cook joint meals to which we added carrots, which we had to swipe from fields, although they grew in abundance.

This people was noted for its hospitality, but it was wretchedly poor and its virtues could not stand the test of the famished hordes of Poles who overran their villages like locusts. For instance, they baked their bread — a sort of doughy cake — in circular clay ovens outside the houses. I often watched women engaged in baking this bread rolling the dough on the calves of their legs and sticking it to the inside wall of the oven. A bundle of cotton shoots would flare up in a strong flame and in a few moments, the bread would be done, warm and fresh. It was customary to invite anyone chancing to be in the vicinity to partake of the bread. The passerby would come over, bend down, put a crumb into his mouth, tarry briefly, say goodbye, and continue on his way. As soon as we Poles learned of this fine custom, we began hanging around wherever women were baking for their household and went from one oven to another. However, in violation of the accepted practice, we would not just put a crumb into our mouths but sit down and eat an entire cake. The natives finally had enough of the Poles' strange behavior and generally stopped extending invitations to them.

Incidents of burglary and theft which had never troubled them before increased. They had never known what it was to lock a house and suddenly they were invaded by this peculiar race. Cries of karabchuk ("thief") became a frequently heard chorus.

Whoever acted properly and not like a parasitical beggar would sometimes be asked to one of the great family meals at which the members of the household would sit for hours eating flob with their hands. The preparation of the flob itself was an undertaking of considerable dimensions. But it was really a dish fit for a king, consisting of rice in oil, chunks of mutton, onions, and carrots. I learned to lick my fingers, literally, with the great virtuosity which music critics could define as "finger technique."

Jews are related to the Kara-Kalpaks as well as to the Uzbeks, Kazakhs, and other peoples of Central Asia: they do not eat pork. Their beards, too, although short and sparse, bring to mind our ancestors a little. I became accustomed to them and somehow, while working in transport, found a living among them. Incidentally, the Kara-Kalpaks had a simple and effective way of making an animal hitched to a wagon go. The driver would walk before it holding a carrot or large beet behind him and the beast would follow him pulling its load until its strength gave out. For some reason or other, this aroused association from the camp of bread rations and the various pots.

The other Poles and I also learned a technique of benefiting from the market in the nearby town. One of us would buy a sackful of tobacco and sell it in glasses. It would thus go from wholesaler to retailer to consumer. This tobacco, called samosad, that is, self-planted, was grown by members of the collective farms in their own plots. We also engaged in other small business activities. But our greatest pleasure did not cost us anything. Nearly all of us roamed through the market tasting the numerous delicious fruits such as apricots, peaches, raisins, and almonds. We pretended that we wanted to buy them and of course had to find out whether or not they were sweet or sour. In this way, we went from one stall to another pinching the grapefruit and gorging ourselves on its rich juice. Each day I went to the market was a wonderful holiday.

These Kara-Kalpaks found it difficult to understand who we were. Their political education had not progressed this far twenty-five years after the Revolution. The following conversation is typical of the interchanges between us:

"You're a Russki?"

"No, Polish."

"Polish? Is that Russki or German?"

I quickly despaired of the hope of explaining that a Pole was something special. They first heard of the Poles at our invasion. Trying to make them understand that I was a Jew from Poland would certainly have been complicated and hopeless. When, in answer to their probing questions, I told them that I was from Warsaw (why give them the name of a smaller town?) they would ask whether it was near Tashkent or Moscow (the two legendary remote cities included in the range of their geographical knowledge).

All this made us smile. However, one aspect of their primitive grasp infuriated me. They would ask questions about world affairs, "Are the Germans good?"

"Bad. Very bad."

But it was difficult to convince them. They could not understand foreign occupation or invasion. I resorted to an overpowering reason, "The Germans are cannibals." But nothing made an impression on them, and they tried to find out whether the Germans were evil according to other criteria. "Do the Germans have collective farms?" When I would admit that the cannibals had no such institution, they would quickly conclude, "That means the Germans are good."

So the days passed and the long-awaited spring came. The river thawed and was navigable again. The months spent at the Kara-Kalpakan collective farm had made me feel more isolated than at Nukus and leaving was actually a second liberation.

I hurried to Kagan near Bukhara where there was a Polish headquarters and announced my wish to join the army like many others. They sent me to a medical board in an army camp. Standing before it, I sensed my difficulty at once. The Polish officers and physicians only looked at the lower part of the body in order to determine a volunteer's fitness for service. They made a pretense of feeling and tapping in several places. However, the decision to disqualify me had already been made. Two black marks — my social origin and my term in prison — had caused the Russians to reject me. Now a third black mark had been discovered by the Polish nobles, lieutenants, and majors which could not be erased — circumcision. My glowing dreams vanished instantly. Among the Jews who had rushed to Kagan to join the Polish Army there was talk of a Polish unit going to Persia. I suddenly recalled a Polish proverb, "No salami for the dog."

How shall I describe my feelings? It would be no exaggeration to say that I felt as if another amnesty had been declared from which I was excluded. After the Polish "gentlemen" had robbed me of prospects of going to Persia, I felt whipped. The perennial question once more arose — where to now?

I wandered around in Bukhara for a few days. I was still hungry for warmth. However, Bukharan heat was too much even for me. It was a blazing April. I saw the natives lying down on the floors of their houses during the noon hours covered with wet sheets which they moistened from time to time. This climatic contrast to the Far North confirmed in my case the Jewish proverb, "I've had it cold and hot," meaning that I had experienced every kind of disaster. Both regions had one feature in common for me: I did not undress or change my clothes for long periods of time. Many nights I slept in the street.

During the day I tried to enjoy the sights of the city and its surroundings and to get into conversation with Bukharan Jews. Despite the fog in my mind and my fatigue and personal agony, it was pleasant to hear Hebrew phrases pronounced in a unique fashion by the local Jewish elders.

Mostly my thoughts were concerned with making contact with friends in Palestine. I said to myself, I won't be satisfied with just dropping a hint in a chance note, which I could never be sure would reach its destination. At Kagan and in Bukhara I began acting in full swing. I sent a cable and several letters — not all at once and to different addresses. One of the letters, written in Polish on the last day of April, 1942, was given to me as a souvenir when I reached Palestine. It appears below:

Dear Misha,[1]

For two years I had no way of getting in touch with you. At the moment I have neither the intention nor the ability of telling of my experiences during this period. At the beginning of last October, I left the Far North and spent about seven months in Central Asia. Several days before I had gone before a Polish recruiting committee which had pronounced me unfit for military service.

I am appealing to you to do whatever you can to make it possible for me to reach Mariana.[2] *I don't think it proper to depend on certain privileges for I am convinced that my wishes are identical with those of all of you. I would like to carry this out at the first opportunity and without delay because I am all in.*

My dear friend, you can't imagine how much I miss all of you,

[1] The letter was sent to Moshe Kol (formerly Kolodny) who later became Israeli minister of development and tourism. He was my group's leader and good friend when I first joined the Noar Tsiyoni — Zionist Youth — movement.

[2] The name *Mariana* refers to the Noar Tsiyoni movement, its members, and Palestine. It's from the name of the Warsaw street where the Noar Tsiyoni had its headquarters in Poland before the war. In time, I also fell in love with the name and even used it to sign certain articles.

*how I long to see you and shake hands with you. Give my regards
to Dr. Kleinbaum* [Moshe Sneh].[3]

I had no return address so I wrote down "Kagan, Proyezdni"
("In transit" — the Russian equivalent of poste restante). Shortly
afterward Moshe Kol and Moshe Sneh sent a joint telegram
to the Jewish Agency representative in Teheran in which they
wrote, "Our cousin Yehoshua Globerman is in adverse circumstances. His address is Kagan, Bukhara, In Transit. Do all you can
to help and rescue him."

I was not permitted to remain in Kagan or in Bukhara. Those
"unfit for service" were summoned to Polish headquarters and
told to go somewhere else. We were given some food, and this
time armed Polish guards escorted us into waiting railway cars
which were to take us to another place.

One of my fellow travelers suggested that we go to Semipalatinsk, a city in Kazakhstan on both banks of the Irtysh near Altai
country not far from China. This was almost at the terminal of
the celebrated Turksib, the three thousand-kilometer-long railroad connecting Central Asia with Siberia which had been the
first great transport construction in the Soviet Union. A legend
was circulating among the men rejected by the Polish army that
in Semipalatinsk there was an acute shortage of labor and living
was cheap there. So, what's the difference? Why not? Let it be
Semipalatinsk. In any case, I needed a permanent address where I
could receive answers to letters I had been writing to my friends.
My idea was to write to Palestine again as soon as I would arrive
in Semipalatinsk. So, my geographical knowledge was to become
enriched with still another region, not far from China.

[3]A prominent Zionist leader from Poland. For a time head of the Haga-
nah Command. Lately a leader of the Communist party in Israel.

All Because of One Little Louse

I never reached Semipalatinsk. Here, I am tempted to write a sort of brief essay on the subject, "A small louse as the cause of a turning point in a man's life." And the strange part about it was that the louse which transformed my life was not even my own but belonged to someone whom I never knew.

This is how it happened. We refugees from Kagan and Bukhara who had been declared unfit for service in the Polish army were traveling in freight cars attached to a passenger train on the way to the Semipalatinsk region where many of us hoped to find happiness. I have already mentioned the fear of epidemics, especially typhus fever, which troubled the authorities because of the large numbers of refugees and evacuees on the roads and abnormal sanitary conditions. Examinations came frequently and supervision increased. This applied to modes of transportation as well. A sanitation board came on the train at one of the stations and inspected shirts in a number of cars, especially those under suspicion as being susceptible, like ours. The men had to take their shirts off and hand them to a nurse or medical orderly for inspection. So it happened that a tiny creature famed since Pharaoh of old slipped into our car and made its way to a shirt of one of the passengers. The order was at once given to uncouple our car from the train, have it thoroughly disinfected, and take all its passengers to a delousing station. The car was to be separated from the rest of the train at a small station called Chu between the district's principal city Dzhambul and the capital of Kazakhstan, Alma-Ata. We were informed that after the disinfection operation, the car would be coupled to another train going in the same direction.

We arrived in Chu. Our car was left on a siding after having been shut on the outside and placed under guard to see that no one left it. We were then all marched off to a bath and our clothing and limbs delivered to the health and hygiene authorities. The delousing finished, we returned to the car to wait for the resumption of our journey.

The large numbers of Polish citizens and former camp inmates living in the town soon heard of the carload of Polish Jews rejected by the army. People began swarming around the car to find out what had happened and look for friends or seek information about people they knew. Loud, lively conversations developed between the car's passengers and the people outside.

A friend of mine from the camps was living in Chu together with his family, which had been banished to Siberia and released under the amnesty granted to Polish subjects. This man, Barukh Gertsulin, also came to the car. It was an exciting meeting. With cogent logic he tried to persuade me to remain in Chu since I had no special reason for going to Semipalatinsk. He insisted that I could find in Chu whatever "fortune" I was seeking in Semipalatinsk. There was also a Polish office in town which held him in high esteem, and many Jews. Why should I go on into the unknown? Somehow I would find help here and get along. In short, I discovered a way of slipping out of the car and stayed behind in Chu with a very glad feeling that I was no longer so alone.

The decisive turning point in my life to which I have alluded was yet to come. Meanwhile, Chu was a station of relative ease on my itinerary. For the first time since my release from the camps, I lived in a real house and slept in an actual bed. My life became a little more stable. In a few days I found a job in a vegetable garden belonging to an auxiliary farm of the local foundling home. Obviously, I was no longer hungry. My job consisted chiefly of watering the plots. The water was diverted from a main irrigation canal to secondary channels by gravity. From them I dug new furrows every day, if it was necessary, distributing it in the fields. The chief tool was a sort of hoe used for digging, shaping channels, taking out earth, and making holes.

Watermelons and cantaloupes were raised on most of the land and the director told me that I had become an expert in growing them. If I should live a million years, I would never eat as many watermelons as I consumed on that farm. I would wash off the hoe well and split the watermelon with it into two crimson halves delightful to behold and taste. We workers used to make bonfires and bake potatoes in them. But there was nothing to compare to our watermelon feasts. I learned how to eat them with salt, bread, potatoes, and onions, and in all kinds of raw and cooked combinations.

My superiors found my work satisfactory. In response to a request I made, together with a hint that I would leave if it were not heeded, I was assigned living quarters with a bed and bedding in the shoeshop of the children's house. There I really had it good. I no longer had to worry much about cooked food and my expenses grew smaller. I also loved the optimism, some of which rubbed off on me, of the shoemaker. A refugee from a small Ukrainian town, he was very proud of the higher education of his children, the offspring of a Jewish shoemaker, and of their high military rank — they were all now at the front. He never complained of his lot, either now or in the past. He told me that now and then he would take his family to the workers' restaurant to make use of his rights as a worker, although they hardly touched the "official" food since they cooked meals at home the way they liked them and could afford. Many did this, he told me, in order "Not to be conspicuous." His friendly and wise counsel was very illuminating: "Be dumb. Our most precious gold is silence. No matter how curious I may be, don't even tell me much about yourself."

Living together with foundlings and abandoned children also taught me a great deal. Stealing among the youngsters was common. I paid considerable attention to the perverted wish-fulfillment dreams children have because of want. I was often amazed at conversations between children of nine or ten about what they wanted to be when they grew up. Children everywhere love to talk about this and usually reveal their hidden wishes and the objects of their admiration in such talk. Their imaginations are aroused by sailors, flyers, athletes, doctors, and craftsmen. Here, at the home in Chu, I heard such desires as cook — "so I could always stuff myself on what I like," or baker — "you can eat all the rolls and cookies you like," or confectioner — "all the candy and sweets you want," or a waiter, and all kinds of other professions and "missions" satisfying desire for satiety.

What prosaic romanticism of a prolonged lack of having enough to eat! It seems to me that if these children from the dyetdom (children's home) had to dress up in costumes for Purim and express their aspirations and envy in their masks, we would see most of them masquerading as cooks, bakers, and waiters.

In time I learned that the memories and experiences of adults also accumulate around food. The culinary memory of Russians I met was amazing. One of them, an intelligent man who had seen a great deal, in telling of his experiences in the huge construction program of the Urals would never forget to describe the schnitzel served in the workers' restaurant or the frosting cakes he ate there at the celebration in honor of the October Revolution.

The outlet must have had a unique magical appeal if an important official placed it at the center of the reminiscences connected with his work at Chelyabinsk, the gigantic industrial city.

Although I worked hard, I was satisfied with my daily existence. My life outside this existence was neither in Chu nor anywhere else in the Soviet Union. My spiritual world was taken up with my ever-increasing contacts abroad. I wrote letters and received answers although I cannot say what percentage of my communications reached their destination and how many stuck to the probing hands and eyes of the NKVD.

In June, 1942, I wrote a Yiddish letter in pencil to my brother in Palestine on half a sheet of notebook paper. I was afraid to write in Hebrew — an obvious identifying mark of the counter-revolutionary.

Dear Brother Leibke,

Not for one moment have I forgotten the night when we kissed goodbye in Vilna for the last time. Lately, we have been separated by thousands of kilometers, but I always see you before me. My pencil is on the verge of writing some words of endearment with love and longing, but I am afraid that you might be offended: you're already a young man of about twenty. Have you been writing home? I have not written the whole time and received no letters. Once I got some regards purely by chance. As soon as possible contact Misha and the rest of my friends from Marianska Street. Keep in mind that only the hope of meeting my relatives keeps me alive.

In another letter from Chu to friends in Palestine, I complained:

Soon six weeks will have elapsed since I sent Misha a wire and several letters and have as yet received no reply. How long will

we remain separated? I want to write still more, but it's impossible.
I would give several years of my life for just a look at you, for a
kiss, a word. Please do something urgently to arrange for us to
meet.

In the same letter I made inquiries about various friends I had
left behind in Vilna when I had departed, including Solomon, my
good, kind friend Shlomo Entin, who, as I later found out, had
died bravely while acting as messenger between the fighting underground of the Vilna ghetto and the fighting organization of
the Warsaw ghetto.[1] I also asked my friends in Palestine if they
had any information about Hayyim and Joseph: "I was with them
for a short time, and we worked together building the railroad.
Then we separated."

The answers I received were very encouraging. My world was
enriched. Every bit of information about Palestine was like a
breath of fresh air. I also received a number of food packages. I
was certain that no effort was being spared to get me to Palestine,
and much was actually being done. Misha left no stone unturned
until he finally succeeded.

However, instead of 1942, I reached Palestine in 1949. . . .

On the anniversary of the Russian Revolution, on November
7, 1942, twenty-five years after the Great October, I was alone
with my country by means of a letter to friends and to my
brother:

Thank you for encouraging me. . . . When I receive a letter
from you, a current of strength goes through me — where shall
I discharge it? So, only my nerves tremble and I cannot find a

[1] Solomon was one of my Pinsk friends who had moved to Vilna. In time,
he headed the activities of the Noar Tsiyoni in former Poland from there,
particularly the coordination of the anti-Nazi underground activities of the
movement's branches in Vilna and Warsaw. His brother, Meir Entin, was
killed in the defense of Nitzanim in the Israeli War of Independence.

place for myself. Today I don't have to go to work because of the holiday, but I don't know what to do with my free time — go beat your head against the wall.

I want to believe that I shall soon find out the results of your efforts on my behalf. I don't know what to think about Hayyim and I am unhappy at the fact that you have no word of him. First we lived together with our friend Akko [that is, prison; Akko is the Hebrew for Acre, where the British had a prison]. *Our friendship withstood the most difficult tests. He is honest, sincere, and bold. We ate out of the same plate, and with him, it was easier. He is industrious and has blessed hands. I don't know how it's possible to find out anything about him.*

Meanwhile, life grew easier for me. When I first began working in the fields, I would often ask the director of the children's home for a raise of ten to twenty rubles a month. I needed money for my expanding correspondence, and more urgently, in order to buy some decent clothing, which was very expensive. The director not only invariably replied with a refusal and an explanation that it was impossible because the table of organization did not allow it, but gave me a kind smile the significance of which I failed to understand. Finally, to my complaint that it was hard to live on my salary, she answered, "You have to know how to live." She told me this two or three times. What had she meant by it? I should have understood the hint. Stupid fool, you're fighting for a raise of ten or twenty rubles; who is stopping you from making much more than this more easily? Finally, I grasped her hint completely. You work in the vegetable garden. Take away whatever you want from there and live. There is enough there for you, too.

I took the hint well. From the garden I began taking onions, watermelons, potatoes, and other vegetables to town and selling them. I gradually improved my pilfering technique. I discovered that the water in the main channel flowed in the direction of town. Putting a whole flotilla of watermelons into it, I would take it easy sauntering along the bank with the fruits seemingly accompanying me. At a certain spot inside the town, I would remove them one by one and storage them.

Afterward, I was promoted. I became the children's house "official" driver, directly responsible to a very pleasant person, who also had "black marks" on his biography. He was one of my greatest instructors in the science of living.

I drove a wagon hitched to a pair of oxen. My superior taught me the simple job of harnessing and driving them. In each such pair of oxen, one was called Tsop and the other Tsabe. My Tsop was brown and Tsabe was red. Tsop was on the right and Tsabe, on the left. When you said "Tsop" and hit him with the whip, he would begin moving toward the right, and Tsabe would follow. If you said "Tsabe," the lovely couple would turn left. It could not be easier. However, there was one secret of which I was not aware when I began my career as a driver which nearly led to one ox killing the other. They became entangled with one another, ran wild and collided, and almost demolished the wall of a clay hut because I did not grasp that the animal on the right was my right behind the oxen and not from the front when I was harnessing them. But I caught on pretty damn quick.

My superior and I would visit bakeries, warehouses, and stores. Our rule was for us to benefit without anyone missing anything. Naturally, we only helped ourselves to reasonable quantities as was befitting each man's station and rank. We did not forget the other officials either. One should not be selfish.

But I have fond memories of my superior not only because of material matters. He was an educated person, well versed in literature. Sitting in our wagon being dragged by the oxen, we would occasionally take our minds off Tsop and Tsabe and perch on some sacks; he would expatiate on Lermontov and Pushkin, his eyes shining with the light from another world. He was an excellent teacher and a good friend.

However, just when everything was going well, I was sent

back to prison. My immediate life — let my lips refrain from sinning — was good. The future seemed brighter. I was establishing encouraging contacts with my friends in Palestine and preparing to go to Kuibyshev where an immigration certificate to the Holy Land was being kept for me at the British consulate, which had been evacuated from Moscow. Then, without warning, this bolt crashed down on me from a clear blue sky.

On December 7, 1942, the director witnessed my arrest. I was with her on some errand pertaining to the farm outside of town. The NKVD men apparently could not wait until our return home and came to the village in which we happened to be stopping. They had a warrant for my arrest as well as a search warrant, both properly signed, with careful attention to regulations. The law, literally, "ran wild." My director was stupefied. However, experience had taught her how to behave in such circumstances and without uttering a word, she acceded to the request to sign that she had witnessed my arrest and search, as the law required. She only asked the maintainers of order if she could secure some food for me from a villager and brought me a loaf of bread and a piece of cheese. The men wanted to know where my belongings were. I did not have much and consented to have the NKVD men fetch them without me. I did not want the children and the other workers in the home to see me being led away.

My imagination worked at top speed, but I could not find a reason for my arrest. My captors could only console me and say that everything would certainly be clarified. The next day I was taken to Alma-Ata, the capital of Kazakhstan, and housed in a confidential prison located under the same roof as the Republic's offices of the commissariat (after 1946, ministry) of internal security and the commissar himself.

This was the great dark turning point which took place — so I can now joke about it — because of the tiny louse which was not even mine that was discovered during the sanitary inspection of the train supposed to take me to Semipalatinsk. Who knows, per-

haps if I had not stopped off in Chu, fate might have chosen another way. Or maybe if there is something in store for you, you
cannot flee from your own shadow.

However that may be, I began to serve an additional sentence
of *five full years:* a complete pyatiletka — five-year plan.

My One-Man Cell—And My Pichugin

After the formal details — medical examination, personal search and the removal of all buttons, bath and haircut, registration and affixing of signatures required by law — of my incarceration at Alma-Ata had been completed, I was locked in a one-man cell, called an odinochka or "oner."

I was already familiar with life in an "internal" prison from Vileika, my first permanent home in the kingdom of the NKVD, but at Alma-Ata I found marked variations. First of all, solitary confinement. Day after day alone inside four solid walls bordering an area of about four square yards. The only faces you saw were those of the kluchnik (the turnkey who was also corridor guard), the woman distributing food, the sentry taking you for a walk in the yard by yourself, the guard taking you in to interrogations, and the interrogator. All around you there was an abysmal quiet from which creatures of the depths crawled forth without a murmur and wrapped themselves around your neck.

In such loneliness and in this silence nightmares of the imagination become alive and grow, as if somebody or something must fill the empty space around you. And there was another conspicuous difference from all my previous quarters: here it was terrifyingly clean, as if they had also deprived you of grains of dust and filaments from a spider's web. The cell shone with cleanliness and you were warned to see that no stain appeared on the floor or walls. This was murderous cleanliness which in the hermetic solitude only emphasized the inhumanity prevailing here. And the order was stifling! You were linked to a strict schedule for all your activities — going to the toilet, food distribution, receiving water . . . everyone lives by the clock, and the time of activities is the clock.

In every cell there were two or three articles of "furniture," every item of which had to be in its exact place to the fraction of an inch; there was to be no deviation, God forbid, by change or variety. Each cell had an iron cot and a mattress which from the time of the official rising had to be folded in half, with the blanket — also folded according to regulations — and pillow on top of it. The towel was spread out on the exposed part of the cot. Your shoes, when you were not wearing them, had to stand militarily at the foot of the cot. There was a table 16″ x 16″ which also served as a chessboard. However, not only did you not have anyone to play with — you could not even play by yourself because you had no pieces.

The construction of the cell added to its terror: its height exceeded its length. The barred window shuttered on the outside was near the ceiling. Across from the window in the ceiling near the door there was an electric bulb in an iron cage. The light burned all night above your eyes, but order required that you not hide from it; it was forbidden to pull the blanket up over your face just as you were not allowed to hold your hands under it — regulations designed to keep the prisoner disciplined as well as to keep him from attempting suicide. During the day you could not lie down at all, and if you were caught violating this prohibition, you were liable to lose the mattress for a few days and sleep on the bare iron slats of the cot.

You were shut in and locked up, alone and isolated in this epitome of prisons. Still, you were kept under surveillance, and every one of your movements was watched. In the thick, heavy iron door there was a hole over which a movable cover had been fixed on the outside. The hole was narrower on the outside and wider on the inside to enable the guard to take in the whole cell with his eye without being seen at all. In prisoners' slang this peephole was called little wolf or eye. Other more intellectual people would refer to it as Judas Iscariot to indicate that it gives away, betrays . . . Many years after Alma-Ata, I was touring Athens and entered a small Greek Orthodox-Byzantine church. Over the door adorned with ritual pictures and surrounded by sacred figures an *eye* had been painted; it was the eye of God watching the actions of men. For some reason, this Orthodox-Byzantine eye reminded me of the prison eye of the NKVD watching and seeing everything. . . .

In the daytime, the cell was shrouded in gloom. A lone beam of light infiltrated the barricaded, barred, screened window and rested on the floor. It did not amuse me. I do not believe that anyone can wax poetic over such a souvenir slipping in from another world. And perhaps my sensibilities to views from nature had been dulled so that not even a trace of them could evoke a response in me. On the other hand, I yearned to hear the voice of a human being, even the miaowing of a cat, the barking of a dog. For what was most harrowing was the *silence*. I am almost certain that it is included among the psychological means scientifically devised by the NKVD (or NKGB, the People's Commissariat for State Security) for softening up prisoners due for interrogation. Strange, I would eagerly have welcomed a lone fly.

But let's leave the cell for now and go to the *interrogator* for our first meeting. It was midnight. I was awakened by the key turning in the lock. The cell door opened a foot and the guard

stuck his head inside. I was asked to give my name. It was really
me they wanted. "Get dressed." In a moment I was ready in
clothes and shoes (they had taken my shoelaces away; it makes it
quicker to put on shoes). I shivered a little — cold or fear? I
rubbed my eyes, enjoining myself not to yield. A little from my
own experience and from hundreds of stories I had heard, I knew
that nobody gets out of here. Nevertheless, I had no idea why I
had been brought here, to the "internal" prison; perhaps there had
been a misunderstanding after all? I was led from one corridor to
another. I remember them all; they are so familiar to me. But
here, they appear longer. We seemed to be walking through tun-
nels and descending numerous floors. We entered cellars within
cellars, until the guard told me to stop in front of a door, examined the number plate, knocked, and ushered me into a lighted,
well-furnished room with heavy curtains draping the windows.

"Good evening," I greeted the man behind the desk. I was
standing erect near the entrance with my hands folded behind me.
I was wondering whether or not at such a time of night the Russians also employed the greeting "Good evening," but I seemed
not to have committed a blunder. "Good night" is said departing
and not on entering. At a wide desk a man in uniform was signing
a receipt that he had received the prisoner from the guard who
had brought him. The balance sheet tallied. Only now did he raise
his head and answer courteously, "Good evening to you."

As soon as the guard had left, the man rose (he was wearing
boots which I had not seen before) and gently offered, "My name
is Pichugin. I shall be your interrogator."

"Very nice."

"You know the regulations? I mean the rules during an interrogation?"

"I think so."

"Ah, yes. This is not your first time at such an interrogation.
You were already interrogated and sentenced once, isn't that so?"

"Yes, I was sentenced by the Os-So to five years' imprison-

ment, but I was released under the amnesty granted to Polish nationals." I immediately tried to point out my foreign origin and
the fact that I was an ally.

"That's not important at the moment. I only wanted to know
if you are experienced with interrogations. Do you know what
your obligations are and how to behave, and, in general, do you
know how our interrogations are conducted?"

"I think so."

"That's good. It will go faster with you, I hope. Sit down,
please."

"Thank you."

I sat down immediately in a chair in the corner according to all
the rules: my head faced the interrogator and my hands were on
my knees.

"What is your family name?"

"Globerman."

"I mean your real surname."

"What are you driving at? My surname is Globerman."

"But I am interested in knowing your *true* family name."

"I understand. My only family name is Globerman."

"You're already being stubborn at the beginning of the interrogation? What is your real family name, I asked."

"What do you mean, my real family name. What other surname do I have?"

"Only *I* can ask *you* questions and not the other way around.
And don't get nervous, my friend. Just answer to the point."

"But I don't understand the question."

"The question is very clear. Your alias is known to everybody,
but we also know what your real surname is. So there's no sense in
concealing it. Say it, and let's get it over with."

"I don't know any other surname of mine. I'm Globerman."

I had certainly not expected such a strange stroke of ill fortune. Who could have invented the idea that Globerman is an
alias? In time I learned that the interrogator's confident questions

and "allusions" had no legs whatsoever to stand on. They were a kind of shot in the dark. And if this shot hit nothing, it would constitute part of the "business" deal between the interrogator and the prisoner: now, he would yield on the point of your "real surname" and in the course of the interrogation, you would give in to him in other matters.

"Okay, let's assume for the time being that your name is Globerman. We'll come back to it. Meanwhile, let's make some progress. You'll see that there's no sense in being stubborn and you'll come and tell me your real name of your own accord."

"But I won't suddenly make up a surname. My family name is Globerman."

"Very well. I told you that for the time being we have finished with that. We don't have any time to remain in one place. Now tell me, why were you arrested?"

"You're asking me?"

"Whom shall I ask?"

"I don't know why."

"We're used to such answers. No one knows why at the beginning. Tell me, why did they arrest you?"

"I don't know anything. I can't even guess."

"What did you do against the Soviet Union?"

"I didn't do anything."

(In an argumentative drawl) "That means that the Soviet security authorities, according to what you say, arrest people for nothing?"

I felt a trap and replied with as much restraint as I could muster, "No, that's not what I said."

"Then what are you saying?"

"It's simple. It could be a misunderstanding, a mistake."

"Cut out the foolishness! The NKVD never makes mistakes. If you are here, it means that everything is known and clear."

For a moment, I forgot my position and dared to ask, "What do you know?"

"That's what you are going to tell us. *You.* We know, but nevertheless, you will say it; you will talk. Generally, you should know that *we* do not need what you can tell us. Everything is manifestly clear to us. You need your confessions [this fine word was already being used in the first interrogation] to make it easier for yourself."

"But, I don't know anything."

(With malicious, emphatic irony) "Right away I'm going to ring for them to open the gate and let you go home. You don't know anything."

"I really don't know anything."

"Stop pretending you're innocent. Tell me about your counterrevolutionary activity."

"What should I tell you about?"

"Everything you did and sabotaged. Speak honestly."

"But I didn't sabotage anything. [I was beginning to get nervous.] I don't know what to say. What do you want from me?"

"Nothing, only the truth."

"I'm telling you only the truth."

Taking a file out of his drawer, he waved it, "The truth is here, *here!* The whole truth. We know everything. I repeat, we do not need your testimony at all. It's you who needs it. I'm simply advising you, speak, for your sake."

"But about what?"

"Try to remember, what you did, your activities, your associates — try and think."

"I don't recall anything."

"I'm telling you to remember. If necessary, we'll remind you. But that will be held against you. And it would be too bad to waste time."

"I can't remember anything, because there was nothing special."

"Special? I know, you're used to things like that. Still, maybe you'll do me the favor of remembering?"

"There was nothing [I was careful to omit the word special]."

"Nothing? So you made up your mind to sabotage the interrogation too. You certainly don't know whom you're dealing with. You don't understand your position. You still don't grasp where you are."

"I know where I am, but I can't tell more than the truth."

"You're being evasive; you're wriggling. I'm telling you honestly, it won't help you. You have nothing to conceal. Everything is written down. And by the way, what you don't say is being told by those who were arrested together with you."

At Alma-Ata when I was being taken from the police detention cell to the internal prison, I was startled to discover in another corner of the same truck Lucia Gertsulin, whose brother Barukh had persuaded me several months before to settle in Chu. Armed guards, in addition to those in the corners of the vehicle, stood between us and watched our every movement so that we could not even exchange signs. I did not see the prisoner, Lucia, again from the time we were together in the truck until I reached Poland in 1948 (six years later). In the course of the interrogation, I learned that she, her brother Barukh, their cousin Noah Eisenberg, and I were linked together in one dossier. However, at the outset of the interrogation I had no idea that my dossier was a collective one and that simultaneously three more of my "partners in crime" were also being interrogated (Noah Eisenberg had been arrested later, but he had already been interrogated before his arrest in Chu, where we had been living). When the interrogator mentioned "those arrested together with you," I only knew of Lucia's arrest. However, I pretended not to know anything about other prisoners and said, "I don't know who was arrested together with me and why I should have been arrested, but no one can tell you more about me than I myself."

"Okay, you tell it."

"But, according to your questions, I have nothing to tell."

"Listen, you'll find out that you have something to tell, and how. Talk like your companions in the other cells have talked."

(I again showed nervousness) "Let them talk! I have nothing to tell."

"Look at him, pretending to be insulted. So capricious."

"I am not capricious, but I don't know what you want from me."

"Listen, young man, I thought you'd have more sense and spare your strength. I thought it would go fast with you. But, if you're mulish — we have time. It seems we'll have to work on you. Go and do some thinking. Go back to your cell and try to remember. But listen to my advice, I'll call you again and drop this comedy! We've seen greater actors than you here. It would be a pity to waste your talents and energy."

He telephoned for the guard to come for the prisoner and then continued, "It would be better for you if we conducted your interrogation peaceably. You certainly understand that we have various ways of conducting an interrogation, but I want it to be done in a civilized fashion. You'll have time in your cell to think it over."

The guard appeared in the doorway. I did not know what time it was. It was difficult for me to estimate how long I had been at my first get-acquainted meeting with the citizen interrogator Pichugin. But I did not fall asleep again. Traces of dawn were already visible in the screened and barred window. Reveille was not far off. And I was a tangle of thoughts, fancies, and conjectures.

We Are Not a Police Force

When would Pichugin call me again? And what should I tell my interrogator the next time? I really did not know what to say.

It seemed that I was the victim of malicious slander. It was a frame-up from beginning to end. What could they suspect me of? And who were those "conspiring together with me" who, the interrogator said, were "talking"? My thoughts were tormenting me, but I could find nothing to take hold of. I tried to reconstruct the sequence of my activities but could discover nothing to which the interrogator had alluded. Over and over again, I pondered upon his words, "false name, real name, you did, you acted, you sabotaged." I had already served a term; I was interrogated; I was sentenced. But then I had been caught, pure and simple. Honestly or not, justifiably or not, I had attempted to cross the border illegally and had been punished. But what was I in for now?

The strange meeting in the police truck with Lucia, of the family from Chu, who was also being taken in the same direction by the NKVD gave me the shred of an idea that perhaps they had been watching me at work in the vegetable garden and on the wagon of the children's home and had detected my pilfering. I would sometimes stop at this family's house and even leave my loot there for a while. But it was difficult to really put any credence in this faint notion since I had been taken to a confidential prison — a highly significant fact. Meanwhile, this was the only idea of any substance in my criminological explorations. However, it was the only point to which the interrogator had made no illusions. Nevertheless, I could think of no other solution.

All indications were that citizen-interrogator Pichugin had been assigned to me personally. The following night, I was again taken to him. I slowly became accustomed to the phenomenon that night marked the awakening of the NKVD and its mysterious duties. The investigation division became alive. Terror and secrecy filled the atmosphere. I was marched into my interrogator's office. It had the same scenery as the night before and the same act was rehearsed. It was not until about an hour later following an exchange of questions and answers similar to our previous session that Pichugin asked me to come to the desk on which lay an official interrogation form. He filled in the date and began writing, "question, answer, question, answer."

He did not fill out more than one page. These were all personal details. He let me read what he had written and handed me a pen for signing. Everything must be done in an orderly fashion. I affixed my signature to the first page of the investigation report. These pages subsequently increased to a volume of about five hundred sheets bound together in a cover on which were inscribed the instruction *Khranit vyechno*, "Hold forever."

After signing the first time, I felt slightly relieved. The interrogator had not listed all his persistent questions about my "real name." He had only put down "Globerman" and had just written a single reply to each personal question (date of birth, place of birth, education, names of parents, etc.). Perhaps he would also give up his other inventions about my activities, sabotage, and so forth. But I was quickly proven wrong. The seesaw began once more.

"Well, what have you been thinking?"

"What was I supposed to think about?"

"You forget that, too? What a short memory! Are you or are you not going to talk now?"

"I'll talk."

"But to the point. Tell me about your activities."

"What activities?"

"That caused your arrest."

"I still don't know why I was arrested."

"We've already known for a long time and you don't know yet?"

"No, I don't know."

"Your only choice is to recall."

"I don't recall anything."

"No sins? A pure soul?" After a pause, "Why do you keep quiet?"

I felt like a person with something stuck in his throat. I could neither swallow it nor throw it up. Perhaps I should also contribute something to the progress of the investigation. I decided to put out a single card but hesitantly and cautiously in order not to hint at too much. After Pichugin again asked, "Why do you keep quiet?" I uttered, "I don't know, but perhaps there was something wrong with my work in the vegetable garden of the children's home."

"What, for instance?"

"I'm not sure. Maybe I shouldn't have . . ."

He interrupted me, urging me to continue, "What shouldn't you have done?"

"Sometimes, going home from work, I took watermelons and potatoes. I didn't think I had to ask."

My Pichugin literally burst into hysterical laughter, but his guffaws quickly turned to fury. "Listen, that's a wonderful story, watermelons, potatoes. You could die laughing. What do you think anyway, that we are policemen? Who gives a hoot for your potatoes. As far as I'm concerned, you could have carted away wagonsful from your vegetable garden. Not a bad story, but it won't work. An enemy of the people like you trying to play the part of a petty thief! Poor pickpocket! Watermelons he gives me."

"Then, what do you want of me?"

"Tell me about your anti-Soviet activities, you blackguard."

Not counting enemy of the people, blackguard was the first insult flung at me during an interrogation. In the course of my investigation, this drop became a flood. I did not react to the epithet and asked quietly, "What do you want me to tell you?"

"Anti-Soviet activities. Yes, your acts against the Soviet state. I want to know about your counterrevolutionary deeds and not about vegetables."

"What counterrevolutionary deeds?"

"Put your activity against the state down on the desk and never mind lousy watermelons."

"I engaged in no activity against the state."

"That means you're sticking to your story. Sabotage is in your blood. You haven't stopped sabotaging the investigation."

I have often thought of these terms "sabotaging the investigation." I always connected real or imaginary sabotage with industry and production. Apparently an investigation is also a sort of economic enterprise, a kind of production. I made an effort to defend myself against the accusation that I was sabotaging this production. I said, "I have no intention of sabotaging the investigation. I only want to clarify matters, and I am telling the whole truth about myself."

"A truth about potatoes. You can sell that to the police, not to us."

I had already discerned a number of times that the NKVD men looked down upon the police, upon the civilian preservers of law and order. Apparently the suggestion that the NKVD had perhaps discovered my pilfering and was interested in my offenses was not only regarded as funny by my interrogator but he had actually been insulted by it. His honor as a member of the secret police had been affronted. He would not stoop to such foolishness. He wanted to hear another tune. "You won't bring us watermelons. All we'd like to know is about your acts against the state and whatever you did against the Communist regime."

"What I did against the Communist regime? When?"

"When? You fought us all your life. But first of all, let's straighten out your recent acts."

"I have no idea what you're talking about."

"You know very well. But you're a consummate counterrevolutionary. That's okay. You'll soften up. We've cracked harder nuts than you. But for your own good, open your mouth of your own accord."

I was becoming more nervous. "Maybe you can tell me what I'm accused of?"

"Very well. I'll help you remember. Are you acquainted with Gerzl?" (He meant Herzl [1]; there's no H in Russian.)

"I know about him. He was a great Zionist leader."

Just then I had a mind to display more erudition. I could finally answer one question properly. However, he interrupted, "Thank God, we're getting on the road. So you know a great deal about *Zionism*. You're quite familiar with Jewish nationalism, aren't you now? Tell me, what did you do for Zionism in our country, in the Soviet Union?"

"I didn't do a thing."

At this point, my interrogator assumed a manner of speaking combining both natural logic and diabolical cunning. "Perhaps you'd like to tell me that you know nothing of Zionism, that you are not interested in it?"

I saw no reason for just pretending and replied, "I am not ignorant of Zionism, but I know nothing of any Zionist activity in the Soviet Union."

"Then, what kind of a Zionist are you?"

"What do you mean?"

"I mean your Zionist activity, exactly that. Perhaps I should remind you what role you played in the Zionist movement? Maybe you have forgotten that you were a member of the Central Committee?"

I pondered for a moment. I would try a legalistic explanation. "I was a member of the Central Committee of a Zionist youth movement in Poland before the war. There, it was permitted. Here I do not belong to any movement and I engage in no activity as the member of any organization."

He grasped at my use of the present tense, "Certainly, here, now, you are not a member any more and you are not active — "

[1] The founder of political Zionism; author of *The Jewish State*, in which he advanced the idea of an independent Jewish state as the solution to the Jews' problems.

"I never belonged to any movement or engaged in any activity in the Soviet Union."

"Again I see that we'll have a little work with you. But it's nothing. We'll remind you of many things. You'll be very much surprised to learn how much we know about you. Meanwhile, go back to your cell and think." He telephoned my guard to come and until the soldier appeared, the interrogator continued giving me friendly advice. "You would do well to think about Persia a little."

Pichugin cast the word Persia into my world just as the sentry entered.

Persia . . . Palestine

Pichugin's final word, Persia, pounded in my head all the way back to my cell and for the rest of the night. The NKVD interrogators possess a sort of mysterious power not just for discovering what you do but also for laying bare your secret thoughts. I really do not know of any act of mine connected with Persia; but going there was what I intensely desired. After the Polish officers had rejected me for military service, my hope of reaching Persia was shattered, but now and then it would come back to life in my heart. Actually, only in my heart. Did the interrogator really know what I was thinking of?

Persia, Persia . . . The word drove all other matters from my mind. What was happening here? It was like trying to solve a crossword puzzle. A package I had received in Chu had come from Persia. I did not even know who had sent it. It had probably been arranged by friends in Palestine. So what? Polish units organizing and training on Soviet soil were openly being allowed to leave for Persia. Why couldn't I, a Polish national enjoying the Polish amnesty, receive a parcel from Persia? But there must be some secret buried here. The interrogator did know something that I had no inkling of.

This time, they did not leave me alone until night came. I was summoned at noon. I was once more in the interrogator's office, tensely waiting to hear more about Persia. However, he was in no hurry to begin the conversation. For a full hour, he was looking through papers, rearranging his drawers, and talking on the telephone. "How was the party in your house? . . . How is your daughter? You have a nice little dog? . . ." Pichugin paid no attention whatsoever to his guest. I was sitting in a corner without moving. He wrote down a few words, drew several lines on a sheet of paper with a ruler, and took his wallet out to count the change inside. Then he took a folder out of his breast pocket and sorted out the slips of paper and bills it contained. Finally, he began looking at pictures. What is this, I was thinking. It was obviously the demonstration of a free, normal life clearly directed at a person who was deprived of it. The telephone rang. "We'll come, we'll be there. Prepare a glass of something good."

Finally, he turned to me, "What's new?"

"Nothing new."

In a fatherly tone, as if he did not know, "What cell are you in?"

I told him the number.

Once more he asked in surprise, as if he did not know, "What, alone in a cell?"

"Yes."

"That's only temporary. When you complete the investigation [I'm thinking, when I complete . . . I'm the one to complete the investigation] you'll be transferred to a general cell. How's the food?"

"Satisfactory."

I really did have enough food at the beginning, four hundred and fifty grams (nearly a pound) of bread, a pinch of sugar, and something cooked twice a day. However, the new situation I was in bothered me and took away my appetite. Above all, I did not want to show weakness before the interrogator.

He continued questioning me, "Is there anything you'd like in the cell?"

"I'd like a book to read. There's a library in the prison which, according to regulations, the prisoners are entitled to use."

Pichugin let me in on a secret. As long as I was being interrogated, as long as my status was that of a prisoner being investigated, the fulfillment of my slightest wish was entirely up to the interrogator. I soon learned that this ruling did not stem from the mere formality of dividing authority but was one of the means of conducting the interrogation. Each morning the officials inspected the cells. One of the higher officers would list the prisoners' requests. It was quite certain that these requests were handed to the interrogators who made use of them psychologically in learning where to exert pressure. Then the interrogator would determine whether or not the prisoner being investigated might receive a book, purchase additional food or tobacco in the prison store, be sent parcels from the outside, or see his family. For instance, just those for whom smoking was everything and who begged for tobacco would not receive it easily and the interrogator would continually harp on the subject. And if a prisoner were a glutton constantly troubled by a sensation of hunger, they waved food over him, as it were, but he would not easily receive additional rations for his own money from the prison store or in a parcel from the outside. The interrogator would quickly find out who of his clients was afflicted with an intense feeling for his family and stimulate it and hold it out as bait in his interviews. Apparently just because I repeated my request for books nearly every morning during the inspection tour I did not receive any. Pichugin, for his part, would promise to see that I was given books, but hinted gently that as a matter of fact, it all depended only on me, on my conduct during the interrogation.

To my amazement, Pichugin did not ask anything else after the conversation about conditions in my cell and my wishes and sent me back. However, the same night I was awakened shortly after I had fallen asleep and ordered to dress and accompany the guard to his office. He was again different from what he had been during the day. In the days and nights to follow, I discovered that this dual, or possibly multiple, personality is a weapon against the prisoner. What astonished me most was the rapidity of the transformations. Pichugin could change the tone of his speech and the inflection of his voice, his style and his entire way of acting, not only from one interrogation to the other, but during the course of a single session as well. This time, he greeted me with a surprise question, "Is it true that you are against the Soviet regime?"

"I am not a Soviet citizen and I have no special views on the regime in the USSR."

"Why are you afraid to say that you love our regime or hate it?"

"I cannot define love or hate of a regime when I am a foreign citizen."

"You're intelligent enough to define it. But, let me ask you something else. Do you like our regime?"

"I like many things. There are some things I'm not used to."

"That means, you hate us."

"I did not say that. In general, I am not used to the concepts of love and hate in relation to a certain country."

"Very well. In your Palestine [for the first time, I heard the word *Palestine* in an interrogation. Previously it had been *Persia*. My thought feelers were leading me to the idea that *Palestine* and *Persia* were tied together in the interrogation plan], would you want a Communist, Soviet regime?"

Stalling for time in order to think a little and formulate an answer, I asked, "What do you mean by that?"

"Well, what sort of regime would you like in your Palestine?"

Still trying to gain time, I asked, "What do you mean *my* Palestine?"

"Then whose is it? Mine?" With a diabolical smile, he said, "Perhaps you have decided to change your mind and deny altogether that you are a Zionist and that you have any interest in Palestine?"

"I do not deny it. However, we Zionists have not discussed the nature of any future regime in the Land of Israel. We claim that first of all we must build up the country and then determine its type of government."

He jeered in amazement, "You don't say! Extraordinary! You're building and you don't know what. But, tell me honestly, isn't it true that you are an enemy of the people?"

"It's not true."

"Then, you love us?"

"Neither hate nor love. In general . . ."

He stopped me, "Quit splitting hairs. Either you're our enemy or our friend. If you don't love us, you hate us. We'll show your true face, you sly snake." His anger mounted, "You'll see yet what we have in store for enemies of the people like you. I'm warning you for the last time ["last times" like this were repeated quite often], better lay your weapons down. That's all you can do once you are in our hands. Don't think I'll dance attendance on you like a nursemaid. Give up, I tell you. Don't look for trouble with us."

"I'm not looking for trouble. But I don't know what you want of me."

"He doesn't know what we want of him, the baby! Tell me, you know what Gorki said?" Again Gorki, like the first time I was arrested in Vileika. It was quite clear that what Pichugin meant was, of course, that same standard phrase. However, I inquired as if I had no idea what it was all about, "What did Gorki say?"

"That an enemy who surrenders is to be forgiven, but a stubborn one must be destroyed."

"What does that have to do with me?"

"O, my little dove, it has a lot to do with you. And how it concerns you."

"I have no idea what you're talking about."

"So innocent! He has no idea. And what about *Persia?*"

"What Persia?"

"You don't know anything, huh?"

"I don't know anything."

"Clever boy! Are you trying to put something over on us?"

"I'm not trying to put anything over on you, but I do not know what you're talking about."

"Really, I'll order your release right away and you'll go directly to your Palestine just as you wish. You see. You have convinced me." He paused briefly and eyed me. "Listen, I'm sick of standing on ceremony with you and I'm telling you clearly, we know all about your organization for taking Soviet Jews to Persia. We have been after you for a long time. Now, tell me all about the methods you use. Who financed your activities? Who took part in them? Telling me that alone can make it easier for you. Your organization has in any case been wiped out. You can no longer save it. But tell me how it operated."

"What?"

"Exactly as you heard. You are being charged with the attempt to organize the flight of Jews from the Soviet Union to Persia for the purpose of helping them reach Palestine."

"What Jews?"

"That *you* will tell us. We really know, but you are going to tell us." He waved a file, "It's all here. But you must tell us. You have to confirm it."

"This is all entirely new to me."

"Certainly it's new. You did not expect to get caught. Pardon us for not notifying you in advance."

"But this is the first time I have heard what you just told me. I did not participate in any organization for taking Jews to Persia and Palestine."

He once more tried to sound logical. "So what. As a Zionist, as an important Zionist leader, aren't you interested in Jews coming to Palestine?"

"Of course, I'm interested. But I engaged in no activity for that purpose here. It never occurred to me to do anything against the law."

"Leave the law to me! I want you to give me the names of all the persons involved in the network."

"I don't know of any network or any names."

He unleashed a flood of curses, "I'll make your dog's blood flow. I'll twist off your head, you bedbug. Vermin! Shameless liar Zionist spy!" He waved his fists but did not touch me. He screamed and his eyes made my blood run cold, "Speak! Will you or won't you talk?"

I stuck to my story, monotonously reiterating, "I don't know anything. I don't understand what this is all about." Finally he said, "Go back to your cell and try to remember."

We'll Organize a Meeting for You

I cannot reconstruct the entire course of the investigation and its division into sessions, and see no need for such a report. Hereafter I shall describe what happened without regard for the normal time sequence.

Nothing new was brought up at many of our sessions. The same arguments recurred in varying forms. The matter of Persia, for example, figured in numerous discussions. I did not deny that I wanted very much to go there, and from there to Palestine to my brother and friends. However, since this was impossible, I stubbornly insisted that I had done nothing illegal in order to leave the Soviet Union. It is quite illuminating that, following many nights of nightmares and threats centering around the charge of organizing Jews to flee to Persia and Palestine and after the interrogator had spoken with such confidence about the network and its members, all of whom had been caught, the accusation was suddenly dropped and was not even entered in the record. The law provides that if the charge is dismissed, the way should be clear to an acquittal and release. But the popular Russian saying is right, "As long as the man is here, a count will be found." With or without Persia, what difference did it make? Now discussions of another sort between Pichugin and me began.

Suddenly I discovered that I was accused of anti-Soviet propaganda. Previous charges of my interrogators (enemy of the people, counterrevolutionary, saboteur) had led me to expect to hear that I had blown up bridges or that I had spearheaded the march of masses of Jews to the Persian border (according to the enthusiastic appraisal of the interrogator). In the end, my image as a saboteur had dwindled to midget proportions and my leading hordes of Jews to the Jewish land had become entirely nonexistent. On the other hand, the charge of anti-Soviet propaganda had remained firm. I admitted it. I had signed to the effect. The bulky file with the words "Hold forever" on its cover had my signature on every page. Had I really conducted propaganda against the Soviets? There is no simple answer to this. It is a question of dialectics and semantics. I had better describe the essential details as they developed during the interrogations.

From the heights of sabotage and magnificent Zionist organization, my interrogators reduced me to the plain of conversation between myself and individual friends and acquaintances. These had been simple talks about commonplace matters. They had included chance remarks made in a private room or during a walk, usually just between two persons. They had consisted of rambling conversations skipping from one subject to another, of jokes, observations, sayings, fragmentary impressions, names of books, talk of food intermingled with views on women, reactions to experiences of the moment, inquiries about news and the health of the other person, recollections of a mutual friend, and reminiscences. In sum, these conversations had really comprised all kinds of haphazard chatter with no definite subjects. However, I learned that my interrogator had complete protocols recording such conversations with friends and acquaintances. He was no longer groping in the dark, throwing in a line hoping to fish out some choice morsel, but walking on almost firm ground. He knew all about conversations which had taken place with all their external features — where I had walked with one friend and had sat with another, when I had reacted in one fashion and when in another, and how I had laughed and joked. The interrogator would describe the situation filling in the background for a certain remark, wisecrack or minor gossip.

I would not even define these conversations, these dialogues, as political. We simply chatted. However, it was only natural that now and then they would touch upon a facet of Soviet life, of the reality surrounding us. Sometimes, we would express disapproval or compare a Soviet practice with a Polish custom. However, the conversations had been without any special meaning, as one man talks of his feelings and thoughts to another, generally in a jocular spirit. But the interrogator, adept at fitting words into patterns, had transformed these conversations into a conspiracy and propaganda. His formulations were actually absurd, if not outright caricatures. The trouble, however, was that that is how they looked to me, whereas he regarded — or pretended to regard — them with grave severity.

For example, I was once sitting in the mess hall waiting for them to serve the miserable cabbage soup. Like everyone else, we had to wait about an hour. I remarked to a friend, "How much time must men who have work to do waste here for this thin soup. See how the waitresses crawl like turtles — what do they care?" That was what I had said, word by word. And one of us had remarked that if he were the proprietor of this restaurant, he would see to it that the customers were served quickly and courteously so they would come back.

This conversation — as others like it — served as a kind of corpus delicti to the charge against me of spreading anti-Soviet propaganda. In its final metamorphosis, it became transformed into "slandering the Soviet Union and its commercial and economic system while marveling at and praising the commercial and economic system of the capitalist regimes." At first I was amazed at this statement and at myself. Had I really said that? And in such a "literary" form? I was simply talking about *my* cabbage soup and complaining that it was not being served fast enough (I was already afraid to reveal to the interrogator a matter he did not know yet, that I had also found fault with the soup because it was nearly cold). But Pichugin simply explained to me the necessity of formulating concepts, or, as he put it, giving a form to things. "I can't just write everything down any which way," he told me, "as if it were a woman talking in the marketplace."

Here is another example. I was out taking a walk with my friend in Chu, Barukh, merely to get some air. We joked, laughed, and chatted. Passing a section of the railroad undergoing repairs, we saw a number of women working hard at digging up earth and loading it on trucks. One of us observed, "In our country [Poland before the war], I never saw women doing such hard, dirty work." (This was not so at all. We had apparently not been familiar with the wretched existence of many people in Poland. On the other hand, we had not seen in Poland women occupying the important positions they did in the USSR.) This had not even been an "opinion" but simply an idle remark. But it had been enough for the NKVD, and Pichugin had mantled it in the formulation of "slandering the USSR by pointing out the bitter fate of the Soviet women required to engage in labor; comparing the Communist way of life with the capitalist system to show that the former does not respect women."

Again I neither recognized myself nor what I was supposed to have said. I had used such an elegant style, as if while taking a walk with a friend I had been composing pamphlets for publication. I protested, contending that they had ascribed words to me I had never said. But, Pichugin reassured me, he was only putting my words into a stylistic framework. One could not write in a disorderly fashion. Meanwhile, he dropped an apparently irrelevant sentence which implied that he could enmesh you still more, so you had better leave well enough alone. "Why, incidentally, did you have to go walking near the railroad tracks?"

Now I am citing these statements hastily in passing and pointing out isolated examples. However, at the time, when such discussions and bargaining over fine distinctions were going on for weeks, I was beginning to give in to the interrogator's will. These talks were accompanied by threats and vituperation, shouts and curses with no end in sight. Finally I became convinced that the whole battle was unimportant, that one word more or less would not change my condition in the least, and every fiber in my being just yearned for surcease from the interminable inquisition.

Moreover, some of Pichugin's concepts became part of my own thinking. What the hell, somehow progress must be made! How long did I want to rot here over a fine point in the statement or sweat blood over every letter and diacritical mark? So I continued attempting to change the protocol here and there, and the interrogator also "conceded" a word or two until I agreed. The deadlock has finally been overcome. I accepted the "joint" statement and signed in the hope that an important phase had been completed.

But again I was mistaken.

For then, damn it all to hell, a new phase began, and then another, and later on, still another. The number of protocols was endless. Pichugin still had many of my friendly conversations in his bag, more or less faithfully reconstructed. My God, how I managed to slander the Soviet Union while talking about a suit or laundry or food in the mess hall or the children's behavior in the home, or some other trifle!

After a considerable quantity of such conversations had accumulated in protocols, I put a fundamental question of principle to my interrogator: "Where was there agitation here? What sort of propaganda was I disseminating — whatever it was I was saying in my meaningless conversations with just a single close friend? Was this agitating?" Then I was vouchsafed a reply which was an instructive lesson for me. It taught me that my interrogator and I were thinking in absolutely different concepts, that we were living in completely separate and distinct worlds, that our thought mechanisms were functioning according to entirely divergent processes. I truly could not grasp what sort of agitation I had engaged in.

Pichugin, however, gave me what seemed to have been a true and innocent answer, "What did you think, that we would organize a meeting for you, take you to Hyde Park?"

In a word, no meeting whatsoever was necessary for an "agitator" like me together with three of his fellows to be sentenced without facing a judge, in accordance with the proper sections: No. 58, subparagraph 10 — counterrevolutionary activity by disseminating anti-Soviet propaganda, and No. 58, subparagraph 11 — the same counterrevolutionary activity jointly with others.

How did information of this "agitation" between two persons reach the NKVD?

First of all, the arrest of myself and the others in the "conspiracy" should be evaluated, to a considerable degree, against the background of the relations between the Soviet government and the Polish government in exile in London. This does not mean that we had any part in the development of such relations, but they were reflected in our fate. The romance between Moscow and Sikorski did not last long. Tension arose between them. There were mutual recriminations which became more acrimonious on the publication of charges that the Russians had massacred fourteen thousand Polish officers at Katyn forest. The honeymoon of the Polish refugees and former prisoners ended. The Russians began treating them more strictly and roughly. Finally, diplomatic relations between the Soviet authorities and the Polish government in exile were severed (we were already in prison when this happened), and the Polish offices in the USSR were dissolved. To a certain extent, we were certainly the victims of an anti-Polish campaign and the charges against us served as auxiliary material to build up a case against the Poles.

To our great sorrow, this auxiliary material was supplied by a woman living in Chu who was also a refugee from the West. She had polished western manners. I myself did not know her well but she used to make herself at home in the house of my friend Barukh, and I had met her there on several occasions. She was dressed according to western taste and I remember marveling at her fluent Russian. Barukh's family was experienced in such matters, and I was particularly cautious about my contacts with people after hearing stories of fathers informing on their children and the other way around. I kept to myself even in the company of people whom I had no reason to suspect. However, whatever I said in Barukh's house or his conversations with the "Western Woman" were so guileless and meaningless, so homey and lacking in social or public significance, that they were uttered with no afterthought. Who could imagine that such a smiling, elegant woman apparently sharing our exile in a foreign land would be devoting herself to collecting our conversations in order to bestow them on the NKVD?

I thought a great deal of this woman and her slander after the interrogation as well. Perhaps we really had babbled too much and our tongues had got us into trouble? But, even with the greatest caution, no one can live for months on end only with himself, hermetically sealed off from society. You cannot go around constantly with a sort of built-in psychological radar to examine each person you encounter and determine his trustworthiness. Life has not endowed us with a perpetually functioning sense of suspicion which assumes in advance that every waitress or salesgirl, every fellow worker and neighbor, is liable to be a secret agent. Above all, you really do not have to talk about politics at all in order to reach the interrogation chambers. Prattle about women and flowers, home and store, a dress and a hairpin, perfume and shoe polish may also secure your admittance to these precincts. Someone will be found to prepare the proper "statement." So is one supposed to padlock his mouth?

To this day I do not know the name of the "Western Woman" and I certainly know nothing of her views and what she thinks. I cannot think of any reason of vengeance for her conduct. I remember her reminiscing with a nostalgic sigh but am unable to say whether or not it was done sincerely or for the purpose of instilling confidence and starting a conversation. The four of us — after we had met once more and attempted to get to the bottom of the matter — ventured a guess that she had gone to work for the NKVD on her own initiative either in order to make a career for herself, demonstrate her patriotism (informing is an honorary act in the Soviet Union), or simply to earn a living. Another theory was that the authorities had forced her to spy on us and report on what we said and did and she could only escape from this role at the risk of her life. Or it may be that she made friendships in all sincerity but at a certain point, the Powers That Be decided to make use of her contacts. Perhaps she herself was not entirely guiltless and had been compelled to act as she did in order to do penance for some crime of hers.

It must be admitted that she did her job well. She reported what she had heard with her own ears and whatever sayings and jokes of mine or fragmentary conversations between Barukh and me which had been repeated in her presence. She also told them details of our lives. I did not talk to her much, but from keeping her eyes and ears open in the home of her hosts, she knew that I lived for the letters I received from Palestine, that I was burning with desire to meet someone from there, and that I believed that sooner or later, I would somehow reach the land of my dreams.

I asked the interrogator to confront me with the Western Woman. I wanted to refute some of the statements she had made, especially the spice that she had added to our talks. My wish was not granted. I had the impression that it was not necessary, either for the interrogator, the Western Woman, or me. Her reports had all probably been formulated with care and polished since words were not supposed to be written down as they are uttered. Barukh and Lucia were individually given the opportunity to confront their "intimate friend." They argued, asked questions, contradicted and supplied proof. But of what use was it all? The confrontation was only a formal ceremony.

Lucia told me how her confrontation with the Western Woman had begun. The interrogator pointed to Lucia and asked the woman, "Do you know her?"

"Yes, we were friends."

"As what do you know her?"

"As a person with hatred of the Soviet Union."

Lucia was furious and shouted, "And I know *her* for a snake in the grass."

However, the interrogator lectured her on uncouth behavior. In any case, her remark was not recorded in the protocol.

What became of the Western Woman I have no idea. Where the road of the four persons who shared the same file led, I shall relate in due course.

Lermontov's Prisoner and the NKVD's Prisoner

My cross-examination lasted about four months, half of them while being located in a cell by myself. However, I did not occupy it consecutively. Apparently Pichugin was playing with me. He allowed me to find out what a general cell was like, but when I did not respond he sent me back to my solitude.

For a while they put another man in my cell and had a second bed brought in. We tried playing checkers with pieces from a broom but scarcely spoke to each other. I suspected him of having been thrown in with me on purpose to make me talk. This is called "planting." It's important to know that even in a prison cell you have to watch out for stool pigeons. A person employed in this role is usually garrulous and talks a great deal about himself. My companion was reserved. Who knows, perhaps he suspected me of having been planted for him? So we played checkers and kept our mouths shut.

What else do you do in a solitary cell between interrogations and during the free hours you have every day? I hummed all the

songs I knew. I silently reviewed chapters in the Bible and stories.
I wrote on the table with my finger, as it were, and "copied"
articles by heart. I counted the bricks on the floor. I did exercises
in arithmetic. I counted the groats in the soup and multiplied the
figure by days, weeks, and months to learn how many I ate in a
single year. A prisoner is like a plant growing in poor soil and
sending its roots very deep in order to suck vitality for its
wretched existence from lower strata. He digs deeply in the layers of his memory for something to revive his spirit. I toyed
with sights in order to kill time, classifying them in my imagination and assigning them to departments according to their nature
and time. I made up intelligence tests for myself; for example, I
formed short words from longer ones such as Pichugin and Djuga-
shvili. I added up the figures representing the numerical value of
words, taking each letter as a number, that is, A as 1, B as 2, et cet-
era. In this manner I performed arithmetical operations with Bible
verses, adding and subtracting figures. I learned all the prison regulations by heart. This was the only literature I was allowed. It
hung on the wall. I added up the number of months, days, and
hours which had elapsed since my birth, and later, since my first
arrest; I tallied up the number of days and hours I had spent in
school. This figuring can also be done in minutes, providing the
sound of footsteps in the corridor does not mix you up and does
not send a tremor through your insides.

Someone is coming. They are calling a name. They are bringing someone. A prisoner is being returned to his cell. Someone is
being taken out. They are putting somebody in. What cell is that?
I hear someone walking, stopping. Doors are opening and shut-
ting. You are taut with expectancy. You merge with the horrors
outside the door.

Once a rare experience came to me from the corridor of secrets and terrors. Putting an ear close to the door, I heard the
voice of the turnkey reciting poetry. I caught the same words
two or three times but was unable to identify them until later,

when I was in the common cell. They were verses from Lermontov's poem "The Prisoner." We also identified the strange warder. My cellmates told me that he had suffered a shock or lost his mind, apparently as a result of his duties, which were too much for him. Anyway, this turnkey disappeared and his voice was not heard again. However, the lines of the poem became close and intimate to me. Whenever I had the chance, I repeated the lines, either in the original Russian or in Hebrew translation.

The song went as follows:

> *Open the bolt and the door for me,*
> *Give me the sun's brilliance,*
> *A black-eyed girl,*
> *A proud steed with a mane of jet.*
> *Then, drunk but not from wine,*
> *I shall kiss the beautiful-eyed one,*
> *Then, quickly on the horse*
> *To the wilderness I shall fly.*
>
> *But the window of my prison is high*
> *And the cell is shut, locked;*
> *The lovely girl is modestly*
> *Sitting, hiding in her attic;*
> *And without a bridle, without resting,*
> *The horse flies, waves in the wind*
> *His tail, as if playing,*
> *And enjoys the freedom of spaces.*
>
> *Sorrow. Gnawing loneliness.*
> *Naked walls surround me.*
> *The fire of an eternal light expires*
> *And is swallowed up in the shadows.*
> *I only hear: Behind the door*
> *In the hush of the darkness,*

With a rhythmic step, a sentry quietly paces
With the seal of silence on his mouth.

But let us leave Lermontov's "Prisoner" for the NKVD's prisoner. Days and nights dragged on. Then Pichugin summoned me once more.

"Good evening."

He did not answer my greeting. Where had his cultivated politeness disappeared to? What would he concoct for me tonight?

"I have to clarify a small matter with you. Where are you actually from?"

"Pinsk."

"Right. That's what you said at the beginning of the cross-examination."

It seemed to me that this was the first time he had immediately confirmed something I had said. So, I was thinking to myself, what is this all about? After my release, I had stopped claiming that I was from Warsaw as I had during my first period of imprisonment. Many people I had encountered on the way knew where I was from and I was afraid to get in trouble. I no longer saw any sense in keeping my hometown a secret as I had done previously in order to keep my parents from harm. I wish I could have received some word of them. Perhaps they had managed to escape from the city now occupied by the Germans. My friends in Chu certainly knew where I was from since they came from a town not far from Pinsk.

Pichugin interrupted my musing. "Where is this Pinsk of yours?"

"In western Byelorussia."

"Ah, I know. The Pinsk marshes."

"Yes."

"What city did you say you were from at your initial interrogation, when you were arrested the first time?"

"I said I was from Warsaw."

"Right, that's what you said. Why did you especially pick Warsaw to claim as your hometown?"

I wondered why he was so anxious to confirm my previous statements. Pichugin obviously had my first dossier. The words "Hold forever" are inscribed on the files for a purpose. My interrogator had doubtlessly sent for my first file. I now resolved to tell him the truth about Warsaw. I would only continue hiding my *mission from Vilna*. Until now, Vilna had not been mentioned in my questioning. That meant they knew nothing about it. I replied, "In 1940 I went to Vilna where my girl friend happened to be. However, when I was caught at the border, I was afraid my parents would suffer because of me. I even thought that if I were considered a refugee from the German occupation zone, I would be forgiven."

During my cross-examinations and in my relations with Soviet institutions, many strange things happened to me. This time, too, the unexpected occurred. Just because I had expected difficulties, pressure, and considerable trouble and I had in my mind prepared all kinds of alternate replies in case of emergency and had planned evasions, Pichugin dropped the entire matter for good. He asked me whether or not I knew anything of my parents. "Who knows," I wondered, "whether they managed to escape; they were old and sick and the capture of Pinsk was very sudden."

And it seemed to me that he was sympathizing with me without uttering a word.

An actual event like my work in Vilna was quickly and smoothly passed over while absolutely meaningless matters generated a great deal of tension between my interrogator and me. During one of our sessions, he demanded that I tell him all about my "ramified" ties with Polish representatives and institutions in the USSR. My connections with them had been extremely cold and I had only gone to them a few times to register and secure some assistance. I had not been friendly with Polish leaders and officials anywhere. But Pichugin continued pressing me to tell him about the activities of the Polish offices and its members, not only in the towns I had passed through but in places to which I had never been as well. I had to suffer a great deal of torment until he finally dropped the matter. But something new came in its stead. It seemed that I had been promoted.

"Who talked you into becoming a spy? What secret name did you get from that person? What did you speak to him about?"

I could not refrain from smiling, "That's all I need."

"You have nothing to smile about, my dear friend. At least tell me who tried to enlist your services as an espionage agent?"

"I have no idea what and whom you are talking about."

"Wonderful. We know and you don't."

With a touch of anger, I retorted, "You don't know anything."

"You're provoking me. Let me remind you that this is not the place for such behavior."

"I am not trying to provoke you. But even untruths need some logic."

"How dare you talk like that [I am omitting his choice language]. Tell me about your espionage activities! That's enough evasiveness. Look at him; see how courageously he lies."

"I am not lying. Why are you bandying around the word 'spy' for no reason at all? Are you saying anything new? For whom could I spy? [At this point I took the initiative.] Maybe for the Germans?"

"I wouldn't be surprised if someone like you would take a spying job from the Germans, too. But meanwhile, you have been spying for the Poles and the British."

"For whom?"

"What are you putting on such an innocent act for? Yes, for the Poles and the British."

"But these are allies of the Soviet people."

"Don't teach me politics."

"I'm not teaching anybody anything, but . . ."

He interrupted, "But you would like to see us defeated, you're looking forward to it."

"How can you talk like this?" I went on with unconcealed anger, "I won't answer any more questions."

"No offense meant, brother. I see through you."

I made up with him, "You see through me that I'm anxious for a German victory?"

"I wouldn't say exactly that. But you would like the Soviet Union to be destroyed also and your Englishmen to emerge victorious. Then you would go back to your Poles, to the *pans*, to the Sikorskis. Isn't that so?"

"I have nothing to answer to that."

"You are hurt, little virgin?"

I did not say a word.

"What is there to be offended at? You don't hate us? You don't love Churchill?"

I maintained my silence. My "strike" infuriated him.

"Listen, are you going to talk or not?"

"I don't know what I'm being asked about."

"You don't look like that kind of a simpleton." He waved a bunch of papers, "These don't prove your innocence either. You had better answer."

"Answer what?"

"What you're asked. Believe me, if you don't talk, you'll rot here. We'll fertilize Soviet soil with your bones. You're being given your last chance."

"What chance? Why?"

"To tell me who the other spies are and clear your conscience a little with an honest, sincere confession."

"I have nothing to confess."

"If you don't confess now, you'll do it tomorrow, or the day after, or in a week."

"I'll never make anything up."

"We'll see."

Pichugin lifted the telephone to make a call. A sentry came to escort me back to my cell.

I waited for the next day, for the day after. I was certain that now a new gear would be applied to my body, that they would send for me day and night without a letup. However, for some reason or another, just after he had put the screws on me in connection with the spying charge, he did not trouble me for more than a week. When I was once more summoned to Pichugin after this respite, prepared to fight him over this asinine espionage charge, and had braced myself for a hail of questions about my "enlistment," the interrogator did not breathe a word about all these supposed contacts of mine, as if they had never been mentioned. I had heard of persons being cross-examined under similar pressure who had attempted to reduce everything to an absurdity and I had told myself that I would do the same. I had intended to tell Pichugin that I had direct ties with the Japanese Mikado and had planned the bombing of Moscow. But this time Pichugin went off on a completely different tack.

Now he wanted me to tell him of my activities in the Zionist youth movement and to hand over the names of leading members.

"What names?"

"All you know, and describe their activities and functions."

"I knew many people at different times. They engaged in the customary activities of a youth movement." I told him of discussions, hikes, camps, collections for the Jewish National Fund, Hebrew courses, and agricultural training farms.

"But *who* are they?"

"What do you mean 'who'?"

"Who were the leaders? Give me *names*."

The demand for names was repeated many times. It was interposed between questions and not especially those directly connected with the subject of the interrogation. "Whom do you know?" Here, there, a year ago, ten years ago. In your hometown, in all the towns you ever visited. You must list, provide details, point out facts. The quest for names began embracing wider areas. He wanted names not only from my movement but from others as well. It was a mad hoarding of names. No normal man can deny that in the course of his life he had neighbors, friends, acquaintances, and teachers. But you must be careful in naming these persons. Who knows what sort of trap they were setting? However, it was ridiculous to stand like a dummy and say, "I didn't know anyone." What you needed was a "stock" of names.

The safest solution was to make up names and addresses as they occurred to you. But this practice could easily trip you up. You yourself would forget the names and addresses and if the interrogator should write them down and later ask you about them again, you would be rattled and you would confuse yourself further. Consequently, a certain amount of authenticity was necessary in your choice of names or you had to be able to recognize them yourself by some sign. I would invent names based on the designations of cities, such as Warsawski, Pinski, Czenstochowski, Minski, or Kharkovski. Or I would give him the names of friends who had gone to Palestine before the war, or the names of people who had died. Sometimes I would move Warsaw people to Lodz and vice versa. But what an unquenchable lust for names this Pichugin had! What for? What would he do with them? He would drown in them. It soon became clear that he himself attached no importance to them. This whole rigmarole was either a pause between leaps or a means of creating a certain mood around you in which you become used to laying bare and scrutinizing all the crannies of your life.

The discussions between one practical question and another about whether or not I was an enemy of the people seemed to be breathers of this sort. They were quasi-hypothetical discussions unrelated to facts. Why was Pichugin so anxious for me to declare and sign that I was an enemy of the people? What actually is an enemy of the people? What would my admission give him?

What would it change? I believe that this, too, was part of the technique of creating a mood about you rendering you vulnerable to the interrogator's attempts to probe into all the recesses of your spirit. Or it may have stemmed from Pichugin's professional pride, his aspirations to achieve outstanding professional attainments. At any rate, he put the question to me countless times, "Well, it's time you confessed that you are an enemy of the people."

"I'm not an enemy."

"But how can you not be our enemy?"

"Why must I be your enemy?"

"Listen, let's speak frankly. How can you love us? We who hate your Zionism, who loathe your entire bourgeois psychology, who cannot stand your nationalism, who do not permit you to go to your Palestine? How can you love us when we hate and exterminate your whole class?"

My class. This was news to me. What class did I belong to? What did my property consist of? Whom had I employed or exploited? It might be worthwhile asking. "Which is my class?"

"You are a bourgeois and the son of a bourgeois."

As far as the investigation and charges were concerned, this had no importance. However, I let myself be dragged into the argument.

My father had employed no one in his shop. My mother's only consolation had been the knowledge that they had no debts. Father nearly always worked from dawn to dusk. It was still dark out when he put on his phylacteries and wrapped himself in the prayer shawl for the morning devotions. At that hour you couldn't find the requisite number of ten men necessary for conducting a public service, and there were some sticklers for tradition who held the belief that it was still too early for the morning service and such a prayer would be considered "bearing God's name in vain." But with respect to certain matters, Father had a sort of religious code of his own: he had no choice but to say his prayers before going off to work. While in his prayer shawl and phylacteries he would simultaneously, for the sake of efficiency, do two other things — boil water in the samovar and roll himself cigarettes.

Pichugin, however, had come to a decision of his own. "Your father was a tradesman, a parasite."

I was irate. "Who gave you the right to talk like this? I'll complain to the prosecutor. I'll write to the minister. Father earned his living honestly. He did not exploit anybody. He worked hard to support his family." I was about to say, Father is more of a proletarian than you and all the others here, you parasites! but I restrained myself. "What makes you think you can insult him? I am the accused here being cross-examined. Talk about me, not him."

"What are you so angry about? I offended your exalted honor?"

"It's not a question of honor but of truth. I'm not going to say anything any more. I won't answer any questions if you continue expressing yourself like this."

I do not know what it was that influenced Pichugin, whether it was my excitement, my threatening to complain, or my announcement that I would not answer any more questions. In any case, he never touched on my father's class affiliation again.

Since I have already alluded to it, I shall say something about complaints and appeals. Writing requests and depositions of various kinds is a constant occupation of the inmates of soviet prisons. Naturally, for this purpose you must be able to secure a pencil and paper from the authorities. The prisoners write requests for clemency and forgiveness, declarations of regret, promises to be an honest citizen, and appeals for reopening files and for a personal meeting. To whom do they write? In my time, they wrote a great deal to Kalinin, the chairman of the Presidium of the Supreme Soviet, who was considered the elder of all Russia, or to the Presidium of the Supreme Soviet itself. Letters were sent to Andrei

Vishinsky, the generation's top saint, to Lavrenti Beria, another symbol of honesty, and to prosecuting attorneys, judges, ministers, party secretaries, and to nationwide and republic authorities. An important address for ex-party members was "Tse-Ka [Central Committee of the Communist Party], Moscow." Many wrote to Stalin himself. I was told that time was when prisoners used to write quite often to the writer Gorki and his wife, who were regarded as defenders of humanism, or to Krupskaya, Lenin's widow.

Opinions were divided regarding the final deposition of these letters. Some said they were never delivered while others held that they actually did reach their destination, where they accumulated without anyone ever paying any attention to them. It is interesting to note that the custom of writing was a prison occupation only. In the camps it was dropped. The prisoner had already received his sentence and, anyway, he had a more realistic approach there.

Interrogation Secrets and Novices

At this point I should like to evaluate the art of interrogation. While I was being cross-examined, all sorts of illusions I had held in common with many others and which are still current in the world crashed. I had given credence to tales of potions, drugs, pills, and hypnosis, and of injections which put the prisoner to sleep, befuddle his consciousness, transform him into a robot and induce him to say automatically whatever he is told. The investigation skill of the NKVD is much simpler, and nevertheless much more effective.

Let me say something about *beatings*. I know that when *necessary*, they mercilessly administer severe beatings. But that is only when it is *necessary*, and the system of striking the prisoners is not resorted to in haste and indiscriminately. I myself was beaten but once, when Pichugin punched me under the chin in the wake of a flood of imprecations and threats. After that blow I said I would not utter another word and I kept my mouth shut in spite of his questions and shouts.

Generally, I doubt that beatings are the most effective means of squeezing out confessions. It seems to me that sometimes a blow even affords a little relief to a prisoner from a feeling of depression, cheers him up somewhat, and fortifies and steels his determination. This is not true in the case of endless, drawn-out degeneration and a gradual decline when a man is methodically reduced to a cipher. Day and night the seeds of despair are sown in you and you are overcome by the realization that you are entirely in the interrogator's hands and everything is predestined and lost. In time you actually become a partner of the interrogator: your stubbornness is fruitless, and your fight is only a waste of time and effort.

I picture the NKVD men as patient artists in mustering every psychological means of breaking the prisoner. They often resorted to flank attacks, touching upon trifles entirely irrelevant to the subject of the investigation just to induce a feeling that they know everything. They are adept at waving all kinds of bait before you, ranging from meeting members of your family to sending and receiving mail and other minor privileges, depending on whatever weak spots they discover in you. Sometimes the interrogator will order a good dinner for you in his office from the personnel dining room, and another time he will offer you first-rate cigarettes. The next day, however, he will forbid you to receive parcels and buy in the store. At nearly every session, he will weave in the barbed question, "Why are you tormenting yourself? What good is it?" This query strikes at your vitals, slowly wearing away your resistance no less than actual beatings.

I said that I had been struck only once. Pressure of another sort was, for example, exerted against me by beating others. This is not a joke. Pichugin would open the door near which I was seated and stand in the doorway while my ears caught the sound of another prisoner being beaten in the next room. Sometimes I suspected that this was staged in order to give me to understand what they were capable of doing here. Since they did inflict beatings when they thought it "necessary," why did they have to stage them? Through closed doors, I could hear performances whose acoustic effects were intended for me. One person would scream blood-thirsty sounds, threats, and curses: "I'll finish you! You won't get out of here alive, son of a bitch! I'll trample you to a pulp, smash your teeth, and break your head! Lie down and don't move! Fascist! Scoundrel! Whore!" and the other would plead, sob, beg for mercy, shriek hysterically, and howl, "Help! Have pity on me! What are you doing? Leave me alone! O, God!" These sounds rumbled in your ears and drove you out of your mind. The beatings from the next room seemed to crash into your belly and whip your face. Maybe it is not fair to talk like this when it was someone else who was being beaten. However, I am not sure who is psychologically affected more, the real recipient of the beating or the person expecting one and listening to its echoes through walls.

So it is an obsolete, oversimplified conception to believe that beatings are the most effective means of extracting information or confessions. The mood of the corridors, nightmares, hours of sitting motionless before a powerful light apparently burning for no reason at all, are stronger than beatings. If necessary, they will put you into a dungeon for several days and let drops of water fall rhythmically on your head one by one. But sometimes the same questions repeated over and over again almost automatically resemble the drops of water wearing down your resistance, drop by drop, day after day, night after night.

The various Pichugins have a special way of seating you across from them for hours with your hands on your knees without asking a single question or even noticing you. You sit like a model for an artist completely mute with your head turning to lead on your shoulders. Finally, your nerves can take it no longer and you begin to squirm a little, wiggling a foot or moving a limb. Once this happened to me and Pichugin asked, "What's the matter with you?"

I actually shouted, "Ask me something. Speak to me!" We seemed to have exchanged roles. I was already just about begging him to go on with his questioning, to press me, make demands, and even curse and call me names — just so he would rip away this terrible nocturnal stillness. But Pichugin, like the righteous man who understands his beasts of burden, drew the silence enveloping him still more closely around himself. Finally he broke the quiet with a question as soft as butter, "Did you want to tell me something?"

"No, I have nothing special to tell you."

"I thought you did have."

And once more, absolute silence. Many hours passed. He was busy with all kind of matters of his own. In the end, he sent me back to the cell. A little while later I was brought to the investigation room again to face a new inquisitor.

When they are at you day and night with their questioning, with or without brief interruptions, they use a sort of conveyor belt system. Is it the interrogator's fault that his client is stubborn and requires a great deal of work? The investigators are changed, but you stay at your post. One of them goes for a rest and another one comes, to be relieved by a third until the first man returns. They are assured by the constitution of their worker's right to rest. At such times, you are rarely in your cell. You quickly bolt down the cold soup and piece of bread and get ready to return to the interrogator. You do not have to wait long. The investigation then becomes a little more varied, depending on the character and temperament of the interrogator.

But the variations are not far-reaching. One interrogator continues where the other left off. Sometimes you hear some new molasses: "Really, I feel badly for you. You could have finished a long time ago and dispensed with all this. What purpose is there in refusing to tell the whole truth?" Sometimes you would be exposed to the whole dictionary of vilification and pornographic language which was an exact copy of what you had heard from another interrogator. Occasionally, the name-calling would be followed by, "Perhaps you'd like something to drink?" or "Cigarette, please?"

"No, thank you. How can I accept your offer when you swear at me and curse?"

"That's your affair."

During my cross-examination at Alma-Ata, I had to contend not only with interrogators but with students as well. This was a special affliction of the NKVD which subjected the prisoner to persons taking courses in the school for interrogators. Here, in isolated basements, they had to conduct experiments, observe, and serve their apprenticeship. In a word, this was their internship. These neophytes were healthy, robust young men who went to school to learn how to wage war against an internal enemy while millions were being killed and wounded at the front. In these basements, they enjoyed special purchasing privileges at a time when masses of people, women and children, were living in want and hunger. They were dressed for show and their glowing faces reflected an easy life. Whenever Pichugin wanted to go out for a while either to the cafeteria or to chat with a friend or when he was ordered to report to his superiors, a student was called in, since I could not be left alone. This man would never be satisfied with just acting as a guard and would always try his own strength as if he were an experienced investigator. This would be actual practice for him after having previously sat in on numerous sessions, listened, observed, taken notes, and certainly marveled at the professional skill of his older companions.

Once an incident took place between a student investigator

like this and myself. He was a burly man with a freckled face. His neck looked swollen and had the appearance of a section of smooth pipe. This was the kind of person about whom camp prisoners would say, "A face asking for a brick." His hair was closely cropped and slicked back as if pasted down with spit. He was repulsive even to meet in the street, without knowing his special status. When I was left alone in the room with him, I became aware of his heavy breathing, choked by an excess of fat. He at once began pacing the room, strutting importantly, and flinging questions at me in the raucous tones of the marketplace and calling me names. He added a personal touch, shouting, "I'll show you right away."

Coldly and resolutely I said to him, "Citizen student, you are not my interrogator and I do not have to answer your questions at all. I am answering you politely because I have nothing to conceal. But if you talk like this, it's all over between us."

The man was furious. He had certainly not expected such an offense to his professional pride at the beginning of its growth. Apparently, as a student in the school for investigators, he had come to believe that he could get away with anything and that success in his profession was based on firm superiority in his relations with the client whom he was supposed to interrogate.

The more I refused to accord him any recognition the redder his face became. He no longer playacted, he stamped his feet, screamed, swore, and threatened. On the basis of this performance alone he would have failed the examinations — poor man — and would not receive the long-awaited degree and diploma of Master of Interrogation.

The student's rantings mounted until Pichugin's return. The latter noticed the tension as soon as he entered and asked the routine question of whether I had related anything of interest. The intern complained that I had stopped talking altogether and had acted with "provocation" (this apparently is one of the expres-

sions taught at those schools). "I'll look into the matter," Pichugin said calmly. I almost began to admire him. Such experience!
Such professional bearing!

After the student's departure, Pichugin inquired what had happened. I told him. I saw that he was enjoying the student's inepti-
tude which he felt as a compliment to his own professional skill.
He smiled briefly as if to say, "We both know what these young
squirts are worth." It was this behavior of his which gave me the
courage to tell him that the student reminded me of the Yiddish
proverb, "It's easy to learn how to cut hair on someone else's
beard."

Take the Whip and Let Me Have It!

I do not, God forbid, want to belittle the professional skill,
resourcefulness, and psychological insight of the NKVD interrogators, but these qualities should not be exaggerated. My impression has been that actually neither the best minds nor the cleverest
men go into this business in the USSR.

During my career as a prisoner, I came to know half a dozen
investigators and I formed the opinion that they operate without
much private initiative but are trained in a uniform curriculum
laid down by a central office. They employ nearly the same methods and make use of the same series of techniques and even
threats, names, and oaths. The formula of their appeals and monologues is almost uniform. Many of their questions are stereotypes,
hammered out in advance as if they had been taken from a manual.

Naturally, a great deal depends on the temperament and character of the interrogator himself, and still more on the client's
character and the severity of the subject under investigation.
However, from talking to hundreds of prisoners with a varied

assortment of dossiers, I did not get the impression that the interrogators' activities were distinguished by excessive originality. I often marveled when people told me that although the crimes attributed to them were as remote from mine as Vorkuta is from Alma-Ata, their interrogators parroted the same statements of "We know all about you" they made to me.

One of the commonest and most widespread techniques, and one which I believe to be highly effective, is to deliberately charge the accused with many many more offenses than he is really suspected of. The purpose of this is to create space for bargaining, interplay, and give-and-take negotiations. In a deal of this sort, the prisoner swallows the bait and gives the interrogator a certain incriminating detail, hoping to get him off his back. But then the investigator demands to hear more hostile acts and charges: "What did you think, that you would fulfill your obligation by telling me a single detail and in this way give the impression of telling the truth?" Then the negotiations begin in earnest.

"I'll forgive your intention to dismember the Soviet Union, as it were, if you tell me all about the spying. What, no spying? Let's compromise and hear about sabotage. All right, let's drop espionage and sabotage, but organizing emigration to Palestine by way of Persia is a fair suggestion from me to you. Good, you yourself were not the instigator, but you were once an active member. We'll let it go at that, and I'll delete it and correct the protocol, but you yourself wanted to go to Persia. You became a victim of this organization and we'll take that into consideration. But you must sign. No? This you won't do either? Well, then let's hear about anti-Soviet propaganda. That's the bottom price and it won't be any lower . . ."

I must admit that what remained of the original charges with their worldwide implications seemed to me like a bargain. Not to concede something trivial like the last proposal was plain piggish.

It seems to me that the investigators' power does not stem either from their intelligence, cunning, or skill but rather from their confidence in their superiority and their control over you. By virtue of the simple fact alone that they hold you — a fact absolutely and demonstratively flaunted on every occasion — they can crush you. You eventually capitulate — that is, confess — because of a fairly accurate consideration: in any case, you won't get off with less than five or ten years or even more. What difference does the length of your sentence make? As Pichugin put it, "What's the use of being a hero?"

It is quite illuminating to learn that the interrogator is even a little interested in your feelings and in your understanding that the cross-examination is to a large extent make-believe. In other words, he wants the client to reconcile himself to pleading guilty and accepting the verdict from the outset, whatever the proceedings and differences between them may turn out to be. For this reason he is not so careful about pretending to search for factual truth. He even enlists the prisoner in a sort of conspiracy, implying, "The both of us know that all this business with you is not so important, but you certainly understand that this is my duty," or "I'm not so stupid as to believe the charges that I myself am making up about you, but I can't escape either from this vicious circle, and you have even less of a chance of extricating yourself from it."

I think that is why Pichugin openly enjoyed a Jewish joke I slipped into the interrogation between questions and answers. This was one of those sessions in which my interrogator, patently bored, mechanically made rapid leaps from one charge to another, as if it were another rehearsal for all sorts of one-act plays which he had previously abandoned. Once more he returned to espionage, sabotage, and organizing Jews for illegal emigration. My replies did not interest him either. They were stock answers to stock questions, as if the two of us had to fill in a certain number of hours together. It was then that I screwed up some courage and told him the story of the duke who owned a number of farms which he leased out to Jews. Once he decided to visit them all, one right after the other, together with his entourage. Coming to the first of his tenant farmers, he said, "Well, Moishe, do you have some good Jewish delicacy to serve up to your master?" Moishe quickly rattled off a list of foods he knew the duke was fond of, "Gefilte fish, roast duck, stuffed derma."

The duke made a grimace, "I come to visit you once a year and you could not have prepared Jewish dumplings?" He then gave an order to have Moishe whipped. When Moishe's son saw the duke's strange behavior, he ran to the next farm to warn Itsik, "The duke is here and he wants dumplings." When the duke arrived and asked for refreshment, Itsik counted off on his fingers, "Roast duck, derma, dumplings —" But again the duke was indignant, "I visit you only once a year and you could not have honored me with steamed udder?" Itsik, too, was flogged. In short, messengers ran from one farm to the other to warn the tenants and tell them what the duke wished to eat. Each time, however, the nobleman asked for a new delicacy and ordered whippings. Finally the duke came to Hayim's farm and put the question to him, "What do you have good to eat?" Hayim answered, "Your grace, I don't have anything except my behind, take the whip and let me have it!"

The moral was quite obvious to Pichugin and required no comment. He took no offense. On the contrary, this time he laughed loudly. In the final analysis, he knew very well that the assortment of charges which he had already leveled and which he would throw at me in the future were only a pretext for a flogging — for a preordained sentence. I just want to add that he could not restrain himself and went off to repeat the joke to his colleagues (after leaving the student with me). He also brought a number of them to look me over because I had told a funny story about a behind.

However — and this was typical — that very same evening, after having enjoyed a good laugh which he had shared with the other interrogators, he suddenly adopted another role in the play.

"Enough joking," he shouted. "We have to get this over with! Let it be clear to you that you must exhaust everything — all your crimes, slanders, and contemptible acts." Then he put in, as if alluding to the interval of relief afforded by the anecdote, "The Soviet government does not joke."

At the same time, he continued to demonstrate that he was only carrying out orders he had to obey. Once in a while he would step out of his role and talk about life in Poland. For some reason or other, he was interested in the advanced textile industry in Lodz about which he claimed to have heard a great deal. These digressions may have been calculated to win my confidence, or perhaps his curiosity had gotten the better of him. Whatever it was, after a brief conversation of this sort he would remind me clearly, "You won't get any bread out of this and it won't give us a protocol." Once or twice, he even paid me a sly compliment: "I swear, I'd only like to have tea with you. It's nice talking to you. But what is there to do when duty comes before pleasure?"

Pichugin let me share his duties and obligations many times. "Listen, we have to go a little faster, we [that is, we "partners"] have a deadline for submitting the file and it's getting closer." Returning to more "relevant" questions, he would ask me, "But don't give me any of your hogwash again; I want something substantial that I can give them without looking ridiculous."

A sense of the melodramatic induces a person writing about cross-examinations or reporting trials to seek out the man under the robe of office — the human being in the interrogator or the judge. I had occasion to witness such revelations only very rarely. To tell the truth, I could get along very well without them. Generally they were annoying. Pichugin's artful, make-believe attempts at reaching a mutual understanding and tearing down barriers troubled me no less than the pressure he exerted; however, this phenomenon was such a rarity that they constituted no problem. I learned from experience that the investigators identify well with their role, whether from the heart or out of a love of the game.

Pichugin even revealed once that being an investigator was not really his work and hinted that he was not happy in it. He said that he had been drafted for the job. And a man had to do his duty, this like all the others, seriously and honestly.

I think I took him entirely out of the game just one time. I was sitting in my corner waiting for his questions. He was in no hurry and was looking in the newspaper. This was the beginning of 1943. I ventured a question, "Citizen investigator —"

He raised his head, "What is the matter?"

"May I ask something?"

"What?"

"What's new at the front?"

"Why are you suddenly interested?" he asked grimly.

Unable to contain myself, I said, "Because in spite of everything, I would like to know how this terrible war against Hitler is going."

With astonishing frankness, he replied, "If I talk to you about such matters, I could be in your place. Understand?"

I entreated him, "Just tell me one word."

"Our side is making rapid advances. Giving them hell."

That was all he said. For a single moment, Pichugin had allowed himself to permit a captive enemy of the people to share his feelings of triumph at the Red army's victories. But it was only for a moment. A second later he lashed out at me with his vicious tongue, "You whore, I'll make you put all your cards on the table, up to your very last counterrevolutionary activity. Carrion, you won't get out of here alive if you try to hide anything."

Getting Closer to the Finale

I became used to Pichugin's language and his threats and to the fists he brandished in my face without ever letting them touch me. When, nevertheless, no progress was made on the protocol and there was nothing to add to it, he resorted to a new, original, syrup technique which I remember no less than his barbs.

One evening when I was brought in to Pichugin, he informed me that the head of the investigation division to which he was attached, that is, his immediate superior (and the man in charge of the separate investigations of the four of us sharing the same file), would like to meet me. That is exactly what Pichugin said, "would like to meet you," which was the kind of invitation requiring my consent. "Of course," I replied. I was there for about another hour. He was writing something, which meant that we were making a little "progress." Then a sentry came in and handed him a note. In almost solemn tones, Pichugin told me, "You have an appointment with him now."

I was taken to a large office literally screaming with exaggerated splendor and spaciousness. Flowers and flowerpots were incongruously conspicuous. This was to be a confidential meeting with the chief investigator.

He rose from his broad desk and invited me to sit with him on an upholstered sofa near an elegant coffee table. Crossing his legs, all calmness and relaxation, he said, "I'm your investigator's superior. But I did not want to meet you for the purpose of talking about your cross-examination. By the way, I'm completely informed as to its progress and am familiar with all the details. However, that does not interest me now. Somehow you will make headway and finish it."

I noticed that he had begun to display a little disdain for his subordinate. In my opinion, it was both real and put on in order to gain my confidence, as if to demonstrate that he was being frank with me about his feelings and his relationships and did not hesitate to run down in my presence the man I considered so important. He continued, "I'll tell you the whole truth. The end of the cross-examination and its results do not especially interest me. I know what should already be clear to you, that you will get several years. I have no wish to calm your fears. It may be three, five, even ten years. We, of course, note our impressions of your conduct and whether or not there is any hope for you in the future, for everyone would still like you to become a useful citizen. We have nothing to say about the penalty. But that's not what I wanted to talk to you about."

My God, all my bones cried out, then what *does* he want to talk to me about? He keeps telling me what does *not* interest him, but what *does*? Why is he getting on my nerves so much?

He calmly went on, "I have read your confessions. I am familiar with what you did. I know everything about your past. But what I want to talk to you about is neither your past, your crimes, nor your acts. And not even your impending imprisonment. I want to discuss with you what will become of you afterward, after you have served your sentence, when you are released, let's say, five years later. I consider you an intelligent man, although you have been misled. I'll tell you frankly, you seem like a clever man to me — refined as well. I know that occasionally the interrogator swears and raises his voice. That's all right; don't let it upset you too much. A job like that is not so pleasant and he sometimes does not distinguish between one man and another, between one kind of prisoner and another. But you ought to ask yourself, 'What is it all leading to?' I mean, you understand, afterward, after your verdict will have been handed down and after you will have served your sentence and been punished for your crimes. I mean, understand what I say, not your settling down but your whole mental outlook, your ideology, your Weltanschauung. What will become of all these? This makes your second term of imprisonment. When it ends sometime, won't there be a third term in store for you if you don't change? You are still a talented young man, but I am under the impression that you yourself are ruining your life. From childhood either you yourself or somebody else filled your head with Palestine and the capitalist way of life and you can't free yourself from them."

What was he driving at? What did he have in mind? What was his aim? All this verbal syrup was unnerving. I had never expected a mess like this. I wished he would come to the point. But he was in no hurry.

"I cannot countermand your sentence. It's already too late for that. The Soviet government punishes, that's clear. A crime is a crime. A sin is a sin. But I would like to help you get rid of your prejudices. Because if you don't, you will spend your life going from one prison to another, with brief intervals of freedom. If you do not throw off your notions and perceptions, you will be like a wolf drawn to the forest. And it will be too bad."

His tones became more fatherly. "You can be very useful in the Socialist society, but you must reexamine yourself and cut off your mind and heart from all your vapid bourgeois, nationalistic sentiments. Just reflect for a while, isn't our Communist idea broader and more attractive and interesting than your narrow-minded Zionism? I look at you and think, here is a young man who has laid himself on the railroad tracks and believes he can stop the train. The train will speed over you and grind your body to a pulp. What are you fighting history for instead of joining humanity's great march toward freedom and a new life?" There was pathos in his voice as he uttered the last words.

I remained dumb. Whoever expected such a concentrated lecture? Generally I responded not at all to the programmatic aspects of his discourse. However, I have to admit that what he had to say about a lost life, a train crushing my body, and wandering from one prison to another — the whole personal perspective that he portrayed for me — hurt me with a scorching agony. But what could I have said to him? Actually, he had not asked for a reply but only suggested that I think about what he had said, that I devote some thought to myself. I believe he wanted to increase my confidence in him in this way. He showed me that he had no intention of forcing anything out of me. That's how he said good-bye to me too, without asking anything and outwardly cordial.

As mentioned, he had not asked me for an answer. Nevertheless, I assumed that he would send for me again to find out how his monologue had affected me, to learn my reaction. I even prepared explanations in my head, on a theoretical plane also: I do not know where I am headed, but, as you say, I acquired my love for Palestine from *childhood*, and so on. However, he had nothing further to do with me and the "refined" young man was once more delivered into the hands of Pichugin, who acted as he did and treated him in his customary fashion, doubtlessly under the supervision and with the knowledge of the fatherly official.

That is how we came closer to the finale. The file grew bulkier as we argued over formulations. Many times I refused to sign, claiming that Pichugin had distorted my replies.

"If you don't want to sign, you don't have to. You'll come begging me yet!"

"I will not sign such a twisted statement. That is not a protocol."

"What, you're going to teach me now to write protocols? I cut my teeth on them."

"I am talking about this protocol. There's something in it that I never said."

Then Pichugin flung at me, "You're petty."

Regarding certain sentences I continued to claim, "I didn't say that," or "That's not how I said it." And he would shoot back, "You're petty, there's no one as petty as you. For a trifle, you're making me copy the whole page over and waste time." For my petty bargaining, he also said that I had a shopkeeper mind.

In the end he gave in. Apparently my signature was still worth something. However, his evaluation was correct. I really was petty. I was stubborn about matters which would in no way whatsoever affect the final result.

The last stages of my cross-examination also included a confrontation with my friend Barukh, one of the three other persons with whom I shared a dossier. The ritual of an interview of this sort is instructive. Both persons are seated some distance apart opposite each other after having been warned that exchanging words or signs is forbidden. Each in turn must answer directly only the interrogator's questions. If either one has a question to ask the other, he can only do so through the interrogator, who will decide whether or not the other person should reply. Naturally, a protocol of this confrontation was kept for insertion in the file labeled "Hold forever."

It's interesting, even amazing, to what extent the NKVD men are anxious for a semblance of legality and judicial honesty in this whole game. The first question alternately put to each person in a confrontation is, "Do you think that he [the other person] had any grounds for a personal grudge against you, for vengeance, and do you believe that he has any malicious intentions against you which may exclude the possibility of his being objective?" The interrogator is prepared to go into detail. "Have you ever quarreled?"

Statements that one prisoner has no reason for suspecting the other's intentions add weight to the testimony they give about each other: not only was it not given under pressure, freely and voluntarily, but relations between the two were normal.

The questions asked at the confrontation had no special value but had to lend corroborative force to the file. We were again asked about a number of meetings and conversations between us. Differences between my reconstructions and his had to be coordinated and the statements in the protocols corrected. How authentic everything was!

I spent entire days and nights reading my file, protocol after protocol, before it would be submitted to whomever it was going. Although I had previously signed each page and protocol separately as well as for every erasure, correction, and addition, I was once more granted the right of checking the whole file. Perhaps after all an inaccuracy had crept in? I was already well acquainted with the protocols. Nevertheless, when I received them sewn together and bound they made a special impression on me and I felt the need of being extra cautious. It was difficult for me to read the handwriting of a language I had learned a short time before without any formal instruction. However, I overcame this shortcoming and read carefully. A number of corrections had been made at my request and the file inscribed with "Hold forever" was ready for delivery to the prosecutor, who, in accordance with the provisions of the procedural code, was responsible for the course of this cross-examination.

At the termination of the cross-examination, you are accorded a personal meeting with the prosecutor in charge of procedure as provided by law. He asks you several personal questions, leafs through the file, and examines the appended documents. He asks you to acknowledge your signature. You now have to sign Section 206 of the procedural code which says that the cross-examination, which was conducted fairly, is finished.

This is the last ritual. Since you will not see a court and judges, this is the final ceremonial act of your trial. However, cynical sadism, or sadistic cynicism, abhors haste. Pretense and make-believe must still celebrate their great triumph. The prisoner has already mentally prepared himself to sign for the last time and be rid of the whole affair. However, the prosecutor calmly and gravely asks you without batting an eyelash, as if he were an innocent observer, "Do you have any complaints against the investigating authorities?" You are astonished. What does he mean by complaints? And he explains what he means simply and patiently. For example, "Did they subject you to illegal treatment?" Again, you are amazed. What does he mean by illegal? He does not spare himself the effort of going into greater detail. "Let's say, perhaps they led you on unfairly, or they may have used physical means of influencing you?" He adds another detail, "Perhaps they threatened, beat you, forced you to confess and sign?"

From numerous stories told to me by fellow prisoners I learned that sometimes during such a meeting with the procedural prosecutor, the prisoner takes heart and says to himself, there is still some honesty, a tiny bit of justice still remains. Thus a ray of light occasionally penetrates the darkness of the inquisitorial night. There are times when the prisoner allows himself to be talked into believing that the interrogator's attitude toward him, and his conduct and methods, were arbitrary and entirely unknown at the top; that, of their own volition, the investigators at the bottom exerted pressure and used force in order to demonstrate their loyalty and skill, but that their superiors are sticklers for the truth, reliable testimony and confessions, and honest documents. And so it happens that such a prisoner, drained of his last drop of vitality, seems to receive a sudden shot in the arm and bursts out, "Yes, citizen prosecutor, they forced me, they tortured me, they threatened me, they cursed, I couldn't stand it any longer, my strength gave out, I didn't care any more and I did not tell the truth but what the interrogator wanted me to say. I was sick of it all and I signed whatever the investigator asked me to."

The procedural prosecutor calmly listens to these specimens of the way the cross-examination was conducted and announces with a sort of cold firmness, "So, I am unable to accept this file and these protocols as reliable." In a word, he invalidates the cross-examination.

Then the investigation is reopened, usually to another investigator or team of investigators. If the prisoner was previously forced to confess without beatings, he is now struck on any and every occasion. If before curses alternated with restrained talks, this time the prisoner, the stinking bitch, is subjected to a shower of vilification and spit and clearly given to understand that this is in payment for his provocative behavior at his meeting with the prosecutor. The renewed pressure is intensive since an additional cross-examination is not allotted the same time given to the first one. The deadline for submitting the new dossier is just around the corner and there is no time for amenities. In this way, the prisoner is quickly brought to the verge of absolute physical and mental collapse and signs the protocols in their new form.

The prisoner is once more brought before his procedural prosecutor. Again, the ritual of terminating the cross-examination in accordance with the provisions of the law, Section 206, is gone through. The prosecutor serenely inquires, "Did they employ physical means of influencing you?" But this time, the experienced client quickly replies, "No, no force, I have no complaints about the way the cross-examination was conducted," and he affixes his final signature.

To this day I ponder upon this matter, seeking an answer to the riddle of why the NKVD needed all this. They could really have done whatever they wished, so why did they have to erect houses of cards and put up windmills? Why did they have to invest so much in a helpless convict like me and tens of thousands of others? Could they not have more easily and simply bestowed upon me the same five years to which I was sentenced in absentia on the basis of a decision of the unknown Os-So? But reflections on this fetish of appearance, of strict adherence to regulations, law practices and details of procedure can lead one to phenomena beyond the investigation chambers. The fact remains that they feel the need to keep up appearances.

Now I should like to relate something of the cross-examinations of the three persons with whom I shared a dossier, just as they told me about them. Naturally the conduct of our investigations was very much alike. But there were a few original incidents worth mentioning.

It turned out that Lucia was especially privileged to have her interrogation conducted by the head of the investigation division himself, the same man who had invited me to visit him for a friendly talk and had delivered an ideological lecture to me. His name was Bikov and his rank was major. I had just had a single session with him and being occupied with his lecture had not paid attention to his looks. Lucia recalled his appearance well. Tall and lanky with a wrinkled face, he had a Puritan air about him, except for his mouth, which flashed gold teeth. He was a veteran member of the secret police, confident and unruffled. In our group of the interrogators he played the part of a father seeking to do good and educate.

The father seeking to do good and educate did not refrain, when the "need" arose, from drawing a pistol during Lucia's cross-examination and laying it on the desk. Jokingly, he told her, "Don't be afraid. I'm not going to shoot yet."

"You can shoot. I don't care," she shrugged her shoulders.

"But if you were to meet me in Poland, you would shoot me on sight."

Lucia also asked in amazement, "What sort of agitation is it when two people converse at home alone."

He candidly replied, "In our country, you can even sit beside the oven [that is, be a housewife who never goes out] and conduct anti-Soviet propaganda."

For a while, Lucia's cross-examination was conducted by a Lieutenant Dubas. He also interrogated her brother Barukh, and it was in his presence that we were confronted. I remember him as a handsome young man whose whole appearance bespoke satisfaction with himself. However, he acted quite sadistically. He liked to probe into the private lives of the prisoners and did not hesitate to use the expression "sly Jew." But he could also speak gently.

"Do you think," he said to Lucia, "that I like this work? Believe me, I have more pleasant diversions."

"Enjoy yourself. Who is stopping you?"

"But certain matters have to be finished."

"Finish them."

"But you have to help me."

"I have nothing to help you with."

"How selfish you are!"

Once the procedure prosecutor came in while Lucia was being

cross-examined and Major Bikov introduced her, "This is the girl I told you about. She is intelligent, educated, and pleasant, but can't stand Communists."

The prosecutor took the hint. "That means she is a Fascist."

Lucia interrupted, "Why a Fascist?"

However, the prosecutor insisted, "So what are you then, a Communist?"

"But you also have people not identified with any party."

At this point, Major Bikov commented, "She doesn't have to hunt for words in her pocket; with her it's really not so easy."

The prosecutor asked Lucia, "What sort of a family are you from?"

Bikov answered for her, "The entire family — enemies."

Noah, who was also arrested with us, had a real class blemish. He owned a printing press. Until the end of his interrogation, he staunchly defended his Zionist views. None of this was entered in the protocol. Neither was the following exchange:

Noah said to his interrogator after he was fed up with the entire procedure, "You know as well as I do that I am not guilty, but, what the hell, I'll sign."

"You're a good fellow, I swear. Shake hands."

A word more or less — all of us later received our sentence from the unknown mysterious Os-So.

The cross-examination was over. I was also through with my solitary cell. Although the common cell was administered by the same regime, it still afforded a feeling of considerable relief. Characteristic of the system is the fact that ten or twenty men, some of whom have already completed their investigation and others still being cross-examined, sit in one room and rarely does somebody ask about or discuss what is going on in the interrogation chambers or the reason for a particular person's arrest. First of all, it is a criminal offense to reveal any details of the investigation. Secondly, you are gripped by a fear of agents provocateurs; if a stool pigeon has not been planted deliberately, someone in the cell is liable to sink so low as to allow himself to be talked into such a job. Essentially, however, there is nothing to say because it is all very personal. When you make someone's acquaintance and become friendly with him, there are topics of conversation of common interests outside the realm of your arrest and cross-examination. There are the cell duties, a certain cultural activity, stories, entertainment, and reciprocal "visiting." The cultural animal does get a little of what it wants.

It was customary in our common cell for those receiving a parcel from home to contribute something for the group. This added a little to my official prison rations, nothing to be sneezed at, since after the tension of the cross-examination had subsided, my appetite increased to a horrifying degree. I also received a little food from the outside. I had a friend in the cell, a Polish Jew. Whenever someone received a parcel, he taught us to make use of it for judging conditions in the prisoner's home. As a matter of fact, a "declassed" society and the families of prisoners are always unfortunate, but, nevertheless, tears shed over a slice of ham cannot be compared with those shed over potato balls.

In the common cell of the confidential prison you are also isolated, cut off from the world. Nevertheless, we managed to hear some echoes from the "outside." Various stratagems were devised for circumventing the precautions taken by the prison authorities. Although they cut open and sliced the bread and salami sent in parcels, crumbled the cheese, and pierced the potatoes, some sort of note did occasionally get by the inspectors. And the commodities and gifts themselves not only brought regards from the sender but often served as an indication of a family event or of steps being taken on the outside to help the prisoner.

Incidentally, Barukh's and Lucia's family left no stone unturned to do something for them after their incarceration in Alma-Ata. First of all they tried to give them some material assistance. This, too, was quite complicated. Sender, another brother, had to secure an "errand pass" in order to be able to bring them parcels in the Alma-Ata prison. He managed to secure such a permit from the health authorities for the purpose of going for an x-ray. He did more than just deliver the parcels. Several years later he told me how dejected he had been following a visit to a lawyer in Alma-Ata. The attorney had told him frankly, "It's impossible to help them. Nothing will do any good." He went on to explain, "If I had an indictment, I could perhaps make an effort to do something for the prisoners but an indictment does not exist, only protocols and more protocols. How could you defend yourself from secret protocols which an outside eye would never see? There is nothing to be done," the lawyer concluded, adding, "and now, in an atmosphere like this . . ."

If the shining ideal had previously been to finish the cross-examination and begin a "normal" life in the common cell, it was now to get out of these walls to a camp. You were anxious for air, movement, activity, something to do in order to vary your life a little.

After I had been in the Alma-Ata prison for about eight months, the cell door opened one day and a warder asked, "Who is under the letter G?" Everyone whose surname began with a G stepped forward, including me. One of the inmates tried a subterfuge and pretending he misunderstood, called out his first name Grigori. The warder squelched his humor at once. They only wanted Globerman. "Get yourself and your things together," the warder ordered. Then he left and slammed the door shut. The creak of keys in other doors could be heard. Everyone in the cell began to speculate. Why? Where? There was general agreement that we were going to travel. We heard the sounds of men being taken out of many cells. There were other conjectures, but the majority held the view that this was a journey to a camp.

I was ready and waiting, having already said my goodbyes, when half an hour later I was summoned to take my bundle and go to an office to hear my sentence read to me. It had apparently just arrived. The Os-So had decided that I should be deprived of my freedom for five years. Five years in five lines. But it must have taken them a long time there in Moscow to deliberate on my case.

After hearing my sentence, I was taken to a crowded cell which, instead of beds, had a continuous shelf around the walls. This room was reserved for those leaving for camps. The same prison regulations were also in force here, but the guards were not so strict. It was noisy with men from various cells meeting.

I was pleasantly surprised at encountering my friend Barukh. He had been sentenced to eight years. It seemed to us that we had enough stories to tell each other for the entire term of our imprisonment. We analyzed what had befallen us. Many details were obscure, but we attempted to speculate about the future.

Lucia had been given three years, and Noah, eight.

In this cell, we had the unusual experience of meeting prisoners originally condemned to death whose sentences had been commuted to varying terms of imprisonment, usually ten years.

That is a story itself. These were generally deserters from the front or slackers. Some of them were vulgar, disgusting characters and others were gay individuals who simply loved life. After they had been sentenced to death, they were kept in a special cell. But, at this point, a curious thing had happened. Apparently, a secret order had been issued not to carry out these sentences. The condemned men were told they could appeal to have their sentences commuted to imprisonment. Even if they did not want to appeal (some said, "I'm sick of living, let them do to me whatever they wish"), the authorities forced them to, going so far as to write the letters for them and making them sign. These requests were approved almost automatically.

Now, the former condemned men were sitting with us waiting to embark on a trip with the same rights we possessed. They told fascinating stories of life in the death cells. Every morning when the prison warden and his staff would come to inspect the cell and list the inmates' requests, the condemned men would ask, "Dear warden, when are they going to hang us? When are we going to be shot?"

The warden, well aware of the fact that the sentences would not be implemented, would angrily retort, "That's none of your business. You'll be told when. When the time comes, you'll be sent for."

The men would reply, "If we're not going to die, give us smokes. If they aren't going to hang us, give us some tobacco, dear warden."

Incidentally, former condemned men like these, deserters under fire and slackers, were released under an amnesty at the end of the war. Paradoxically, they were the first prisoners to benefit from victory. Traitors who had stood in the shadow of the scaffold were set absolutely free, while those who had chatted a little too volubly, like all the "anti-Soviet propagandists," remained in prison until the end of their sentences.

We were finally taken to the railroad. I was at last on the way out of the city with the poetic name of Alma-Ata, which in Kazakh means Father of Apples. I had spent about nine months in this capital of a republic and had no idea how it looked. It was supposed to be one of the most beautiful cities in the USSR. Perhaps that is so. For me, it was the Father of Misery.

An Established Camp and
Its Class Divisions

Each prisoner was sent off to a camp and I, together with the two other men who shared my file, was brought to the Aktyubinsk labor camp, about six miles from the city of the same name, in the northwestern region of the Kazakh Soviet Republic. This country is considered a sort of extension of the Urals and is rich in minerals, including petroleum and coal, nickel, bauxite, cobalt, chromium, copper, and gold. Until a few years earlier, no attempts were made to extract them from the earth. However, a giant plant for smelting iron and numerous auxiliary industries had already been set up near our camp. It was said that Aktyubinsk was included in the sweeping plans for wartime industrialization and production for Socialist construction in general. So it was natural for us prisoners to be here.

It can always be worse and every unlucky person can use a bit of good fortune. Sometimes, not the length of the sentence but the camp one happened to be sent to decided a person's fate. Excluding special strict camps, there were differences from one camp to another in the ordinary network of such establishments. The same regulations were binding on all of them, their uniformity was centralized, and they were directed and supervised from above. But they varied from one another as, let us say, an advanced country differs from a backward one. There were differences in the atmosphere and the relations of the officials to the prisoners and variations in food and clothing and living quarters and hygienic conditions. These were important differences affecting every aspect of living.

Compared with the northern camps, the one in Aktyubinsk was up to par. Most important was the fact that the camp was already well established when I arrived there and did not require pioneer acts of creation. Buildings for living quarters, services, warehouses, and offices were ready for use. It was possible to undress and go to bed from the first night. I recalled how many months had to pass in the North until the standard of living was high enough for us to receive sacks filled with sawdust for mattresses; here a straw mattress was no problem. Rumor had it that our living conditions were even much better than those in the camps of the Karaganda oblast (district), bordering on the Aktyubinsk oblast in the east, which were famous chiefly for their coal production. Let me add that generally the living quarters and food at Aktyubinsk were superior to those I had at the Kara-Kalpak collective farm.

Until now I have discussed the general situation. At Aktyubinsk I learned that the prisoners' society was divided in numerous classes, a many-runged ladder with numerous social levels ranging from those eating from the common pot to others who never touched it. As a matter of fact, the camp population did not represent a classic example of equality in the North either, but there among the great mass of wretched slaves only individuals had advantages and privileges.

B.C. & P. (before camps and prisons) I thought there could not be greater brotherhood, truer friendship, more internal solidarity and sharing than in a prisoners' society in which all the members had been deprived of their basic rights. However, this notion quickly faded away. Especially in this vale of tears did I come across man's wolfishness. Whoever said that suffering purifies was taken in by commonplace bombast. The struggle for survival among the condemned and the miserable has no inhibitions and often substantiates the favorite expression of hardened criminals, "You can croak today, and me, tomorrow."

For instance, one prisoner will steal another's hallowed bread ration. There are all sorts of deceptions and small tricks over a soup spoon. Lying is rampant. Flattery and obsequiousness flourish everywhere about you. The strong trample the weak. And, perhaps more than outside, it is whom you know that counts. Bribery is prevalent. If you want to live and get along, you have to make much use of your elbows and keep pushing all the time.

Not only do the way of life and conditions differ from one group to another, but — in a labor camp — there are prisoners who loaf or work half the time and others who are actually employers! The men mostly resort to flattery, pull, and bribery for transfers from one job to another and for securing food — the two basic factors which determine the prisoner's ability to hold out.

A poem by Nikolai Nekrasov comes to my mind: "Who Is Happy in Russia?" which attacks the social regime in the Czarist empire. Who has a good, happy life? In Nekrasov's poem, seven peasants answer one after the other, the landlord, the government official, the priest, the paunchy merchant, the noble, the minister, and the Czar. If Nekrasov were to ask the same question about the camps, his peasants serving sentences there would point at a line of other privileged individuals — the director of the warehouse, the store manager, the cook and manager of the bakery, the workers in the pharmacy (who can secure spirits for themselves and their friends), the bread-cutter, and the commandant (the overseer of the work group heads), and engineering technicians holding key positions inside the camp or in production outside.

Under these circumstances there were people in the camp about whom it was said, "They never had it so good at home." They indulged themselves, showed off, lorded it over the rest, gorged themselves, had good times and entertainment, lived with women, and quaffed the sweet intoxicant of power over others. As for the rest of us, our situation was comparable to that of the beggar whose greatest dream was to have all his benefactors living in one huge apartment house so he could go from door to door more easily. The dream of the miserable and the hungry was for others to receive food parcels from the outside or to rise to privileged positions so that more of the government soup would remain for them. Not one man used to wait for his "aristocratic" neighbor to let him wash his eating utensils in which there were remains of the food he had either prepared from his own supplies or had received because of his connections with the kitchen staff.

There were various classes in Aktyubinsk. However, in contrast to the almost static condition prevailing in the northern camps, there was considerable mobility. Few remained in the same class for any length of time. At Aktyubinsk, movements up and down on the social ladder were frequent. As their personal experience, length of time in camp, and proficiency increased, most prisoners moved upward.

First of all, progress was in the direction of lighter and easier work. You became a Stakhanovite and then advanced to "excellent worker," to "two hundred percenter" (one who fulfills two hundred percent of the quota), and to "record-holder." In time one could become a "recorder" or a "checker" making lists which required no technical knowledge or administrative experience. And one could be appointed squad leader and group head. You could even achieve a true administrative or technical rank such as project planner, calculator of work quotas, and bookkeeper.

There were opportunities for advancement at Aktyubinsk. Construction work and industry in the vicinity of the camp required skills. Bureaucracy needed people to do the paper work. A whole network of small industries grew up in the camp around the production of consumers' goods. There were workshops for clothing, shoes, and tanning. The camp produced ceramicware, woven goods, and ink for the outside market. Even shops for reparing timepieces were established near the camp and served the camp officials as well as chosen people from the locality.

Cultural and educational activities also developed. The head of the Department for Education and Culture was a young Jewish party member, a decent sort of fellow from Odessa who knew how to strike a balance between his humane feeling for the prisoners and his official position which required that he remain aloof. We had a movie hall where films were frequently shown. Tickets were distributed according to a scale of priorities. The "excellent workers" were first. However, in practice they were preceded by all those who had pull and knew how to shove. There was also a need for artistic talents for painting slogans, decorating the camp, and embellishing reports and announcements.

In time, a sort of propaganda group was organized consisting of both professional and amateur actors, singers, musicians, and even a magician garbed in a full dress suit and top hat. This troupe used to put on revues for the entertainment and encouragement of human hearts behind barbed wire. The performances included passionate patriotic numbers, anti-German sketches, and humorous and satirical acts based on life in the camps.

The prisoners at Aktyubinsk had the good fortune to be joined by the Yiddish acting team of Shimon Dzhigan and Alter Shumacher (who died in Israel in 1961). Each of them had a five-year sentence for having been found guilty of trying to leave the Soviet Union illegally for Persia. At the beginning of his sentence Shumacher fell ill and was transferred to the sick area; Dzhigan succeeded in finding work in the sewing room. Later, the two of them became the backbone of the actors' troupe. They conducted performances and were responsible for most of the directing and acting. For Shumacher, the camp actors' group was a full-time job, whereas Dzhigan continued to sew artistic patches on the clothing of the prisoners while also being active in the theater. Dzhigan and Shumacher managed to weave in numerous Jewish songs and acts in their programs: a wedding, musicians, and small-town tailors. Nostalgia for each one's small hometown would spread through the hall and tug at the heartstrings. These numbers aroused the enthusiasm not only of the Jewish prisoners; after Dzhigan and Shumacher would accede to the requests for an encore, shouts would go up in various parts of the hall, "Davai svadbu! Davai portniazhki!" — "Give us a wedding! Give us tailors!"

The curious situation of key positions occupied by prisoners was exemplified by a Jewish lawyer of noble appearance from Moscow who had been sentenced to ten years for counterrevolutionary activities. He was the camp's legal adviser. It should be kept in mind that the camp was a commercial and economic unit with interests of its own. Even though everything belonged to the state, there was much litigation in the Soviet Union between various bodies and numerous financial claims of one institution against another. In such instances, the various units needed the services of a legal adviser. Everyone who knew about it was proud of our legal adviser whose talents made it possible for him to win nearly every case in which our camp was involved with other institutions, chiefly as a purveyor of manpower. This lawyer would be escorted to the courthouse in town under armed guard in order to represent the camp authorities and return under guard crowned with the wreath of victory.

I should like to add to what I have written about the relations of various institutions to each other that, despite the fact of everything belonging to the state, local patriotism and particularism are common. In our camp it went as far as the camp directors' encouraging the prisoners to steal various materials from nearby construction jobs. The features of a good official were measured by his ability to "organize" the misappropriation of coal for heating the barracks stoves or to find ways for the prisoners to lay their hands on some outside plant's oil paint in order to improve the appearance of the camp's buildings. For a certain period my own prestige mounted in the eyes of the camp authorities because my position in the nearby construction work gave me a chance to transfer some of its materials "home."

However, all the ranks and positions I have enumerated and all the privileged jobs and professional rights which I have described do not exhaust the full scope of the camp's possibilities for advancement and promotion, and even for actually becoming rich. In Aktyubinsk mobility upward was based on two more economic activities, trade and stealing.

I do not exactly mean hard-working small traders who would run around seeking to barter bread for soup or tobacco for fish or trying to buy and sell their own and others' possessions. I don't mean "merchants" like the Jewish boy who specialized in selling herrings. Even those who did not eat them, either for reasons of health or because they did not need them, knew that he was the central agency for their purchase and sale. (I can't help relating how sometimes the boy, glowing with satisfaction at his business success and a good turnover, would say in the tone of a merchant, "They sugared my herring today," that is, there was a big demand for them.

I am referring to large-scale merchants, to retailers with initiative, vision, and scope. A whole enterprise was developed in the camp for the transferring of cloth, thread, and ready-made clothing, and their transfer outside from the sewing room, by means of connections with free employees whom the prisoners would meet on the plant's premises.

The camp's workshops also used to receive private orders from the outside, and the proportion of the raw materials supplied by the purchaser to the quantities used in the finished product was very flexible. For example, if an ordinary rifleman on guard duty day and night should kill a calf and bring its hide to the tannery, he would receive less than the quantity that could be produced in order to build up a reserve for something else. However, if somebody important ordered a suit, the tailors did not limit themselves to using the cloth he himself had brought officially.

It should be kept in mind that commercial relations of this kind find fertile soil for growth in a society where want is common. The Russians' language when they talked about the most basic staples attracted my attention. They would enunciate the words toilet soap, leather boots, or woolen pants lovingly and tenderly. It's no wonder then that whoever could provide these luxuries would be a person of privileges with the ability to maneuver, make friends, and establish contacts.

In time the prisoners at Aktyubinsk also developed a small underground industry. Buildings designed for the manufacture of heavy equipment also housed independent workshops for producing goods out of pilfered materials, waste, and remnants. The products included tin cooking utensils, pails and kettles. Some of the inmates also set up a complete soap industry.

Aktyubinsk commerce throve. There were prisoners who found ways of sending money to their families, in addition to living on a grand scale in the camp and keeping mistresses. But in order to keep these businesses in operation it was necessary to cheat, steal, finagle, and invent all sorts of subterfuges for the books. Actually, enterprises of this sort were impossible without robbing the rank and file of the prisoners. If, for instance, you used up in every winter coat the whole requisite quantity of cotton batting, where would the cotton for extra sewing come from? This is where a glaring paradox became evident. People were sent to the camps to be reformed, and instead they were afforded a tremendous area for black-marketeering and swindling. This black-marketeering became a part of the landscape. Swindling became a normal, accepted phenomenon, something natural and legitimate which no longer aroused attention. There were instances when so much had already been stolen from the warehouses and workshops that it became necessary to overturn a lamp in order to start a small blaze and make it possible to file a report claiming that much more had actually been destroyed by fire.

But even these tricks did not exhaust the camp's quota of ethics and honesty. Cases of plain theft and burglary were not uncommon at Aktyubinsk. One such incident led to a show trial in the camp movie hall in order to deter further acts of this sort. It was a remarkable performance and one of the most instructive entertainments I have ever witnessed.

Before describing the trial itself, I should like to say something about the judge. He had come from the oblast capital for what is called a "mobile court session." However, until the trial began, during the recesses, and after it ended, he moved around like quicksilver from one institution to another and made courtesy visits to the various workshops. In one place he left an order, in another they measured him for some article of apparel, in a third he left something to be repaired, and somewhere else he picked up an item he had left at a previous session of the mobile court. Nimble as a squirrel, the representative of justice managed to complete all his errands. When the trial opened he was seated in the movie hall facing the audience of camp inmates.

A handsome young man was sitting in the prisoner's dock. He was one of the camp's upper crust. With a long past, he was notorious for his professional skill. All sorts of thieves trembled at his name and admired him; he was the god of the petty criminal.

The judge, constantly rolling his eyes with cunning and self-satisfaction, first of all cross-examined the prisoner for the purpose of determining the kinds and quantities of articles stolen. This part of the trial was conducted as a friendly dialogue. The judge would name the article and ask, "You took this?" The prisoner would answer, "Yes." The judge would inquire, "How much?" And the other would name an exact or approximate figure. Thus, the prisoner acknowledged that he and his gang took so much meat, so much sugar, so many cans, so many cookies, and a long list of our food products out of a certain warehouse. This idyllic interchange continued until it was the salami's turn.

At this point, the prisoner made his first denial: "No, I took no salami." After the affirmative answers which had succeeded one another almost automatically, the single negative reply struck the spectators with amazement. A violent battle broke out between the judge and the prisoner over the outraged salami. The judge called the prisoner over and asked him if the signature affixed to the preliminary charge sheet in the presence of a police investigator were his.

"Yes, that's my signature," the man announced.

"So how can you now say that you did not take the salami if at the indictment you admitted the theft and plainly signed to that effect?"

"Citizen judge," the prisoner began addressing the court with enviable eloquence, "tell me yourself. Do I have any reason for concealing a piece of salami from you? What can this negligible piece do to change my circumstances? I admitted and I repeat once more that I took meat, sugar, spirits, jam, preserves, and cookies. Do you think I would be afraid to admit taking another miserable piece of salami? But this is a matter of principle, of honesty. My conscience does not permit me to lie for no reason at all. What I took I took. And I told you exactly what. But what I did not take, it's not fair for me to say that I did."

"But if it's a matter of truth and honesty," the judge persisted, "why did you say at the preliminary arraignment that you took it and even signed that you did?"

"Citizen judge," the prisoner continued to declaim, "I shall tell the whole truth here, in all honesty. I was fed up with the investigator and could not bear his face any more. I gave him whatever he wanted, whatever I had to give. But he was as stubborn as a mule. He would not let up. 'Give me salami,' he stuck to me like a leaf of a bathhouse broom to the body, 'Give me salami.' So finally I did give him the salami and I hope he chokes on it."

A loud guffaw rolled through the hall. The show had just about reached its climax. If the judge had not hastened to silence the spectators, enthusiastic applause and demands for an encore would have filled the hall. While ordering the audience to be quiet, the judge permitted himself to display his own companionable sense of humor. Stressing the prisoner's expression "I gave him," he commented, "Perhaps you really should have given him something." The audience burst out into a loud laugh again and the presiding judge joined in.

At the time, I enjoyed the show without thinking about it too much. The prisoner's appearance was actually charming. However, those in the know explained to me the real meaning of the investigator's pressure on the thief to add "a miserable piece of salami" to the list of stolen commodities. If a burglary had already been perpetrated, it should be exploited also for subtracting from the inventory items that had not actually been stolen but had daily been sticking to the hands of various officials and privileged prisoners. The theft would make it possible to account to some extent for articles that had long been missing.

Much later I came across an issue of the Soviet humorous periodical *Krokodil* in which there was a cartoon reminding me of that trial. It showed a food warehouse in which a rat was gnawing at some commodities. Opposite it sat an official filling out a form listing the damages caused by rodents. Deep in thought and greatly worried, he was saying, "and now what shall I do about the vodka? The rat doesn't drink."

In brief, the camp was like a miniature state. What exists in a large country is to be found in a small one, too. It is no wonder that a number of those who had done well remained after their release to work either there or in the plant outside it as free hired workers. Often there simply was no place to go back to. The family had fallen apart anyway. The wife was only flesh and blood. She tired of waiting. Perhaps experience had taught her that it was useless to believe that her husband would ever return from prison. It may be that she feared persecution because of her husband's crimes and decided to sever all ties with him. (Sometimes an interrogator attempted to persuade a prisoner to forget going back to his family. He tried to convince the man that his wife had given him up and had gone off with someone else. Of course this, too, was a psychological form of pressure.) A person who has spent many years in a camp is sometimes afraid of unfamiliar conditions either in a new place or in his old environment. He is liable to be kept under constant surveillance and everything he does arouses suspicion and exposes him to further imprisonment. But here, in the camp or near it, he already has his place. He has a name, ties, relationships, rights, and prospects. In fact, here he will have more real freedom than anywhere else.

Before I say anything about my own condition in the small "state" of Aktyubinsk with its numerous classes, I feel it necessary to talk about its *Jewish* community. First of all, in this wolves' existence the conduct of the Jewish prisoners could generally serve as a source of comfort. We loved our ghetto. We found spiritual support in it and the material support for the needy was also considerable. The attraction of the Jewish community was also a defense against certain hostile attitudes of the environment. I would not say that anti-Semitism, in the common sense of the definition, prevailed here; but we encountered manifestations of envy and hatred. Even Russians who had become friendly with Jews used to joke with a mixture of envy and maliciousness, "What does the Yevreichik [Sheeny] need? One hundred grams of bread and a carload of butter." Our communal solidarity and brotherhood, our helping each other, aroused admiration and also hate. There was a petty official in the camp who used to help Jews because they helped him, but when he was asked to do someone a favor, he would grunt, "What, another Aida?" (a play on the word *Id*, meaning Jew). And I was never sure what he meant by this remark: was it envy or kindness?

Like beams of purity, memories of Jewish togetherness on traditional holidays have remained etched on my memory. At such times we did not talk much. The common dejection also found expression without words. But sometimes we managed to seal our unity with the trace of a symbol. For instance, a piece of matzo (unleavened bread) which someone had received on Passover was distributed among friends as the token of a covenant and of hope.

Once a special commission of the "Four Letters" (that is what the Jews called the NKVD) came to us from the capital of the republic, and the Jews were treated to an unforgettable experience by one of its members. This big shot came to the room in which Dzhigan and Shumacher conducted the rehearsals and where many Jews used to congregate. At first we were startled and stopped talking; we suspected that someone had informed on us and had told the security authorities about our meetings. But he immediately dispelled our suspicions. A living, broken Jewish spirit was hidden under his uniform. Our conversation flowed for one, two, three hours and he remained unsated. The representative of the regime clung to the words of his prisoners with childish innocence, and the signs of his effort to restrain his tears were evident on his face.

It is impossible to forget the atmosphere of excitement which was generated as we crowded around the guest — at first uninvited, and very dear as the encounter lasted — and brought up memories of days not too far in the past, about Jewish life in the countries we came from and about Palestine, which were almost archeological discoveries for him. This man, who by virtue of his official status was associated in our minds with investigations, arrests, and sentences, trembled in our presence with the wealth of his new emotional experiences.

We also had agonizing experiences remote from our daily existence. German war prisoners were brought to our camp. They were housed in a separate area but we had a good idea how they lived. On the average, they were much better off than we. There were also German women in their prison area and love affairs between them and our Russians were not long in developing. Our depressed feelings did not stem from the authorities' concern for the German prisoners but rather from their very proximity to us which outwardly symbolized our equality in the eyes of the law and the state; both we and they were enemies.

How did I personally fare at Aktyubinsk? At first I was at the very bottom of the ladder. I was employed as an unskilled laborer. My clothes were rags. For some reason or other I cannot forget the summer shoes I wore my first spring in Aktyubinsk. There was hardly anything left of the soles and the toes peeped out inquisitively. What good did these shoes do me? They reminded me of the Jew who used to put on glasses without lenses in order to read the newspaper. When he was asked about this, he replied, "It's still better than no glasses at all." It was not out of admiration for hard work that I would sometimes respond to the call of a fat cook for volunteers to cut wood, peel potatoes, or scrub pots. These were my circumstances until a few of my close friends were successful, I myself began receiving parcels from the outside, and my personal guardian angel, in the guise of a Russian, appeared in the gray skies of Aktyubinsk. I shall tell about him in the next chapter.

Pavel Grigorovich Shornikov

In the corner of my heart I shall always cherish the name of Pavel Grigorovich Shornikov. He was one of my employers at Aktyubinsk.

What do I mean by my employer? Most of the prisoners at Aktyubinsk worked for the nearby smelting plant, Ferro-Splav. To this day I do not know the secrets of the metal produced in this factory. I heard that a valuable steel produced by the addition of nickel and chromium (or their alloy, called nichromium) to iron was manufactured in the huge furnaces. This steel alloy was used for armored cars and important parts of airplanes. In short, this was a top priority plant. This factory "purchased" our labor for which it paid the camp management. The prisoners worked on the plant's premises either in actual production or in auxiliary jobs and construction work.

Pavel Grigorovich Shornikov was a sort of subcontractor in the plant responsible for jobs connected with thermal insulation. The production of iron alloys required considerable electric power. The electric power station was consequently the nerve center of the entire plant and was constantly being expanded as the enterprise grew. It may sound funny, but to this day my knowledge of electricity does not go beyond the stage of knowing how to change a burned-out bulb; but at Aktyubinsk I helped run the turbines because of Shornikov.

The high temperatures involved in generating electricity and producing iron alloys required that all kinds of machines, pipes, and accessories be insulated. By chance, I was attached to a work group which Shornikov employed in thermal insulation jobs. I must admit that at the outset the very words thermal insulation were a technical mystery to me. For many months a layman like me was not even permitted to approach the professional altar. My work was limited to preparing the proper mixture in the right proportions of insulation material such as asbestos, sawdust, clay and so forth, and of bringing it to the skilled workers in my group. Many days I lugged heavy pails or raised them by rope to the men on the scaffolds.

My group also installed the electric ovens and then I had to bring the bricks. These were fireproof bricks capable of withstanding temperatures of hundreds of degrees centigrade. They are heavy, some of them weighing about twenty pounds each. However, sometimes their varied shapes would be amusing. They were adapted to the internal and external structure of the furnaces and to the forms of the numerous pipes and fittings on which they had to be fixed. If you imagined these bricks much smaller and lighter, you could liken them to the geometrical figures used in assembling some children's games.

I often noticed that the relations between this official, Shornikov, and his prisoner workers were quite friendly. They talked not only about matters pertaining to the work but also exchanged pleasantries. I cannot say that I was excluded but I did not allow myself such intimacy. When I had to speak to him, I did not address him as the others did by his first name and patronymic,

Pavel Grigorovich, but called him Citizen Director. I suppose that unconsciously I was influenced by the fact that I was a Jew among several scores of husky Russians. The only other Jew did not dare speak on familiar terms to the official either but he had an edge over me because he was a skilled worker. While I dragged sacks of wet sawdust from one scaffold to another or handed heavy bricks to others, he was seated on a pipe with a trowel in his hand like a respected specialist. Nevertheless, I was content that I was at least untroubled by the nightmare of general duties and no one was telling me to work faster. I was also nearly certain of receiving my daily ration of bread, soup, and mush in this group.

However, one day an unexpected change in my status occurred. There was heavy frost outside and everyone in my group except me worked inside the power plant. I was preparing insulation mixtures. My hands as well as the materials were frozen. As much as I tried, I could not prepare the quantities being used up by the group. The official went to see what was holding up the work and came out to me. I had actually never seen him acting brutally or coarsely, but I expected a chewing. To my great surprise, he inquired how I felt. Then he asked a question in which I could detect no anger or rebuke: "This work is hard for you?"

Since this dialogue was the beginning of the turning point which took place in my life at Aktyubinsk, it still resounds in my ears. I do not know which of two contrasting emotions guided me at the moment, a feeling of honor or latent expectation for a favor. Maybe it was a little of both. I replied, "I'll admit frankly that it's not pleasant to say hard but if I say that it is not hard, it would simply not be true." I assume that my accent immediately told the official that I was not a fellow countryman of his. He asked me a few more questions about my origins and my past and told me to come into his office some day during the noon recess or another convenient occasion.

I waited patiently for some such occasion when I would find

him alone in his office. And until that time I worked harder at
every job that was given to me. A tiny voice whispered to me that
an improvement in my position was imminent, but that I should
make a dignified appearance before the official and not as someone
on his last legs begging for a handout.

I shall not go into detail describing our conversation when I
came to him. I should only like to say that he showed so much
curiosity about my previous life, my family, my environment,
and my work that for a moment I suspected that it was his intention to inform on me. It was an absolutely groundless suspicion,
the fruit of a sort of bestial instinct which had lodged in me and
become part of my being. I made an effort to be careful about
what I said, but I apparently did not have sufficient self-control. I
lost myself in describing the past in glowing colors. I did not express any opinions, but the nostalgic note in my words was
enough to trap me. In any case, I talked too much. However, I
had an alert listener. At the end of our conversation, I felt that at
least a relationship based on respect and confidence had been established.

It was not long before I was afforded concrete evidence of the
correctness of my feeling. As a member of the thermal insulation
group I was transferred by Shornikov to the job of night watchman. I soon learned that this had been done in order to make it
easier for me. It was my duty to guard the temporary headquarters, which had been divided into two small rooms. One of them
served as an office and the other was a kind of storeroom for tools
and materials. Actually, there was nothing special to guard there.
They could certainly have done without a night watchman.

This was one of the happiest periods of my imprisonment. I do
not hesitate to repeat, a *happy* period; and the theory of relativity
seemed crystal clear to me.

I could be alone for a while. Everything in the world is relative. In the solitary cell of Alma-Ata, I missed some sort of company. Being alone with myself had become a nightmare, and I was

ready to accept anything just so I could escape the loneliness. But here at Aktyubinsk, I longed for an hour of solitude. I was anxious to run away a little from people.

During this period, I recovered a little from my physical weakness. I slept in the camp during the day and also snatched forty winks during night-watching time, although Shornikov had warned me for my own good not to get caught.

And I was not hungry any more. In addition to the "pot" (a night watchman could also be a Stakhanovite), I supplemented my requirements by all sorts of minor services which I had time to perform inside the camp, helping out in the kitchen, bakery, and so forth. The others in my work group did envy me a little, but on the other hand, they derived some benefit from the fact that one of their number stayed at "home." I would run errands for them. I took their clothes for repair or to the laundry, received their bread rations before they came back, and similar matters. And actually, what did they lose?

It was also a time of passionate devotion to reading. I had almost forgotten that there were books in the world. Shornikov brought me one after another. Suddenly I found myself in the world of Russian classics from which he selected most of the books for me. Now and then, he would even bring me a newspaper. On the wall of the office there hung a radio set, if the instrument could be honored by such a term. The Russians dubbed it the frying pan because of its shape. It had no station selector and no dials. When you switched it on, you got only Moscow. However, I enjoyed hearing music from the frying pan and the voice programs helped improve my Russian. More important than any of these, however, were the various news broadcasts which became an exciting and encouraging occupation since Hitler's downfall was now clearly imminent.

What else does a prisoner need to be happy?

But it was not long before I was banished from my nocturnal paradise. And it was not, God forbid, because of the Tree of

Knowledge, from which I had actually eaten a little, but as the result of something entirely unrelated. The number of night shifts at the plant was reduced and the prisoners' part in them grew constantly less until there was no sense in maintaining a large armed guard around the plant in addition to the camp area itself. Indispensable workers for night jobs at the plant came from the free hired help or from those prisoners who could be made liberatees. The liberatees constituted a special category among the prisoners. They were persons sentenced to short terms or prisoners whose release time was approaching. Political offenders were never included in this category. So Shornikov had to do without my night work. How indispensable I was can be proved by the fact that the position of night watchman was abolished.

A camp inmate must be ready for any surprise, even worse than those I had already experienced. However, fate did not abandon me entirely. It is true that I once more had to do backbreaking work, but it seemed that Shornikov was still taking care of me. I began working for him as part secretary, part bookkeeper, part supply supervisor, and part errand boy. In addition to these jobs and partial jobs, I had other strange and varied duties such as measuring, recording, drafting, taking inventory, copying blueprints, arranging the archives, filing, filling out forms, helping make calculations, preparing reports on work projects, transporting materials from the main warehouse to other warehouses and to the various labor groups, taking care of tools.

During this period, I also became a sort of outside representative of Shornikov's. I would contact various plant directors for him. I became acquainted with persons holding jobs with which cars and luxurious offices came on the one hand, and with a sweat and subsistence level on the other. What I saw did not always confirm the slogan "He who does not work, does not eat." I often had to go to the office of the assistant manager in charge of commercial matters for his signature and I always left with a strange feeling. He looked pampered and dandified in a dark blue suit. Occasionally he would refresh himself with some perfume from a little bottle on a shelf beside him. He and his perfume both filled me with disgust in spite of the expensive cigarettes he offered me. I had similar feelings when I discovered that the plant's managing directors had relaxation rooms next to their offices, with soft upholstered furniture. If you got tired, you shut yourself up and rested. The prisoner's fancy not only saw the thousands of workers around him but extended as far as the battlefronts, and the soft upholstery looked to him like an offense against man and his sacrifices.

Slowly I acquired some theoretical knowledge about thermal insulation. I read a number of technical works. I learned which materials and combinations were necessary for what temperatures of the insulating accessories. I began to make sense out of the charts and tables and I would occasionally dare to suggest a substitute for a material we did not have, or some other compound. This profession even began to attract me. And what was most important, I had nothing to complain about. People say that there is little benefit from many trades. However, under the circumstances and as far as I could understand and wish for in those days, my diverse jobs were a boon.

Of my entire varied gamut of occupations, one deserves special mention. After a while Shornikov had me make daily summaries of the work done by the entire labor group and by each individual. This job approximated the work known in the Soviet Union as the calculation and determining of standards and output quotas. It was extremely important because on the degree of completion of such quotas depended the worker's wages, premiums, chances of advancement and, in the camps, it literally determined the size of the prisoner's bread ration.

I have already mentioned how in the northern camps I had completely despaired of fulfilling one hundred percent of the work quotas. It was only now that I learned that it was nothing at all to accomplish. You only had to know the proper technique and it might very well be that all that was required was a bit of artistry with the pencil. If you had a little good will for the workers at your disposal and knew how to finagle, you could satisfy your superiors and make sure those under you had enough to eat.

Shornikov would be thoroughly prepared before presenting a formal work plan to the director of the power station on a special form describing in detail what had to be done. The form's area of maneuverability depended on the descriptions of the auxiliary jobs necessary for the implementation of the main task. Let us say, for instance, that a pipe has to be repaired. First of all, who is going to check the exact extent of the damage? Therefore, on the form you increase it. This expands the scope of the repair work, and incidentally makes it possible to order more materials than necessary. Then all kinds of scaffolds and special equipment for transporting the materials are needed. Access paths to the place of work must then be cleared, lighting installed, waste carted away, and the materials brought and handed to the workers using them. In a word, there is fertile ground for the creative imagination involving distances, special difficulties, transportation problems, several stages of loading and unloading, transferring materials and equipment from one worker to another and from a truck to wheelbarrows, and many more such operations. Naturally, the power station director had to approve all these jobs for Shornikov, who, in turn, had to okay them for the work group. And every day I would submit my progress reports to Shornikov.

I derived a great deal of pleasure from this work. To tell the truth, sometimes I employed too much resourcefulness. In addition to my desire to do the men a favor on my own, I was guided by a delicate hint once made by Shornikov. "Yasha [that's what everybody called me because it was easier to pronounce than Yegoshua]," he said, "see that the men have enough to eat. That's more important than anything else."

There was a tacit division of work between us. I saw to it that the men "completed" one hundred fifty to two hundred percent of the quota while he, Shornikov, made it his business to cover up the percentage in his dealings with those who contracted for labor with him. Before going to ask the station director for his signature, he would telephone the man's secretary and ask her, "Valichka, what sort of mood is Pyotr Ivanovich in today?" Generally, Pavel Grigorovich would return from Pyotr Ivanovich with a radiant face. He would proudly lay the signed form down on the desk, run his hand over it and say, "He's all right, this Pyotr Ivanovich, but it's really necessary to clamp down a little on the work." (He would say "work" and not workers.)

Once I presented a fantastic work report for the group with the help of snow. I exaggerated to the point of absurdity. Shornikov, glancing at the sheet with his experienced eye, noticed at once that with such a report we would give ourselves away; there were logical limits even to imaginary work records. But the sense of humor of this man who loved life did not abandon him. "What is the matter with you, Yasha?" He raised his eyebrows and laughed heartily. "How much snow did you put in here — all of Siberia?" In my relations with Shornikov, I always made an effort to have us understand each other, but I was careful not to have us look like open partners in some sort of tricky deal. So I replied in mock seriousness, "That's right. But what can I do? The snow keeps coming down without a stop. We clear it away and it piles up again and then the same process all over again. If we wouldn't do that, we could not have done a lick of work today." That day the whole group actually happened to be working outside. The men were insulating pipes for conveying hot water from the cooling mechanism of the turbines to the quarters of the plant's workers. However, Shornikov was not convinced by my descriptions of the snow. "Still, Yasha, we cannot make fools of ourselves." Using a popular computer, he proceeded to show me that my figures for the day's snowfall would have been adequate for an entire year.

Shornikov was not only my guardian angel, he was also one of my most important professors in the science of living. He taught me a good deal about another aspect of life in the USSR. Sparing as they were, his stories of the various construction jobs were very interesting.

When I first knew him he was a bachelor. At least, that is how I and others regarded him. He was turning forty. I never heard him mention a family, parents, brothers. On the other hand, he would occasionally make witty and brilliant remarks, which he himself enjoyed, about women and relations between sexes. I considered him a distinct type raised by the Revolution. He may even have been one of the rootless people advancing in society by virtue of the construction jobs which made it possible for him to travel from one place to another easily. Perhaps he was a craftsman who acquired technical knowledge from his own experience and later on supplemented his technical knowledge by taking courses in some workers' institute. At any rate, he was one in the Soviet cadres which came into being with the Five-Year Plans and their projects.

He was conventionally well dressed in a shirt with a broad leather belt, woolen riding pants, and calfskin boots. In the winter he wore a leather coat and fur hat. He was tall and erect and wore a square case on a belt diagonally crossing his chest. He was nearly always carefully shaved. However, sometimes he liked to put on overalls and go inside a dusty, sooty furnace being repaired. For an hour or two, he would work together with the men. This made a strong impression on us, and still more on his superiors. Like many other free workers in the iron alloy plant at Aktyubinsk, Shornikov had been released from wartime military service because he was indispensable for production.

Shornikov had considerable technical skill. But I believe that most of his achievements were due to his knowledge of human nature and his understanding of the characters of people with whom he came in contact.

In time he came to rely a great deal on our work group not to put anything over on him, a little on the group head to keep his eyes open, and a little on me and the bookkeeper (former inmate of a women's camp) who worked in his office. He believed that everything could function properly without the need of his constant supervision and uninterrupted presence. And he really could depend on everyone. The entire work group felt an obligation toward him. After all was said and done, he saw to it that we were well fed. He even made sure (in the reports and accounts that he submitted) that all of us received the additional "assembly ration" given to important technical specialists doing assembly work.

After getting married Shornikov relied upon us still more. I was perhaps the first man in the work group to whom he revealed his intention to wed. This was a further indication of the friendship between us which we were both careful not to demonstrate too much. As is often the case when one has had many women during a long period of bachelorhood, he became a model husband and immersed himself completely in his family and his home, and afterward in the child who was born. After his marriage he began to absent himself frequently or to come late and leave early.

This conduct was a result not only of his altered family status and concomitant change in his mental outlook but also of practical considerations. He had begun to build a house and was doing much of the work, he told me, by himself. At that time the whole work group participated in this activity. Certain materials saved by the men from jobs in the plant strayed to the house in Aktyubinsk as a covert accretion to the authorized materials he bought officially. In our little warehouse we kept some materials which were very hard to secure in those days, such as paints and paint oils. We received them for finishing the insulation jobs and they also sufficed for the manager's house.

Although I continued to maintain a formality in our relations as much as possible, I knew all about the progress of the new house. He seemed actually to live its building. My inquiry, "How is the house getting along, Pavel Grigorovich?" was almost a habit. He used to describe it gladly and sketch the development for me.

When his absences increased, I received instructions from him which proved quite instructive. "Yasha, when someone asks for me on the telephone or wants to know where I am, tell them that I've gone to the work sites." Soviet propaganda used to denounce the managers who kept to their offices or their seats and called them office rats. Contrariwise, it would highly praise those who were personally involved in the work and would go out to the workers and take an interest in all the details of the job. The managers who went out to the work sites were presented as the opposites of the bureaucrats and were awarded decorations and premiums, not to mention glory. Shornikov quickly got the idea. I do not think his prestige ever soared higher and he was never so admired as was the case during the period when he preferred to stay home altogether instead of coming to work. And it was all because of the announcement which I repeated countless times, that Pavel Grigorovich "had gone to the work site." Naturally, Shornikov was always at another site and not at the one to which officials came looking for him.

I learned a great deal from Shornikov's wisdom and enjoyed his kindness. I shall mention more of this later on. Now I should like to describe our final parting.

Shortly after my release from the camp in December, 1947, I was staying at Pavel Grigorovich's. My first free steps outside the barbed wire fence without an armed guard were in the direction of quarters of the plant workers, not far from the camp, where I had several friends. Then I went to the city of Aktyubinsk where I would continue my journey. Even before my release Shornikov had invited me to stay with him as long as I was in Aktyubinsk. "Don't look for any place. Come to my house. We'll manage." He welcomed me with Russian simplicity, without any ostentation but with an abundance of sincere warmth. I surveyed the house in whose building I had been a minor partner. It was a small modest wooden structure conspicuous in its newness. The furnishings were sparse. We chatted a great deal, chiefly about my plans for the immediate future. Fresh reminiscences were frequently diluted with glasses of vodka which we continually emptied and refilled. Pavel Grigorovich was very tactful and did not pry. To tell the truth, I myself did not know clearly what I wanted. My head was full of many conflicting ideas and not a little confusion and blankness occasioned by the riddle of the days to come.

Shornikov had not been able to secure an extra bed for his guest and the day came to an end with his wife sleeping with the child and myself sharing a bed with the official. Only a few days had elapsed since my release and the two of us were already equal "citizens."

There seems to be a Russian proverb for every wonder and every kind of distress. Now, too, Shornikov had a saying for this hospitality of his, "Crowded, but without offense [V Tyesnotye da nye v obidye]."

The next day, we shook hands firmly and said goodbye. "Send us little cards sometimes," he added. "I'll see," I said and the two of us understood that I would not write. How could I in any way jeopardize his position? Did he need any ties with an ex-convict who had been sent up for counterrevolutionary activities? However, I could not suppress the agitation choking me. Perhaps in the final analysis I was nothing to him while he had been the staff of life to me. More than that, he had been a sign from heaven for me that there was still a ray of hope. "I will not forget you, Pavel Grigorovich," I whispered and a tear dropped on my cheek, a very rare tear indeed, for I had been weaned from weeping. I bade him "do svidaniya" for the last time, which in Russian means "until we meet again." But I never saw him again.

Ten years later my friend Barukh, with whom I had shared a dossier, managed to secure permission to leave the USSR where he had been living as a free citizen since his release from the camp. I met him at the airport upon his arrival in Israel and we talked a great deal that first night together. One of my first questions had been, "How is Shornikov?" From him I learned that Pavel Grigorovich had taken his own life because of a love affair of his wife's. He had not been able to recover from this betrayal.

Who knows the secrets of a man's soul? But that it was a good soul, that I knew for a certainty. And when I am in a sentimental mood, I take a cluster of Hebrew words, alien and strange to the person whom it concerns, and transform them in my imagination to a cluster of flowers and place them with deep gratitude on the distant grave of Pavel Grigorovich Shornikov — in the city of Aktyubinsk, the city of the "White Hill." [1]

[1] The name "Aktyubinsk" comes from a fortress Ak-Tyuba, which in Kazakh language means "White Hill."

A Review in Two Acts

I should now like to write about a special category in the prison camps, those for whom crime is a craft and culture.

Act One

While I was still in Kotlas, the gateway to the northern prison camps, I learned something of this group. Two or three hardened criminals, for example, could terrify scores and even hundreds of other prisoners. It is difficult to discover the secret of their authority but it was undisputed. I often wondered: they had been deprived of the same rights and freedom as all the rest of us, so what was the source of their power? There was a sort of advance admission of their supremacy, of their authority. Perhaps it can be likened to the submission of natives to the supremacy and domination of a few white men for hundreds of years. The more I observed this phenomenon, the greater the enigma became. I saw how even proud, brave fighting men, former army officers, yielded to these criminals.

The criminals, called Urkachi, exacted absolute obedience and complete recognition of their privileges. This began first of all with the small details of order and equality. Let us take the lines to the mess hall, the barbershop, or the bathhouse. It never occurred to them to stand in line. But their power also assumed the forms of outright terror, violence, and robbery.

I remember the first surprises experienced by westerners at meeting the criminals either in the North or on the way there. They regarded themselves as naturally entitled to share in our bundles. Now and then they would compel us to hand over handkerchiefs, stockings, or shirts. In order to conceal any inviting article from them, many of us were in the habit of taking our bundles apart and putting on whatever possible so that we would be wearing an extra shirt or another pair of pants. Since it was cold at night, this stratagem served the dual purpose of protection against cold and against thieves.

But even wearing articles of clothing did not save them from the criminals. They would simply order you to take off and give them what they wanted. It was a gripping performance to watch them work over a man in his sleep; they called it shaving him. It did not necessarily have to be done at night. Daylight did not disturb them at all. After a train journey, the prisoners would drop off to sleep in a hut or in the transit camp's yard. The convicts would then skillfully rob them in the presence of a spellbound audience. We would breathlessly watch an artist of this sort cut a man's pockets with a penknife or razor blade in order to reach the inner stitches of a vest or a pair of pants to extract some concealed articles while the owner did not budge, as if he were a patient being operated on under ether by a surgeon. We would look on tensely with a combination of fear and curiosity, and, to tell the truth, a hint of admiration. The only one who remained unruffled was the surgeon himself. He went on with his work quietly and calmly, sometimes even smiling good-naturedly at his audience. It would not have seemed out of place if he would have taken a bow like an actor completing his number.

That is how these experts operated as long as those standing around kept quiet. If their admiration did not interfere with the work, let them have a good time. But if they began talking, whispering, and pushing, the magician would turn on the audience, "What is this, a show? What's all this crowding around? Ain't you ever seen people? What's all the noise about? Let a man work, please." If these appeals did not help either, he would resort to a popular method of dispersing a curious audience. He would take off a boot and brandish it in their faces.

They would go around dressed according to the last word of fashion, that is, in the best clothes brought by the latest shipment of prisoners. After we westerners arrived, articles of our clothing slowly joined their wardrobes. They were either stolen, taken by force, given as ransom money, or handed over in exchange for a promise to bring something to eat. Suddenly the criminals appeared in vests, coats, hats, and silk scarves, but they were especially charmed by tight-fitting jackets. They strutted around like dandies with exaggerated ostentation, their hands thrust into their small pockets, and looked for all the world like figures from an old family picture album.

In time I gave up my belief in the prevalent legend about the underworld characters that they would take anything from somebody else except one thing, which is the bread ration, or as it was called, the blood ration. Actually, they would not touch it as long as they did not need it, and usually they were not short of bread. However, when they too had difficulty obtaining bread and it became nearly the sole staple and very important, its immunity was abolished. The morality of thieves has limits.

The criminals had wonderful notions of honesty and logic in their relations with others. I rubbed up against this during one of my shipments. On such occasions the prisoner is given bread for several days in advance upon starting out. I and those like me employed every effort of willpower to divide up the rations equally for a certain period of time, well aware of the fact that tomorrow or the next day we would not receive any. But such an idea never occurred to the criminals. They always lived only in the present, for the passing day, and they were not at all capable of thinking about the distant future following in the wake of the setting sun. However, on the next day they "invited" themselves to eat with those who had kept bread from their own mouths in order to have something for the morrow. Their arguments were very cogent, "Where is your conscience? Where is there justice? You have a bagful of bread and I don't even have a crumb!"

Of course, they had no desire for bread, soup or a spoonful of mush from the general pot. Their tastes and stomachs were too refined for that. However, when the others did not receive any parcels and their own special sources were cut off, they would also clap their hands on someone's ticket for his official camp meal and leave him standing near the kitchen with his empty plate.

I mentioned their dandified strutting in "fashionable" clothes. Their natural skin covering was also mostly a work of art. Some of them did not have a piece of unadorned skin on their whole body and transformed every surface from the soles of their feet to the tops of their heads, front and back, into artistic canvases. I am referring to their tatooing. You could view entire scenes populated by women in all kinds of poses, but especially with disheveled hair or with curls hanging down to the feet. There were figures of animals, with snakes, butterflies, ferocious tigers, and cooing doves. Among the representations of trees and flowers the most popular were lilies and roses. There were many sketches of ships and anchors, skeletons and skulls, spears and flags, hearts and chains, crescents and stars, and mythological figures and folkloristic motifs. If these canvases could talk you would learn that they embodied hectic incidents or soaring fancies. Some of them reminded you of sentimental New Year's cards. Not a few bore on their chests passionate love scenes with dates, names, signatures, terms of endearment, poems, and declarations of love and devotion such as "I will never forget you."

They had certain enviable qualities. Men of violence, they were also gay and enjoyed life. They knew how to live and had confidence in themselves. They did not know the meaning of depression and apprehensions and cares were beyond their understanding. They took fistfuls of life for themselves. They were happy with their lot, to which the lots of others also belonged. And tomorrow never came for them. This was even reflected in such a superficial characteristic as the way they took care of their daily bread ration. They never wrapped their hunk of bread in a cloth or put it into a bag but simply thrust it into their pockets or the shelves behind their beds. They acted in this fashion not only because they were confident that no one would steal from them but because of the fact that they really did not regard the bread ration with the same reverence in which it was held by wretches pinched with hunger.

They were not content with bread alone (not even bread with something on it or sumptuous meals). *They* had to have bread and *amusement*. First of all came cards. No one asked whether or not it was permitted. Where did the decks come from? Don't be silly. They could smuggle into the camp, as necessity dictated, objects that were larger and more strictly forbidden and dangerous than a miserable deck of cards. As a rule, cards did not have to be smuggled in. The camp dispensaries had a black ointment used for certain kinds of skin diseases. The criminals discovered that if it was good for the skin, it was also good for the spirit and could be transformed into a stable color for marking cards. Occasionally an ambitious camp commandant would decide to put an end to gambling and determine to confiscate every deck of cards. His searches and efforts were in vain. The commandant would catch them playing but would not be able to put his hands on the cards.

One of the techniques employed during a rigorous search was for someone to slip the cards into the pocket of the commandant himself with amazing skill while he was frisking the gang. A prisoner who had already been searched would then nimbly extract the deck and hide it on his own person.

What did they play cards for? Whatever was available — money, food, and articles of all kinds, especially those belonging to someone else. Once they played for my boots. I did not know about it until the game ended. I had a pair of Polish officer's calf-skin boots that were still quite shiny, with stiff shanks and tall backstays. Because of the boots, I was nicknamed none less than Pilsudski and they drove the convicts mad from the moment they laid eyes on them. So they sat down to play a game of cards — for my boots. The loser had to deliver them to the winner. In a little while, he came over to me. "Take off the boots and throw 'em over here!" I was still wondering what had happened when he repeated the order, "Hand over the boots. What are you putting on an innocent face for?" I still wanted to know, "What is this all about?" Then he calmly explained that he had lost my boots. When I looked at him in amazement and asked, "What do·you mean, you lost?" he became impatient with my brainlessness and began applying the wonderful conceptions of honesty and logic of his kind. "You get it. I promised them to a man and I lost. You see, I can't be a rat." That's right. It's not nice to break a promise. Nevertheless, I was still in no hurry (perhaps, in spite of everything, he could still postpone paying his debt). In the end, he did not get the boots from me and not because I acted courageously but simply due to the fact that while he was pulling them off my feet, he and his pals were told to go to the office.

While on the subject of my officer's boots, I might as well finish their story. I was in any case unable to hold on to them for long. I actually wore them in my sleep, for fear that even under my head they would not be safe. However, once I went to sleep wearing boots and woke up in half shoes. It seems that some of the "boys" tried to remove them and failed. They had become wet and dried on my feet as if glued on. The "boys" had to at least get some payment for their effort and so they had quite elegantly cut off the entire upper parts; it was good leather, real calfskin. The criminals preserved their strength. This also had some logic and justice. Their imprisonment was not temporary but almost consecutive. They would leave the camp for a short recess and return. They would joke, "I had just gotten out and then I took someone else's suitcase by mistake." Many of them did not even enjoy a brief recess. They would often stand trial inside the camp for some matter in which they had been mixed up and would be given an undetermined number of additional years. If the sentences of some of them were to be tallied up, they would add up to a hundred years. However, the accepted legal practice was to enforce only the last sentence which would incorporate all the others. In a word, their contention that this was their home was really so. Consequently, they had to be more careful about conserving their energy. They kept their physical fitness through strict hygiene, gymnastics, and exercises. But most of all, they loved massages.

They did little work. They were especially allergic to any exertion. On the other hand, they stuffed themselves. However, when the authorities proclaimed a record day accompanied by all kinds of slogans and concrete inducements, the criminals were the ones to be enlisted to show what could be accomplished by goodwill and zeal. One day a month they could serve as an example. The camp authorities helped them by sending them to an easy place, providing them with good tools, and seeing that they had favorable technical conditions. Under the circumstances, the wellfed criminals easily achieved superhuman quotas. They faithfully acted the role of labor hero on display and then, crowned with praise, returned to their loafing and gluttony.

Once we nearly died laughing when one of these goof-offs overplayed his part and ruined the show. One record day, he went to work carting dirt excavated in the course of constructing the northern railroad. He was given a large wheelbarrow with easy-to-hold handles and a well-greased wheel and assigned to a stretch of soft ground. The boards on which he would have to guide the wheelbarrow were selected for their smoothness. He was assigned several husky assistants to help him load properly and make it possible for him to push the wheelbarrow without unnecessary bending. Naturally, they did not forget to prepare water for him to drink when he felt thirsty and cookies to munch on. All the props had been set up to make it possible for him to achieve a quota of two hundred percent if not more. So he, the labor-hero designate, took off his cotton vest and remained — in the northern cold — in his shirt. His helpers quickly loaded the wheelbarrow and now and then leaped onto the load of earth to press it down well so the man could transport more at one time. The hero-to-be spat on his hands and rubbed them together. Then he bent over a little to lift the handles of the wheelbarrow with its truckload of dirt to get it started. He raised it up and put it down again. What had happened? "Come here," he called to the foreman, "what sort of wheelbarrow did you give me?"

The foreman paled. "What's wrong here?"

"You should ask! Where's the motor?"

"What motor?" The startled foreman asked.

"You, what did you think, that a man could make a vehicle of this sort go without a motor?"

Act Two

During my second term of imprisonment, I saw more gripping performances by the criminals. I was already familiar with the internal code of their autonomous courts and the severe sentences they summarily carried out. They were especially watchful of those who sometimes attempted to leave the gang and begin a new way of life. Less than anything else would they stand for one of their number going soft. A man who would begin to reveal signs of penance and take steps in the direction of the straight and narrow path was said by them to have taken to whoring. They would, however, release someone from membership if they were absolutely certain he would not give them away. Generally, in the camps their numbers increased and did not grow less.

These men whom society had regurgitated created a society of their own. An act of reprisal took place in Aktyubinsk which dramatically showed how the laws of this society operated. One evening a gang like this dispatched one of its members who had turned out to be a squealer. The sentence was carried out symbolically. They cut off his feet because he went where he should not have gone; they cut out his tongue because he said what he should not have said; and they severed his hands because he had stretched them out to accept favors from the authorities in exchange for his whore's services.

How did the camp authorities react? Naturally, one of the gang was arrested and faced a trial and punishment. But it seemed that in their heart of hearts the camp officials were not disturbed. Although they wanted people to inform they also loathed informers.

My second term of imprisonment brought me in closer contact with professional criminal elements. In the North I was part of a mass of westerners who were usually separated in their daily routines from the small groups of criminals. In Aktyubinsk the barriers were down. From the outset they had been obscure. There were many borderline cases among us. They were not actually intellectuals but neither were they gangsters. Living together and belonging to the same work group were effective in hastening assimilative processes.

We were infected by each other. No one saw any rhyme or reason for being conspicuous by appearing excessively courteous.

Two opposing sayings clashed inside me. One was from a Jewish source, "Where there is no man, try to be one." I did make an effort as much as possible. But then, "When in Rome, do as the Romans do." Sometimes it was necessary simply for survival. We are also told, "If someone comes to kill you, slay him first." But perhaps we were more modest in such matters. A sheep among wolves must sometimes assume the guise of a wolf.

This mainly found expression in connection with the boys' vocabulary. I bandied it about quite freely as if I had grown up in it, but not always and not everywhere, only when I felt I had to avoid being considered a sissy. (By the way, I often enjoyed the folkloristic richness and picturesqueness of this vocabulary.) Experience had taught me that being a sissy in a camp invited molestation, bullying, and insults, while a certain amount of toughness called for consideration and respect.

Once my technique resulted in a striking victory. Whenever I received a parcel, the boys would get what was coming to them, but only the way I decided. As time went on, they were grateful to me for my concern and my attempts that they should always have enough to eat from their percentages of work quotas. Once I received a parcel from Teheran. I took it apart and shared it with the others as I had always done. It contained a strong pair of army shoes. I had not yet decided what to do with them, whether to keep them for myself, sell them, or exchange them for food. That same night the shoes were stolen from my bundle. I did not react as if a great tragedy had befallen me but went over to one of the ringleaders of the group and angrily said to him, "So this is how you pay me back?" He had not yet heard about the theft and when he learned what had happened, he was furious. "Yasha, don't worry, take it easy." A little while later he brought me the shoes with the petty thief who had taken them. Some of the others immediately began beating this man up in my presence until I told them to stop. They then resorted to preaching instead

of kicks, "Do you know who you took them from? You don't
shit where you have to eat."

I became friendly with one of the boys. He took me into his
confidence. Not that he suddenly had any regrets, but stealing
simply began to bore him. He would borrow my books and read
them avidly. Once the pusher came around to get everyone out to
work. My friend was absorbed in a book and would not move
from his bed. When the pusher shouted at him, he retorted, pointing to the book, "What is this, you can't wait? A man just got
killed here." Sometimes when I think of this criminal, I am a little
envious of the pleasure he derived from reading.

"In Rome, do as the Romans do." I found this rule especially
useful when I was suddenly sent off from the Aktyubinsk camp
to the prison at Penza, where I spent about a month. How did I
get to this city in the middle of the Volga region? Some vicious
demon was on my heels all the time I was in Russia.

A young man who had worked in my movement before the
war reached Russia during the fighting. He was eventually arrested, for what reason I never found out. When they were
searching him, they found my name and address on his person. He
had received them from common friends who were corresponding
with me. He was imprisoned in Penza and I was brought there
for testimony. I was again cross-examined. Officially, according to
the protocols, I was witness. I never saw him in Russia and he was
not shown to me in Penza. The investigator just showed me his
pictures and asked me if I knew him. I had nothing to add because
I had actually had no contact with him for five years. Meanwhile,
before I was transported back to Aktyubinsk, my knowledge of
prison geography and life increased.

At Penza I was at first kept in a small cell together with several
others. Later I was transferred to a large, noisy room. It was full
of scores of prisoners who were constantly being changed. It was
a regular prison, not a confidential one, and life in it was entirely

different from what I was familiar with in my other jails. My cell was a good example of this way of life. Whether for good or evil, life or death, it was completely dominated by several gangs of criminals ruling together. Their rule was absolute and no one dared question it; the guards and warders outside did not dare interfere.

If a new notorious gangster arrived, a place of honor was immediately found for him. The rags of whoever happened to be occupying the spot were flung somewhere else and the newcomer moved in. If they wanted to, they could take away whatever you owned and you had to be thankful yet that they did not tear you apart. Everyone else in the cell tried to walk on their tiptoes near them and generally endeavored to keep out of their sight.

Actually, they did not need anything, for they had whatever they wanted. About ten parcels a day were sent to prisoners in the cell by relatives. The recipient of such a parcel had only one function, to sign that he had received it. The parcel would then immediately be taken over by the boys. They would extract everything of value and leave some trifles or leftovers, saying good-naturedly to the owner, "Keep the rest for yourself." And woe unto the prisoner who, upon finding out what went on, tried to get word to his family that he really did not lack anything and they should not send any more parcels. The gangs would not forgive anyone being such a bitch and a whore and would not allow it. The murder in their eyes told you right away that they were not joking. Killing and strangling were nothing new in their careers and they discussed them naturally and without malice. And if they promised to pay you for some vile act of yours, you could depend on them to keep their word, it was a word of honor. So it happened that unfortunate families who had lost their mainstay of support and were perhaps depriving themselves were feeding these scoundrels.

As soon as I entered the cell, its rulers beset me. First they wanted to sound me out if I had any money, then they asked if I had anything hidden away. However, they soon learned that they were barking up the wrong tree. They quickly found out that I was no neophyte. I was not frightened and announced, "My second sentence, boys."

My courage was induced by the fact that I really had nothing of interest to them since I had not arrived directly from the outside. Without going deeply into an analysis of social theories, I learned through personal experience that a destitute person, someone who has nothing to lose, is capable of bravery. However, what mostly gave me the strength to stand up to them were the five semesters I had left behind me. To tell the truth, I was a little proud of the years I had served. I already knew how to brandish my extended index and middle fingers in the form of a "V" in someone's face, like a pitchfork ready for stabbing. I could also hurl back "whore" with relish.

They let me alone and all I had to do was calmly observe their ways and habits. I witnessed some fascinating shows.

Reveille did not concern them. Sensitive souls that they were, they continued to hover in the world of pleasant dreams. On the bunk above them, they hung two sheets to keep the rising sun from disturbing their sleep of the just. They had no reason to hurry. The prison breakfast did not interest them. Going to the latrine and washing, however, were another question. They always went with the last group and then returned for a snooze. Then they woke up, rubbed their eyes to banish the last vestiges of sleep, and did some calisthenics. One of them, a fattened ox, would then, like a muezzin, recite his own morning prayers from his bed. With his eyes closed and making the appropriate gestures, he would chant them with concentration and devotion, carefully accenting each syllable. The hanging sheets had already been raised, like stage curtains, and we all listened in silence. Unfortunately, the prayer loses much of its original picturesqueness in translation but it went approximately like this:

What is this wonder? What do I spy?
Ivan is on the roof up high.
He speaks to all the people, the most remote:
Instead of freedom — a prick in your throat.

Each and every morning, at almost the same time, there was this poetry reading. Afterward, they all sat down to breakfast. I could not overcome my curiosity and often passed to glance at their royal banquet or, perhaps, diplomats' reception. A servant waited on them and when they finished eating, he handed them a bowl and water to wash their hands. They did not hurry to get up. They still had something to talk about, some scintillating conversation to sharpen the mind. From their corner, laughter filled the room. This was veritably a kingdom amidst slavery.

They had some current matters to arrange. Soon the cell window began moving. The parcels had arrived. Once more they were occupied. They had to take in the parcels, sort them out, store the articles away, and also throw the real owners a crumb.

That is how the morning passed. Then came lunchtime. After that they took a nap. When they awoke, a servant brought them wet towels. Now it was time for a massage. Afterward, a period of intensive cultural activity began. They were embarking for the world of the spirit.

They could afford to keep a storyteller in their court. Generous nobles have always encouraged artists. The criminals conferred this honor on an intellectual, who not only had to be familiar with literature but also had to know how to tell a story well. They demanded eloquence. For hours they liked to listen raptly to "novels." They never tired of this. They were votaries of epic creations on a grand scale. The story could be told in installments. There was plenty of time. What counted most were the fascination of the story and the talent of the storyteller.

In order to find a way to their hearts, the storyteller also had to call short stories "novels." The word had a magic sound. And if the story was still very short, the storyteller had to fill in with his own imagination in order to stretch it out and make it touch the heart and pinch the soul.

The two central motifs the underworld characters liked most were the suspense of a murder story and melodramatic sentimentality. Their meat was blood and tears. Naturally, it all had to be well spiced with love and adventure. Alexandre Dumas was their king. "Oh," they would sigh in admiration, "that was a writer. That one knew how to write." (Such admiration usually found verbal expression in words like "whore" and "goddam it to hell.") Novels by de Maupassant and Somerset Maugham did not go over badly either. They did not really have to be the "novels" actually written by the two authors, but it was advisable to attribute the works to them for the sake of advance advertising and stimulating the listeners' anticipation.

The stories were only for them. However, culture tends to spread and penetrate. The human spirit cannot be imprisoned. So outsiders able to hear the storyteller's voice also enjoyed the divine spark. I clearly remember the beginning of one of these "novels" (many other beginnings as well, for they were all alike, just like their plots). "At the stroke of midnight, a black limousine with its lights out sped through the brightly lit-up streets of the English city of Paris. Locked in a tight embrace inside were white-handed Masha and Mitya with the golden fingers . . ."

Someone from the gallery could not restrain himself and taking advantage of a pause, called out, "Hey, buddy, Paris is not an English city."

"Cut the comedy!" was the retort. "Anyway, it's in America."

As time went on, the stock of the permanent storyteller supported by the criminals gave out. They began to invite amateurs. Anybody could volunteer, depending on his knowledge. But it did not have the same shine. A number of inmates took advantage of the criminals' gracious invitation to get something off their chests, and if they knew nothing of literature, they talked over their lives and adventures. Whether the stories were true or not made no difference. They only had to have suspense. Life's unfortunates were afforded the possibility of compensating for what they lacked in reality and perhaps transforming wishes and fantasies into actual occurrences. One man, an emigré who had returned to Russia, had actually been to Paris. His stock was very high, although you did not get the impression that he was as acquainted as he pretended to be with the dens, bistros, and gay night spots he had been asked to tell about.

My turn also came. They heard I was a westerner and immediately assumed that I had read a great deal. So why be modest? "Give out, Polack, tell us a story. Don't be ashamed," they insisted. If I had remembered something by Agatha Christie, I would have lived well and acceded to the ranks of the nobility. However, I had to be satisfied with a story by the Hebrew writer David Frishman which is full of action and suspense, a head is cut off and replaced by a cushion and the narrative packs a wallop. However, one change was inescapable. I had to attribute the story to Maupassant.

Life Goes On Everywhere

The place of women in the camps is a complete story in itself, providing valuable material for the sociologist and psychologist and legal and medical discussions. I shall only cite a little of what I myself saw and heard.

My prisoners' landscape was first varied by the presence of women in the Aktyubinsk camp. I hardly encountered them in the northern camps. There, men did all the work in the kitchen, the laundry, the dispensary, and the bathhouse, and cleaned, sewed patches, and performed all sorts of inside services. On rare occasions we saw solitary women doing certain kinds of housework. There, too, we also heard of special women's camps just as in the prisons we were aware of the existence of women's cells without ever seeing their inmates. On the other hand, Aktyubinsk had a whole women's section. Women's work groups would go out to work at the nearby plant, and many women inmates were employed in the camp's services.

Even if you yourself were a human caricature looking like a

scarecrow in your ripped clothing and appearing ridiculous and disgusting in your rags and patches and the can swinging from your waist like a sidearm, you could not help shuddering at the sight of a women's work group going out to do odd jobs. It was especially heartrending to see them in the winter passing like shadows wrapped in tatters of cotton batting. The fair sex — what a bit of linguistic irony! We witnessed a phenomenon which could perhaps be defined as defeminization, creatures from which every bit of femininity had been squeezed out. You looked at them and pity dominated every other feeling. My friend Grisha, a young engineer from one of the Baltic countries whose wife had been arrested together with him and sent to another camp used to say that nothing broke his spirit more than seeing the women — that's how his Lydochka must already be looking.

Becoming acquainted with many of these women added disgust to pity. I was already used to obscene language but I could not yet stand the sewer language of women. They spouted terms and names for the genitals and sexual activities with virtuosity that was enough — in my opinion — to make a dog blush.

I had already become adjusted to the prisoners' language, which seemed flat without words like whore and the oath "I should be a whore." The conjugations and various grammatical forms for sexual phenomena and their incessant use at the drop of a hat, whether for expressing affection or anger, already sounded natural to me. Such expressions had already become so interwoven with my own speech that I scarcely recognized their vulgarity. Nevertheless, when they issued from the mouths of women, it was nauseating to hear.

The female prisoners included robbers, thieves, prostitutes, and shady characters of all kinds, professional criminals all. These harmoniously fitted in the society of male Urkachi. Like the men they fostered respect for their rank, did not soil their hands with much hard work, and terrorized everyone in their immediate vicinity; in a word, they had found their own kind. But among them there were also chance offenders and innocent victims of circumstances. These lambs had to live among wolves. They were hardly able to preserve their human, feminine form.

I cannot forget my conversation with a woman prisoner, a former student from a good family. She was complaining that the bread ration was insufficient. She received eight hundred grams (a little under 1¾ lbs.) a day but finished it all in the morning. I told her to try overcoming her morning hunger once or twice and leave some bread for noon and evening in order to get used to a "rational" division — advice for someone else which I could rarely take myself when I had only the official rations. At this point, the girl retorted with the expression, "No matter how slyly the monkey covers up, his prick still hangs out." The saying was very picturesque but all of a sudden I did not know how to hide my blushing face.

Our discussion of women should have some bearing on men, or, to be more exact, virility. In addition to defeminization, there existed in the camps a phenomenon which may be termed desexualization. Oh, how we made fun of ourselves! Someone said that it was a miracle of nature that we had to urinate (and in our weakened physical condition, this happened quite frequently during the day and night), otherwise we would forget we had a sex organ. In short, all sex attraction vanished. We could proclaim, "Sex — , nobody home." This was before Brigitte Bardot but one man announced, "Even Jadwiga Smosarska (a famous prewar Polish actress) could lie down beside me without anything happening." I think a striptease artist would have died of hunger. Even Lysistrata would have failed. To such an extent did lust disappear from our lives that one of the most popular sayings in the camps was, in reply to an inquiry whether or not one could live like that, "You can live all right but you won't want to fuck."

What did the male prisoners dream about at night? Strings of onions, baskets of bread, bowls of soup, sacks of potatoes, piles of mush, meat, and fish, but a woman's body never appeared. Don

Juan himself could have become a scrupulous monk here. Some men talked apprehensively about their impotence, fearing it would last all their lives.

However, nature quickly eliminated this worry. The condition of many prisoners quickly improved in Aktyubinsk. They became adjusted, "got along," discovered loopholes in the regime's authority, and received food parcels and help from other prisoners. As soon as the hunger pangs were dispelled and a man improved his health a little, sexual desire returned from somewhere. His dreams again became varied and Jadwiga Smosarska could no longer be sure of her immunity.

Love affairs in the camps exemplify the clash between law and life. Actually sexual relations were forbidden to the inmates. As I mentioned before, the camp was divided by sexes and one needed a special pass to go from one section to the other. Fences separated both sections and there was a guard of soldiers and civilians at the connecting gate. However, those with love on their mind found a way. In addition to the official passes which could be secured even if one did not have a vital duty to perform in the other section, there developed a two-way infiltration through the fences. Some guards also received a percentage from a number of women prisoners — "taking it out in trade," we called this transaction.

In some way, female infiltrators would sometimes find shelter for the night in our barracks. A blanket pulled up over the heads of the participants would cover this stolen love. In any case, many prisoners, especially those for whom crime and arrest are their whole world, love to sleep with the covers over their heads. Explained psychoanalytically, this is their way of being alone, of isolating themselves to demonstrate their being "mad" at the whole universe. In the case of an infiltrator, it was two alone against the world. Now and then, sighs of tenderness would issue forth from under the blanket.

The camp authorities knew about these romantic adventures

but closed their eyes to them. Once in a while some official wanted to demonstrate his existence and would put in an appearance at night and pull off a blanket from a couple of lovebirds. Duty is duty.

Then an argument would develop between the representative of the authorities and human dignity. First to take the floor was usually the guest. She would not only refuse to apologize but also speak up for her rights. The feminine argument, "You have taken away my freedom but you will not deprive me of my nature," actually came into everyday usage.

Romance under such conditions was only possible for the few, for the privileged. Most of those who wanted it were not — and could not be — discriminating in their choice of time and place for love. It was always the proper time. And any secluded spot either inside the camp or on the plant's premises was suitable.

I remember the love nest I discovered in Shornikov's brick stacks. It was padded with straw and concealed by rows of heavy bricks. One day, my work group needed just those bricks and when I came to get them, Romeo and Juliet threw me a coquettish look; I went elsewhere for my bricks.

Little by little, the westerners were drawn into the game. One of our men came back shocked from such an adventure, the first in his career as a camp inmate. He tried his line, spoke tenderly, dropped hints, and she, the woman he hoped for and tried to conquer, dragged him immediately to an improvised bed and chided him, "Don't be a show-off."

The reverse also happened. There came a turning point when the woman rebelled against her partner's desire for physical satisfaction alone. She was no longer satisfied with clandestine meetings. Love, like justice, must also be seen; the act itself is not enough.

Generally, the initiative in sexual contacts in the camps was taken by the man. The woman was simply more helpless in this jungle. The primitive struggle for survival brings her with ease to the arms of a man, especially someone tough and privileged. She not only satisfies his lust but also provides him with a normal life. She cooks, washes, and takes care of his health and appearance. He, in turn, protects her from the conditions of the "common pot" and "official" trash.

The general feeling is that female prisoners give themselves willy-nilly. However, there were women in the camp who wanted sexual relations because of advanced biological conviction. They asked themselves, "How long shall I preserve my virginity? I cannot escape my fate as a prisoner, but who is forcing me to be a nun?"

This biological conviction would sometimes cause misunderstanding. A Russian acquaintance, a nice man who had a girl friend, told me how careful he had been not to get her pregnant. To his amazement, however, he discovered that she played a trick on him and avoided his precautions because her one desire was to have a child. How long would she wait without passing on her life!

However it was, in the camp in which contact between the sexes was forbidden, a new category of prisoners appeared, the Mamki, mothers who brought their children into the world behind barbed wire. It is quite certain that one of the factors involved was the practice of allowing the Mamki to take a little time off from work both before and after parturition. Occasionally the babies were the result of an "unfortunate accident." But in many cases, the outcome had been deliberately planned, stemming from an unconquerable maternal instinct.

So there were in Aktyubinsk men with common-law wives who acted like husband and wife. Both the prisoners and officials referred to them, for example, as "Kolya's Katya" or "Katya's Kolya." And woe be unto Katya if she were suspected of or caught in an act of betrayal. Unfaithfulness was Kolya's privilege, but at the same time he was jealous and beat Katya unmercifully. Katya too was jealous, but she would bow her head and keep quiet.

However, the camp couples could not be sure of family stability. Prisoners were being shipped out frequently and there was no avoiding separation, "divorce," and new "marriages." Sometimes a Mamka would be released and go out into the world with three children, each one by a different father. It would also happen that a common-law wife would be set free and remain in a job near the camp only for the purpose of being near her latest lover and helping him. How does the heartrending song I heard from women prisoners go?

> I shall put on a new white dress;
> At the camp gate I shall press. . . .
> I shall go on loving a thief,
> Bring him parcels in deep grief.

At the Aktyubinsk camp, the female inmates also had to compete with rivals from the outside. Not a few of the female hired workers in the plant were hungry for a man and the prisoners satisfied them. Naturally, for the prisoners it was worthwhile. And sometimes even both parties would nurture the glimmer of a plan for marriage after the man had served his sentence. "Where and to whom shall I go when my day comes?" many prisoners wondered. Was there a wife still waiting for him or had she left him? And here many of the hired women were unmarried or widows, or had been abandoned by their husbands.

Each one made his accounts, and then there were impulses and instincts. There were also stormy, heartbreaking sentimental love affairs full of pain and flowing with tears. All these stories of love and sex came back to me after my release from Aktyubinsk during a visit to the famous Tretyakov art gallery in Moscow. One painting I saw there has special meaning for me. It showed a prisoners' car, probably part of a shipment. A group of prisoners were peering through a small barred window. Pigeons had perched on the window ledge and the prisoners were feeding them crumbs from their meager bread rations. The women at Aktyubinsk then came into my mind, chiefly because of the picture's name, *Life Goes On Everywhere*.

Many Friends and One Who Was Close

In this chapter I should like to write about certain aspects of my life at Aktyubinsk which I kept a deep, concealed secret during my sojourn there. It was an episode which I felt that not even my most intimate friends should know about for their own safety. It was so precious and intimate that I hesitated to disclose it to another person.

But now the time has come to release the story. From the time I was first arrested, the members of my movement were greatly concerned for my welfare. Attempts were made to secure my release by appealing to various people and pulling strings. Friends of mine looked for me in Russia and tried to trace my whereabouts. When they did succeed in locating me, we established a lively correspondence. They tried to keep up my spirits and sent me parcels.

My friend Moshe Kol wrote me the following letter, in Hebrew, in the latter half of 1942:

Dear Brother,

We hope to hear good news from you. I fear for your well-being very much. The British Consul in Kuibyshev has your immigration visa for Palestine. We are trying to arrange for you to get there. Our uncle, Raphael Shafar [former head of the Palestine Bureau in Warsaw] *is endeavoring to help our family from the Polish Consulate in Teheran. He is doing whatever he can to assist those in trouble. We have common friends and acquaintances in the ranks of the Polish army units which have reached Palestine. We want to hear from you, and we are still more anxious to see you. We want you to know that we are very much concerned about you. No news in our family. It is quiet and progress is being made in all fields. . . .*

Unfortunately, I did not know the contents of this letter until seven years after it was written, when I saw a copy of it upon my arrival in Israel. It seemed to have been delayed en route to me in Russia and remained with people not so concerned with my welfare. Other letters must have vanished in a similar fashion. I only heard about my immigration certificate at the British consulate in Kuibyshev in a roundabout fashion (however, then it was already too late to go there and find out what my chances were of being able to leave the USSR). But ties with my friends in Palestine were not entirely cut off. They could not really know all the details of my life but they understood what my feelings were from a letter I sent to a group which later founded the settlement of Nitzanim. I wrote, "Do not be surprised that the sole subject of my letters is my desire to see you, for thoughts about you never leave me for a moment."

My talks with Pichugin, my investigator at Alma-Ata, were already well under way when my friends in Palestine began to feel certain that it would not be long before I joined them. Dr. Nahum Goldman included my name in a list submitted to the

American department of state by the World Jewish Congress for forwarding to the Russian commissariat for foreign affairs for the purpose of attempting to secure exit visas from the Soviet Union. In April, 1943, Moshe Kol had sent the following wire to Dr. Goldman in New York.

This is to inform you that I have received information from a reliable source that Yehoshua Globerman was arrested again several months ago. Please do whatever you can at the Russian Embassy and the State Department to at least have him released because his life is in danger.

That was the beginning of a frequent exchange of letters and cables and much was done to intervene on my behalf. All these efforts turned out to be completely wasted.

In 1943, two of my friends, Hayyim Feld and David Pomerantz from Poland, finally located me in the Aktyubinsk camp. They were both working in the Soviet "Labor Army."

In the middle of 1944 Feld wrote to friends of his in Palestine:

I often hear from Yehoshua. He has been ill many times since he left Pohulanka.[1] There were times when his life was in serious danger. As you know, he was never robust. Nevertheless, he has acted very courageously. He suffers mostly from his separation from Mariana.[2] His love for her is as strong as ever. He talks constantly of her beauty and wisdom. He says she is the most beautiful woman in the world and without her, he will never be happy. Sometimes, his longing for her drives him into a depression. Generally, however, he is undaunted. When he and Mariana were

---

[1] A street in Vilna where the members of the Noar Tsiyoni movement met after their flight from Poland.

[2] As already mentioned, a term for the movement and Palestine, based on the name of Marianska Street in Warsaw, where the headquarters of my movement were located.

*separated, he went to Uncle Frontclose[3] with Hayyim. This uncle
did not receive them courteously and sent them off to live with
Uncle Acre.[4] Yehoshua complained from time to time about this
uncle, too, and his attitude toward him. Relations between them
improved later on. It seems Uncle Acre took pity on the children
who had been left without a place to live.[5] Yehoshua became so attached to Uncle Acre that he returned [6] to live with him an extended separation. Please, Uncle Moshe [Kol] and Mariana, leave
no stone unturned to ease his suffering. And first of all, no
stone should be left unturned to have Yehoshua's health restored.[7]
Mariana must know that in spite of everything, Yehoshua has remained faithful to her. I believe that Mariana will also remain true
to him. He absolutely deserves it.*

Several months went by. Another year passed. The war ended.
It was 1945 and Poland had been liberated. Friends of mine in
Palestine wrote to Dr. Emil Sommerstein, a former Sejm deputy
who had been in prison himself and after his release became a
member of the Polish National Liberation Committee, asking him
to help set me free.

When the repatriation of Polish nationals from the Soviet
Union began, David Pomerantz wrote me that he had already
been offered an opportunity to go to Poland among the first
transports but that he did not wish to leave Russia as long as I was
imprisoned there. He told me that he would wait until we could
depart together.

I was of course very much moved by this letter and felt quite
proud. However, in the reply I wrote him immediately, which
was full of gratitude and feeling for his friendship and nobility, I
told him peremptorily to get the idea out of his head and return

[3] A closed frontier.
[4] Prison. The British Mandatory Government maintained a prison at Acre.
[5] Amnesty for Polish nationals.
[6] My second arrest.
[7] To have him released.

to Poland at once. I expressed the hope that somehow we would see each other again. I warned him not to let his naiveté and loyalty involve him in unnecessary dangers and gave him to understand that there was not a chance of what he was intending to do being able to help me in the least.

Whether or not he was influenced by my letter, David Pomerantz went to Poland. Before leaving Russia he sent me a letter which contained a mysterious reference to which I at the time attributed no special importance. He wrote that he felt that he would yet see me reunited with my family and my friends. A while later he sent me a letter from Poland. The return address was poste restante. It contained just a few words: "See you soon," and there was an allusion to our meeting again in Russia. From all this correspondence I gathered that he was preparing to do something for me. Through a letter which I did not send through regular channels I told him not to do anything rash and to be careful. Apparently he never received this final letter of mine.

A short time later we saw each other in Aktyubinsk. I think that if I were to forget everything that happened to me during my imprisonment, that hour would remain forever engraved on my mind.

It happened in January, 1946. A Pole, one of the free hired workers in the iron alloy plant who worked in the fire department and was always on the premises, began to sound me out one day. Would I like to meet someone very close to me? And, generally, would I try to escape? I became extremely cautious, fearful of an attempt to frame me. However, I did not break off all ties with him. Perhaps? In the course of the day, the fireman indicated in all sorts of ways that he was involved in some great undertaking which concerned me directly. Finally he asked me outright, "Does the name *Pomerantz* mean anything to you?" In a last effort to preserve my equanimity, I replied with studied indifference, "I know him, so what?" When he informed me that Pomerantz was close by with the sole express purpose of seeing me and that it could be arranged, I again told him cautiously in a tone of disbelief in order to leave an escape route open, "Have it your way. Bring me a note from him." In my heart I was already picturing David's presence not far away as a fact. The fireman's efforts to sound me out dovetailed with David's last letters, especially the one I had received from Poland.

The man brought me the note I had requested. It was David's signature beyond the shadow of a doubt. And the style of the message was his also; once more, it conveyed the same note of mystery arousing vague hopes and much confusion. "Your day of freedom is near."

On the basis of this note, the fireman arranged a meeting between us in his room in the plant's area. He would either call me or give me a sign.

To make it easier to understand the technical problems involved in arranging such a meeting, let me describe the layout of the camp and the adjacent plant together with the way in which it was guarded. The camp was a square area fenced in with barbed wire and surrounded by watchtowers and searchlights. Special guards patrolled it. On one side it faced the alloys plant. Before work groups emerged from the camp on the way to the plant, it is also hemmed in by guards. The camp and the plant area then became a single guarded compound. In the evening, after the work groups returned to camp and the roll calls indicated that no one was missing, the armed guard was again withdrawn only to the camp area. At the same time, a guard consisting partly of civilians was posted around the plant and at its entrance gate facing the city. This guard was quite strong but did not have the characteristic signs and appurtenances of prison camps. For example, the watchtowers equipped with searchlights were nearly empty.

What did David do at the fireman's advice? Since he could not secure a permit to enter the plant area, he quietly approached its perimeter fence and climbed up one of the unoccupied watchtowers, then jumped inside, clearing several rows of tangled barbed wire. Inside the plant area, he was met by the fireman who hid him in his room to await my coming the following morning when my work group would be taken out of the camp. Pomerantz was to leave the plant area the next night the same way he had entered.

In order to meet Pomerantz, I had to overcome one minor difficulty, getting away from work for a few hours. I was then working for my good "angel" Shornikov. But what could I say to him? Finally I told him simply and slightly abashed that I had to go "somewhere" for a little while. Since I did not specify what I had to do and where, he understood that it involved a woman. That was not a bad joke. He still believed in my powers. In a word, Shornikov let me go with a grimace which implied that a vital errand of this sort superseded any kind of work or duty. As for the work, he said, "It's not a rabbit; it won't run away." So, trembling with anticipation, I hurried off to my rendezvous. Who knew what this hour held in store for me?

We met. For several minutes we simply stood with our arms around each other without being able to utter a word. But we had to pull ourselves together and take ourselves in hand. We were saying to each other, "That's enough, take it easy," but neither of us began to speak. Who knows how long we would have stood this way overwhelmed by our emotions if I had not been pressed for time. "David," I said, "I must go right now. If I'm away too long, they'll become suspicious." I could not forget that my time was limited. In a few hours, the work groups would return to camp. Our excitement had to be curbed.

Even before I heard what plans he had in mind for me, I was filled with amazement and admiration at the boldness of his deed and at the very organization of the meeting. He had come thousands of miles to see me. He was wearing the uniform of a sergeant in the Red army covered with numerous decorations. It turned out that he had come to Aktyubinsk under travel orders issued by a Soviet army unit stationed in Poland. He had come with another man (whom I neither saw nor got to know) in the uniform of a top sergeant. They had several addresses in town. David began looking for a way to reach me — and here he was with his head in the lion's mouth.

His plan was as follows: he had travel orders made out to an assumed name and a complete uniform for me. In a few days I too would become an officer or NCO. David talked to me of bribing the guards, cutting barbed wire, securing a death certificate made out in my name, and snatching my corpse during the funeral, as well as similar activities.

How could I tell my dear friend David who had risked his life to rescue me that from the point of view of the camp setup, these plans were unreasonable. Perhaps others had observed the matter differently, but I recalled what I myself had witnessed. I had seen isolated, desperate attempts to escape from the camp. They had ended in bodies being brought back to camp either riddled with bullets or stiff with cold and emaciated hunger. Sometimes the prisoners would be brought back alive, beaten and wounded, bitten by dogs and almost tortured to death. There was a case at Aktyubinsk of a man who had tried to escape in a load of excrement. Somehow, he was not suffocated. For weeks, however, they did not take away the increased military guard around the plant at night and combed an area of hundreds of square miles all around. In the end he was discovered and triumphantly returned to camp still breathing. Nor could I banish from memory some of the funerals I had seen when, after all the papers and certificates had been issued, the corpse was jabbed with sharp instruments or an autopsy performed. I could also vividly picture the fate of uncounted prisoners, especially Jews, with whom I had made friends, if I were to disappear.

I had to assemble all my mental powers and enlist every bit of logical argument in order to convince David to drop the idea. He contended that he had no right, that he was unable to return to Poland without me, as if all other roads were closed to him and his life would no longer be worth living. So it was not a matter I could dispense with by a single refusal. I tried to get him to see things my way. I argued that an attempt to escape now would be tantamount to premeditated suicide. I also pointed out that I had served nearly two-thirds of my sentence and it was senseless to exchange a reasonable prospect of release in less than two more years for such a risk.

In short, we dropped the matter. Now we spoke freely about what friends were doing, Palestine, life in Poland — Poland without Jews after the great slaughter — and about what the survivors were thinking and doing.

I hungrily listened to every word of David's. When my turn to talk came, I gave him a thumbnail report of the course of my life in the six years since I had left Vilna in the beginning of 1940. I asked him to deliver regards and messages to several people and to look after certain matters for me. In the end, we decided on ways of communicating in the future.

David insisted that I take some of his money for the purpose of improving my health. It was settled that I would ask a free hired woman working in the plant who lived in the nearby workers' quarter to take the money in order to buy me food and clothing from time to time.

And so the bittersweet rendezvous came to an end. It was time to separate. The woman agreed to take care of the money — without knowing where it had come from — and help me. Materially, a great change took place in my condition. I also aided friends of mine with cash and food. I did not care about saving any money and the sum David had left was considerable and appeared fantastic to me. However, I could not permit myself to look like a spendthrift. That was liable to attract attention and cause people to wonder, let alone cause their placing me under surveillance. In any case, people noticed that my standard of living and my generosity were unconventional even for the camp's "rich men," — the recipients of parcels, tough guys, and privileged characters. I was suspected of black-marketeering and stealing. So I really had to be extremely careful in spreading my bounty.

I began feeling more dispirited each passing day. David Pomerantz had vanished without leaving a trace. I did not receive a word from him for a long time. Many months later a card arrived. One line of the return address carried the terrifying information. It had been sent from a northern concentration camp. He wrote that he had been sentenced together with several friends of his; he could apparently not disclose why or with whom. He had been regarded as the head of the group and had been sent up for *ten years*. Some of the others came off with lighter sentences. He asked me not to blame myself and not let my conscience bother me. When he had left Poland on his way to Aktyubinsk, he had also considered the possibility of arrest. He ended his note with the words "Be strong and of stout heart."

How exalted had his mission been. His was the tragic splendor of self-sacrifice for a friend.

What could I say to myself? My good friend who had attempted to rescue me and take me away from my torment to a place of safety was now suffering somewhere in the frozen North, in the land of the white death where I had been in 1940–1941. The bottom dropped out of my world. Despite my early efforts to dissuade David from carrying out his plan, overweening guilt feelings gnawed at me because of the disaster which had befallen him.

I tried to reconstruct what might have happened. Piecing together fragmentary remarks I had heard from him during our meeting, I could well imagine that on the way back, he had attempted to pick up others to take back to Poland with him. Apparently he had failed or had been betrayed.

In the midst of all this mental agony, one question harried me. What was my fate to be now? I found it difficult to believe, after all the experience I had had with the efficiency of the Soviet security services, that the whole matter of David and his companions would pass me by without involving me at all. However, for the present, the facts were that David had certainly succeeded in deceiving his captors and cross-examiners and concealing any connection with me. Now, first of all, he had to be helped in some way. With the assistance of someone outside, I sent him a parcel. I could not pack it myself and I could not send it in the post office, but my whole heart and agony were in it.

Meanwhile, I tried with extreme caution to maintain my ties — indirectly, of course — with friends in Poland and Palestine. The fifth and final year of my sentence began. In a letter I sent to Palestine at the end of 1946, I wrote about my "studies."

The letters from Uncle Misha [Moshe Kol] *make me very happy. I was always glad to hear of your accomplishments. I should like to tell you a few things about myself, if you would like to hear about my life. I am continuing with my studies and I believe that I am making good progress. I should like to finish earlier, receive my diploma, and go home to begin working on my own. I am already enrolled in my fifth course. Next year, I shall take my examinations and then, we shall see what will happen. Naturally, a great deal depends on my relatives and on circumstances. Right now, I must devote myself to my studies and afterward, if my relatives help me, I shall go to them.*

However, several days after I managed to get this letter off (it did reach its destination), I no longer had any doubts that the authorities knew about David Pomerantz's connection with me. One morning in December, 1946, I was in line with the other members of my work group before going out to work in the alloys plant. As we approached the gate where the guards were already waiting to count us and pass us through, one of the officials responsible for our departure called out my name and told me to return to the barracks. My work group left without me. All sorts of conjectures crowded my head but they were all pushed aside by the one almost certain notion that the Pomerantz affair was back, even though it had been a little late in coming.

In a few minutes I had become a knot of nerves. I was once more faced with a trip into the unknown. The unknown? On the contrary, it was all quite distinct. If I had to be interrogated and sentenced for a third time, I was finished. The authorities would consider me incorrigible and I myself could not take it. Now, in my fifth, my *last* year of my *second* term, must I start everything from the beginning again? Grim thoughts frantically ran around inside me and reached fatuous deceptive conclusions. Now and then the hint of a doubt would glimmer briefly, perhaps I had nevertheless been detained for some other reason?

Under such circumstances, it is generally better not to reveal everything, not even to the friend in whom you have unlimited confidence, in order to eliminate the possibility of his being put to the test. However, I had to share my "prospects" with a single friend, as if I required at least one witness during the last moments before I would disappear over the horizon. As it happened, Barukh, one of my best friends, had remained in camp that day. I spoke to him in a subdued manner but in a tone of farewell. Moreover, I sounded as if I were communicating my last will and testament to him. I told him the whole Pomerantz story. I asked him to pass it on to certain people, if that were possible, and to remember some names and addresses; perhaps he would sometime be able to tell friends of mine about my fate. He tried to comfort and encourage me to the best of his ability. However, none of his arguments went beyond the vague straw of optimism he held out to me, "You never can tell."

These were long, difficult moments. Why hadn't they come to call me yet? I had already sorted out my possessions and knew what I was taking with me and what would remain behind. My bundle was ready. How much time had elapsed since I had been sent back from the gate? It seemed an eternity — and it had been only two hours. Time was corrosively creeping along and spinning nightmares about me.

I was finally summoned to the office. In one of the rooms I was confronted by a man in the uniform of the MGB, the ministry of state security. He asked for my surname and told me to sit down. I was almost sure that I was in for another cross-examination. He only filled out the questionnaire and entered some formal details. It was becoming clear that this was to be "orderly" and "legal." Once more, the saying came to my mind, "The law runs wild and order runs wild."

I did not leave the office without a special guard, although I was still inside the confines of the camp, which was fenced and guarded. The soldier came with me to the barracks to get my belongings. He was polite enough but asked me to hurry. They must be waiting for me impatiently, I thought. From the barracks, he took me and the sack of my possessions to the gate, showed a paper to the guard, and after an exchange of signatures, I was taken outside. A spacious, beautiful car was waiting. In addition to the driver, there were three men in uniform in the car. No one said a word. One of the uniformed men sat next to the driver. The other two sat on either side of me in the back seat. Where to now? I had a strong desire to know, but what was the difference? You were in their hands. Tomorrow you would see other faces, but the method was the same and so was the force; it was all the same circle. Meanwhile, goodbye to the Aktyubinsk camp, in which I had also had good days.

I was brought to a prison in the city of Aktyubinsk. All my guesses were coming true. It was because of my part in the Pomerantz affair. I was again a prison inmate. Once more the cross-examinations began. These were intensive investigations. I was inundated by countless questions, threats, gentle persuasion, curses, and seductive promises. Everything came in an indiscriminate flood. And, of course, the *protocols*. Why are they so interested in writing down questions and answers? Even in moments of horror an amusing notion occurred to me, my "collected works" were being enriched with another volume. I was familiar with the technique. I knew all the formulas. There was very little originality in the new interrogator's approach. It followed an almost standardized pattern. I could have conducted my cross-examination myself. Perhaps it was possible to introduce a sort of "auto-investigation"?

But I can no longer be caught with either honey or a scorpion's sting. We, the interrogator and I, are decent toward each other. He knows and even alludes to it a little in his attitude — what a life! And I in turn commiserate — what a profession! Neither of us can escape.

Nevertheless, the cross-examination with all its basic features and incidental phenomena goes on for days — and, especially, many nights. We return to various subjects and chew over numerous matters, variations of questions, and statements. And protocols and more protocols. Will they again be bound together in a file inscribed with the words "Hold forever?"

The cross-examination in the Aktyubinsk prison had several angles of attack. First of all, they wanted to know "What sort of a person are you that whole organizations deal with your case and people risk their necks for you?" I had to force myself to minimize the political significance of the devotion to me. I told them that it was to be attributed chiefly to feelings of friendship. Pomerantz and I and others had been members of the same movement in which the idea of rehabilitating Palestine and rebuilding it through our own efforts was combined with a life of brotherhood. Friends of mine who survived the Nazi slaughter still consider me one of them. They are dear to me and I am held in the same regard by them. What was wrong with that?

"So dear," the investigator interrupted, "that one man by the name of Pomerantz was ready to risk his neck for you? Would he do that for everyone else in your group?"

I also had to compel myself to belittle the greatness of David's undertaking, "After all, it's the age — youthful romanticism."

At this point, the investigator spoke some of his thoughts aloud. What he had to say had no bearing on the course of the interrogation and filled me with pride, "What a man that Pomerantz is! What a friend and what courage!"

To this day, I have no idea whether or not this investigator knew David personally or had just learned about him from copies of the protocols of his cross-examinations and the files of his trial. However, we both agreed on the character of that man Pomerantz.

At the outset of my investigation, I had already learned that the free hired worker with whom a sum of money had been left for me had also been arrested and cross-examined. The interrogator simply asked where the money was that was missing from the sum deposited with her. Careful not to involve friends of mine in the camp, I did not breathe a word of my help and had to present myself as a drunkard and glutton, a common phenomenon among prison inmates, for the sake of the balance sheet. I explained that as soon as I had the chance, I stuffed myself with all kinds of delicacies. Actually, the missing money did not constitute an insuperable problem. The various articles brought to me were purchased on the free market at high, unfixed prices. The money discovered in the woman's house had been taken away (I never found out whether or not the money had been officially confiscated; in any case, it was not returned). I was very glad to find out that she herself was only held for a few days. Apparently, it was easy to be convinced that she had become involved in this affair by chance and in all innocence.

However, the matter of the money served the interrogator as a pretext for asking again, "Who are you?" Perhaps he really did believe that they had a "big shot," or he may have been ordered to elicit information necessary for building up other accusations. "You are pretending to be modest," he said, "while they are squandering sums like this on someone like you. You know, with this money you could support several Zionist institutions in Poland." I discovered that the interrogator was well versed in postwar Jewish affairs in Poland and I even learned from him of the union of various parties into a single federation.

A lengthy, stubborn duel was conducted between us in connection with my refusal to agree to David's escape plan. "Why didn't you really go with him, after he actually suggested all sorts of possibilities?"

I felt that this was my main line of defense and I must gather all my strength to keep it firm. However I saw no sense in displaying my goodness and explaining that I simply did not want to commit another offense. I told him the truth. I said that I had not been free of fear but had been chiefly influenced by concrete practical considerations; I had not believed in those possibilities and I wanted to take no risks, especially since most of my sentence was already behind me. But the interrogator insisted on going into a great deal of detail regarding these points. It seemed as if he actually wanted an expert opinion from me on every aspect of the alternate escape plans. I contended that I had not gone into the details with Pomerantz. However, the interrogator continued piling up the questions. In the end, he formulated an interesting query, "Why was Pomerantz so sure of the success of his plan while you did not even believe in it one percent, as you claim?" I think that my reply hit a view my interrogator shared with me. I answered, "The difference between Pomerantz and me stems from the fact that I know you, that I am thoroughly familiar with the Soviet security service, whereas he had no experience with you until he came to see me and was not sufficiently acquainted with you."

I should like to mention an incidental aspect of my Aktyubinsk interrogation. My investigator liked to listen to music during the course of a cross-examination — a sort of accompaniment to the service. The radio in the room was turned on during most of our sessions. My senses and thoughts were not attuned to the sounds at all. However, occasionally I would be attracted by a certain melody. Once he noticed it and inquired, "Do you like music?"

I answered, "A little."

"Do you know what that tune is?" he asked.

I do not know much about music but the melody that was broadcast is so popular that it is difficult not to recognize it. It was a selection from Tchaikovsky's *Swan Lake*. It was followed by a violin number. At this point, the investigator delivered a whole tirade, "And now do you know who is playing? *Oistrakh. David* [he stressed the name] Oistrakh. Oh, is he a genius! He is a miracle from heaven. His talent is legendary. And he is a *Jew!* One of *you.* This is where a Jew can make a career for himself and reach great heights."

It was neither a question nor a remark. It was a monologue delivered by an interrogator to a prisoner. Whether it was indirectly calculated to affect the cross-examination or simply an innocent soliloquy I shall never know. Anyway, the career of the great, charming, legendary Oistrakh was ineffective against my Zionist obdurateness which the investigator termed my mania.

I spent a few more months in the Aktyubinsk prison. Apparently my cross-examination was over. I was not called again. I waited. In my heart of hearts I had reconciled myself to the possibility of receiving a new sentence. It was true that I had not asked anyone to come for me and I had not run away from camp. I had actually not been requested to sign Section 206, which ends a cross-examination. However, you had to be a complete idiot in order to believe that I would get out of this business. I told myself what I had said to the interrogator, I know you. As soon as I resigned myself to my fate, I felt less tense. My head was once more dominated by tattered clothing, tobacco, and several hundred extra grams of bread.

I was in a mixed cell which contained persons charged with various offenses. The criminals did not molest me. They knew from my manner of speaking that I was not a neophyte. If someone annoyed me with his arrogance, I reacted like an old hand. I played the games that were distributed to us or that were made with pieces of doughy bread, listened to stories, and enriched my stock of jokes. I even told stories to a limited audience. And I continued counting the remaining months of my sentence, eleven, ten, nine. . . . I was already considering this a former sentence, and my reckoning was mechanical and useless. I was certain they would add to it. The question was, how much. Actually, what difference did it make? And sometimes, in the course of my reflections, the thought would occur to me that I would see David soon. And I waited.

Until one day the cell door opened and I was told to come out with my belongings. I knew what to expect. My new sentence would be read to me. I would sign, and the third-time recidivist would be sent away somewhere.

However, to my surprise nothing was said. To my amazement, I was brought back to the Aktyubinsk camp that same day. One of the first to meet me was a friend of mine much older than I, a well-mannered cultured gentleman. He said hello, extended his hand, and did not utter another word. I stammered, "Nothing, they did not add a thing." His reply was, "Okay, but not a sound to anyone, not even to me." I discovered that after I had been taken away, my friends not only feared for me, but also for themselves.

For a few days I walked around as if stunned. I could not believe it. It seemed like a dream. I began feeling at the Aktyubinsk camp as if I had come home.

I am literally in love with Russian sayings and proverbs. Those current in the prisoners' world are full of insight, truth, life's experiences, and picturesqueness. One of them says, "Let there be bones and meat will grow." That's how it was. Slowly, flesh appeared on my body again. I became stronger. Friends generously helped me as much as they could. For a while I worked hard as a general laborer. However, my guardian angel, Pavel Grigorovich Shornikov, again "invited" me to fill jobs he was responsible for. I was once more transferred to the thermal insulation work group, in which I spent the remaining months of my second term in the Aktyubinsk camp.

If I did not "pay up" the Soviet authorities all the "years" I owed them for my first sentence and was released under an amnesty for Polish nationals, I did serve out my second sentence, in the words of a Russian proverb, from "bell to bell" — until the very end. I "owed" them nothing. But, as I have said, everything is relative. After five full years in prison, my release was still a bargain, a miracle I did not believe in until the last moment. I surmised that on the threshold of the hoped-for date, I would be read a decision extending my sentence until further notice. This happened often to persons charged with "counterrevolutionary activities."

To this day I regard my release and the fact that my term was not extended as fortuitous. Perhaps the only logical explanation for this is that MGB authorities of various ranks and in certain regions considered the Pomerantz affair and David's journey from Poland to Aktyubinsk a personal offense and failure. For this reason, they themselves were interested in glossing it over and ending it instead of delving into it more deeply. Whatever happened, it was a curious development.

Kaddish over a Grave in Alien Wastes

Somewhere in the northern polar region where lakes merge with the Arctic Ocean, in frozen alien soil, David Pomerantz lies in his eternal resting place. His grave was hewn out of the hard ground outside the Inta camp after his death in a coal mine. On the bitterest of days, clods of earth as hard as ice covered him. An Arctic blizzard mercifully and angrily howled the kaddish[1] and a white mantle spread over him.

This chapter will be about the final road of one man. It must be kept in mind that this road is to be viewed against the historical background of Jewish life after the war, a life seeped in the slaughter of millions on the one hand and a determination to survive, no matter what, on the other.

The Beriha (literally, flight) was operating on the highways of Europe, orphaned of its Jews. This was a vast movement of refugees fleeing from a land of graves and heading for redemption over impassable routes even before the establishment of the state

---

[1] The Jewish prayer for the dead.

embodying it. The remnants of Jewish survivors in Europe were gripped by an Exodus fever. Mourners became emboldened people possessed of an unquenchable desire to reach the Holy Land. This whole shapeless, surging mass was cast into organizational forms and directed in planned, methodical actions. The Beriha and unauthorized immigration to Palestine became twins, and their operations were supervised by centers, "brains," and headquarters of varying echelons. This became a mighty self-disciplined volunteer movement conspicuous for its devotion, courage, readiness for sacrifice, and a great deal of competence, intelligence, and ingenuity.

This was an epic concerned with illegal border crossings, forged papers, unofficial diplomacy, contacts with friendly non-Jews, deals with groups interested in getting rid of Jews. It was an epic fashioned by the joint activity of emissaries from Palestine and firebrands rescued from the conflagration, of soldiers in the Jewish Brigade and fighting men and women who had fought in the ghettos and the forests of Eastern Europe, of experienced underground workers and simple enthusiasts.

The repatriation of Polish citizens from the USSR infused the Beriha movement with a new spirit. At the end of 1945 there were only about one hundred thousand Jews in Poland. The leaders of the Beriha, excited at the prospect of the arrival of approximately another one hundred fifty thousand Jews, made plans for caring for them and providing them with guidance. In view of the overwhelming national disaster, the members of the Beriha movement were strongly imbued with the literal implications of the Talmudic saying, "Whoever rescues a single Jew is considered as having saved a whole world." Consequently, scattered individuals who did not come under the repatriation plan were not forgotten by the Beriha either.

In this vast undertaking I myself was passively involved from a distance while David Pomerantz was an active worker engaged in actual operations. Another of the Beriha's active workers was my friend Joseph who had also been in the northern camp with me. He had not benefited from the amnesty for Polish nationals in 1941 because they could not find his file. However, he had been released three years later and repatriated to Poland.

Many years afterward Joseph told me that my name had often come up in discussions of various levels of the Beriha. However, they did not have much information about me. While they were seeking ways to help, David appeared. He not only knew more than the others but was also feverishly interested in coming to my assistance. At his very first meeting with Beriha leaders, he was told there was a plan to save me and when he was asked if he was ready to lend a hand, he immediately consented.

Properly briefed and outfitted by the Beriha, David set out for Aktyubinsk.

After his departure from Aktyubinsk, David safely reached Lwow, where he went to the address of Mulik, another Beriha worker, who had been arrested by the Russians a short time previously. David fell into a trap and was also taken into custody. Everyone who came to the apartment was arrested by the security police. David came to the house clothed in the guise of a repatriated Polish national with papers for himself and the members of his family accompanying him. He had previously shed the army uniform and gotten rid of his military documents. This was the end of February, 1946.

As prisoners, there were already in the house comrades of ours who had more than once faced death and had been rescued from several sieges. The war and postwar activity had taught a great deal. Here, too, they at once thought how to get the best of the situation and began making plans. But some characters were sauntering around and searching with their eyes and sniffing. And they had little time at their disposal — several days later, they were already taken off to prison.

Another man arrested together with David later told me that on the way to prison, my friend wanted to throw himself in front of a streetcar. He said, "I'm afraid I won't be able to stand the torture and I'll talk." The others, however, cheered him up and dissuaded him from taking his life.

Several months later, David and the others arrested in the Lwow apartment appeared before a military tribunal because martial law had been proclaimed to deal with the subversive activities of Ukrainian nationalists. The court consisted of three judges, a captain and two lieutenants. The captain seemed to be drunk all the time but nevertheless conducted the trial with complete assurance. He did not permit the defendants to speak much and often threatened, "If you talk too much, we'll put you in solitary confinement and try you in absentia." The room, which was located in the prison, resounded with anti-Semitic comment.

Naturally, the trial had been preceded by an intensive cross-examination. There was a chest full of all kinds of "educational" tools in the room of one of the investigators. These included a rubber truncheon, wires, and ropes. David informed his cellmates by way of a drainpipe communications system that they beat the prisoners severely. The attitude toward the "Palestinophiles" and the pressure on them was not much different from the treatment of the Ukrainian nationalists.

At first they were accused of planning and attempting to overthrow the Soviet regime or dismember the country by armed violence. No more, no less! This offense was covered by Paragraph 58, Section 2. However, no arms had been found on any of the men and these charges were not only imaginary but silly. The interrogators had to come down in price. So they attempted to saddle several members of the group with an espionage charge, but that would not stick either. A more reasonable count had to be devised. This was supposed to be the charge of belonging to a fascist-type Zionist organization. The defendants protested. They accepted the Zionist organization but rejected the implications of fascism. Finally, the following formulation of the offense was agreed upon: "Membership in a petit bourgeois Zionist organization and ties with the international bourgeoisie."

The defendants carried on a debate with the judges. The presiding judge would interrupt, but silencing them was difficult. The government lawyer who was supposed to defend them literally trembled when he mentioned the word *Zionism*. His entire defense was exhausted by the argument that his clients had committed serious crimes, but, nevertheless, some consideration should be shown for them. Mulik, in whose apartment the arrest had been made, would leap to his feet in anger at hearing the vindications of the defense attorney or the remarks of the judges. He himself had been a captain in the Red army and had performed a number of bold exploits at the front for which he had been decorated and which had been reported in the Soviet press. He would become especially furious at the jeering tone in which the words "fighting Jews" were uttered. They may possibly have taken his past as a combat officer into consideration and despite the fact that his apartment had served as a rendezvous, he got off with only an eight-year sentence.

Another member of the group argued excitedly, "Important Soviet leaders welcomed the national liberation movement of the Jews and you put us in prison." Asked directly about his underground activity: "How did you dare to expose yourself to so much danger and go straight into the lion's mouth?" he replied, "A member of Zoya Kosmodemyanskaya's[2] people should not ask questions of this sort."

When David Pomerantz was asked for the meaning of his actions, especially the reasons for his journey to Aktyubinsk, he answered, "First of all, I am like a soldier. I was issued orders and did not do much questioning. Secondly, we have an ancient oath,

[2] A Russian girl who was captured behind the German lines after blowing up a supply depot. Despite brutal torture, she gave out no information and was hanged.

'If I forget thee, O Jerusalem, let my right hand forget its cunning.' "

After the trial when each had already received his sentence, the members of the groups were reunited in one cell together with numerous other men, including anti-Semitic Ukrainian nationalists and fanatical priests. David drew the Shield of David on the wall. Near the inverted triangles he sketched two hands with outstretched fingers in the pose of the ancient Jewish priestly blessing, and under the drawings he inscribed the oath engraved on their hearts, "If I forget thee, . . ." Every evening members of the group would face the drawings concealed from the others and softly sing the anthem of Jewish rebirth, "Ha-Tikva" ("Hope").

Benjamin, one of the men who had been up for trial, convicted, and sentenced to eight years' imprisonment and who had been with David in the northern camps for a long time, had this to say, "Many people loved him." He was sensitive and always neat. He was an esthete who kept himself clean under all conditions. Non-Jewish prisoners also spoke of him with affection and admiration. Some called him "David the Singer" or "David the Painter," for he had a fine voice and used to sing a great deal, and painting had been his hobby for years.

The first camp David was sent to in the Far North was Izhma on the Ukhta River in a region I knew well. From there he and a friend wrote to the Jewish Anti-Fascist Committee in Moscow (dissolved not long afterward) for reading material. The letter never left the camp but someone took note of its contents. This occurred during a period of increased vigilance in the entire Soviet Union (the second half of 1948), especially the camps. Special camps were established, mostly for "nationalists" of various origins. David, of course, was sent to one of these.

A camp of this sort had a regime of its own. No one was permitted to leave the barracks after nine o'clock in the evening. This meant the return of that charming prison institution, the slop pail. Each inmate had a number sewn on his sleeve, the back of his coat, and his pants. The windows were barred. Letters could only be sent twice a year. A prisoner could receive parcels only by special permission of the camp commandant. In addition, there were many other stringent precautionary measures.

However, David and his friends did not despair. On the contrary, they were able to impart some of their confidence and faith to others. They themselves found some consolation in other Jewish inmates who opened their hearts to them. There were many Russian Jews there who had been in prison since the thirties, many of them Communists. They welcomed the "Polish Palestinophiles" (any western Jew was called a Pole) with open arms. As old-timers, they helped the newcomers and briefed them. They clung to this new source of information of what was going on in the Jewish world, in Poland and Palestine, like famished castaways. Their assistance and enthusiasm for Zionism were touching.

To show the power of longing, faith, and friendship — strong ties developed among the men arrested in Lwow and between them and Zionists in other camps of the Far North. David succeeded in establishing tenuous contacts with Palestine.

From the end of 1950, David was in a special camp near Inta called a minlag, that is, mineral camp. After a period of backbreaking work, he was appointed dispatcher, responsible for transportation to the mines, and he had it easier. However, this did not last long and he became a gas checker. It was his duty to go down in the mines equipped with a flashlight and instruments to check on the presence of subterranean gases liable to cause an explosion.

In mining operations, descending and ascending are carefully regulated. There are separate exits for the men and the coal. Naturally, miners are in a hurry to get out as soon as their work is finished, and in their haste some of them forget to observe safety regulations. In the minlag the miners' elevators were not enough to take up the stream of men anxious to leave and there were lines and bottlenecks. The impatient ones would ascend with the coal to get aboveground sooner. One day David tried going up with the coal and was killed by lumps falling on him. One version says it was an accident; another view is that he was murdered by Lithuanian anti-Semites who had collaborated with the Nazis during the war. David was taken to the hospital and operated on, but it was already too late.

When Mulik was released, he was not permitted to leave the district. Like the others of his group, he was sentenced to a sort of exile, although he could move freely within the area. In time, he managed to locate a grave which seemed to answer to the description given to him by a man who had been present at David's "funeral." Mulik carved out David's name on a board and placed it over the spot. I am sure that in the Arctic blasts of the North even this feeble physical reminder of his existence was soon swept away. But in my heart there is a warmth for him that will live as long as I am on earth.

Last Stops—Spring in the
Middle of the Winter

During my last months in the Aktyubinsk camp, nearly all the Jews were in spirit living far far away from the barbed wire fence. A few of us had some form of contact with the outside world. We managed to receive newpapers, among them the Yiddish paper *Einikeit*, the organ of the Jewish Anti-Fascist Committee in Moscow, and *Britanski Soyuznik* (The British Ally), a weekly published by the British embassy in Russian. This latter periodical contained reports of parliamentary sessions in which the Palestine problem figured conspicuously. We were excited and tense with expectation. This was the "Gromyko period" in which the Soviet representative at the United Nations spoke out in favor of a Jewish state in Palestine. We avidly listened to the radio and the antennas of our hearts were tautly waiting to receive good news.

I shall never forget the Russian Jew incarcerated in the same camp who came out to meet me as I was returning with my work group on November 30, 1947. I had scarcely passed through the

gate when he laid his arms on my shoulders and whispered tremu-
lously, "There is, there is . . ." This was just one week before
the end of my sentence and I was feverish with hopes and apprehensions in anticipation of my day. I thought my friend had
learned that they were already preparing my papers. However,
the good news he brought me was from Lake Success. "There is a
Jewish state," he uttered in a shaky voice and tried at once to
suppress his excitement. Walking away from the gate, while
everyone was hurrying off to the barracks and the kitchen, we
slowed down. He began speaking in an exalted stage voice, "Today, the world's justice has righted the historic wrong to the Jewish people."

A week later, my personal good news arrived. "Globerman,
get ready to leave; tomorrow, December seventh, you will be
released." This was a personal spring coupled with a feeling of a
national springtime in the very midst of winter.

On light feet I ran from one institution to another and from
office to office to settle accounts, return what I had to, and receive
papers. I packed my bundle, but have no recollection what was in
it. But I shall never forget that I took with me many farewells and
appeals of "Don't forget . . ."

I was already hovering over other, distant worlds. Meanwhile,
however, I had to decide one small practical question. Where
should I go from here? Together with the identity card issued to
former prisoners, I had to receive a paper stating my place of
destination. I told myself that I would ask them to enter my
hometown of Pinsk. Maybe something survived there? In any
case, I had to see it. A foolish voice inside me also whispered, get as
close as possible to the western border, as if leaving Russia were a
matter of geography.

So I asked them to enter Pinsk as my domicile. They refused.
Pinsk is the capital of an oblast. Although I had been set free, I
still carried a hump. I had no right to live in Moscow, the capitals
of republics or oblasts, and in border areas. As a substitute, I told

them Luniniec, a small town near Pinsk. Three of the people with whom I had shared a dossier at Alma-Ata came from there. I would go to Luniniec and from there to Pinsk.

But first of all, on the way to Luniniec I had to stop off at Moscow. There, I went directly to the Polish consulate and, registering as a former Polish national, filled out a request for returning to Poland. The organized mass repatriation of Polish nationals had already ended. The allotted period had expired. However, I tried to explain in accordance with the facts that during the repatriation period, I had been in prison and unable to make use of my right to return to Poland. I had at the time appealed to the camp's prosecutor and argued that I was a Polish national (according to the terms of the repatriation agreement, I had lived in Poland until the deciding date, September 17, 1939) and I was entitled to enjoy this right. The prosecutor had replied that this also applied to me, but I had no rights. But when I would be released and my rights restored, it would be too late to be repatriated. The prosecutor's answer had been, "You should really explain this matter to them after you are released and they will certainly take it into consideration." When I had asked him for written confirmation stating that I had spoken to him about my repatriation, which I could use when the time came, he had refused; "I have no authority to issue such statements, but they will surely understand. It's quite logical."

Now I was in Moscow to collect my debt of logic.

Was This My Hometown?

I was traveling westward. As soon as I registered in Luniniec I went on to Pinsk. The truth of the matter is that the closer I came to the region in which I had been born and brought up, the less excited I was becoming. The terrible certainty that destruction and death were complete and absolute took possession of me. The few Jews I met in Luniniec knew for a fact that almost nothing remained of the Pinsk Jewish community. But I was going there anyway. What I saw simply confirmed what I already knew.

The hand of fate seemed to want to increase my misery. All the houses on my street, which extended from the Pina river to a marsh at the other end, were undamaged. They stood like tombstones, monuments to the tenants who had gone. But in the entire street, only a single building was missing. Our house was not there. We did not even have a house tombstone. It had been completely wiped off the earth. There was an empty lot there. There was nothing from which I could scrape off a bit of plaster for a memento. Only several trees from the adjacent yard belonging to a Christian family (one of two on our street) sent their branches over our land. Perhaps I should ask them for information?

I wandered around town not knowing why or where I was going. Was this my hometown? I peered into places where I had spent my childhood and my teens, the houses of friends and schools. The buildings were still there; but the desolation was screaming. It was all one graveyard. Before the last war people used to point to certain persons who had lost their minds and say, "This happened during World War I," or "This came after the pogroms." Or they would whisper about a woman, "She became this way after the horrors of being violated." Now, not even a madman remained.

My foot led me to my father's synagogue. Of all the Jewish houses of worship in town, this was the only one that survived. I found a handful of Jews there. Some were originally from the town and there were about ten Russian Jews who had settled there after the war. I sat mute in my father's seat opposite the ark of the sacred scrolls and could not answer anyone's greeting. The tears choked me and my lips refused to utter a prayer. Why had all this happened? Parts of the service seemed such a mockery. Emaciated survivors rocked in prayer over the prayer books. The memorial chant for the dead echoed as if in a wasteland. Someone, either the warden or the beadle, asked me to recite the kaddish. No, I could not say kaddish. I could not lie to my wounds.

I had not yet become familiar with the hellish machine of the Nazis, how they had devoured and seduced, slaughtered and pacified, murdered and allowed their victims to toy with hopes. This was before I knew anything about Satan's diabolical cunning. Then I still wondered, how did this happen to *you* — you young men and ex-revolutionaries, or at least, you husky teamsters and butchers and porters before whom all the anti-Semites in the neighborhood trembled and who struck terror into the hearts of Polish sailors daring to offend Jewish honor? The only reply was from the pits outside the city mutely eloquent.

I returned to Luniniec. I had to become absorbed in a job. I found work with a lumber plant after I told them that I knew something about lumbering (the North) and bookkeeping (Shornikov — Aktyubinsk). They showed me a little and gave me some help so that I caught on. My duties consisted chiefly in making out the payroll of the drivers who brought in the logs from the neighboring forests.

Together with two former inmates of prison camps, I rented a room in the house of a seventy-year-old woman whom we called Babushka (Grandma). We helped her chop wood, clean the yard, and bring water, and she cooked for us. Sometimes I had the chance to make a little additional money. Peasants from the vicinity whose relatives had been arrested and exiled came to ask me to write petitions for them. In their names I wrote to top government officials, and especially to the merciful landlord himself, none other than Papa Stalin. No one knew better than I that ninety-nine percent of these appeals were a complete waste of time at the very beginning. However, these unfortunate peasants — mothers and fathers, sons and daughters — were very grateful and paid me back in eggs and butter from the farm. So my roommates and I were not living too badly.

I wrote brief letters to my friends in Aktyubinsk. It was quite a surprise for me and a stirring experience to receive a letter from a Russian with whom I had made friends in the camp. He was a young, energetic, and charming engineer who was always gay and optimistic. We had talked a great deal, but I had never told him about my part in community activities. It was apparently not until I left Aktyubinsk that friends of mine had told him about me, and he was indignant about my having concealed certain aspects of my biography from him and that I had not told him about "the new life being created in Palestine." He added, "Anyway, now I congratulate you on the heroic times your people is going through and it will certainly prove its greatness in the future as it has reaped glory in the past."

The Stone and the Pitcher

In the middle of January, 1948, I went to Moscow again to try to find out if there was anything new concerning my situation at the Polish consulate. As chance would have it, Solomon Mikhoels, the outstanding actor and art director of the Jewish State Theater in Moscow, was murdered at the same time. It was January 13, 1948. In the Soviet press a brief item appeared that Mikhoels had "perished in tragic circumstances." What the "tragic circumstances" were, the newspapers did not specify, not even the Moscow Yiddish paper *Einikeit* which devoted whole columns to eulogizing and delineating Mikhoels. I saw Jews reading the brief cryptic announcement with signs of sorrow, amazement and apprehension reflected on their faces. A rumor quickly spread that Mikhoels had been murdered in Minsk, where he had come from Moscow on an official mission. Somewhere his cold body had been found. There was a strange feeling that the "tragic circumstances" were not an automobile accident. In time, the Jews realized that Mikhoels' murder had been a bad omen.

Several months later, I came to Moscow again and went to the Jewish State Theater, which Mikhoels had nurtured and created with his inspiration, to see a performance dedicated to his memory. This was already one of the final performances of the theater before its liquidation together with the rest of the Jewish cultural institutions, before the onset of the great wave of terror and killing against the bearers of Jewish culture and the cream of its literature.

When I came to the theater, I was still under the influence of impressions I had received the night before at a gala performance of the "Bolshoi Theater." In contrast, the Jewish theater was not striking in its external form or its dimensions. It was located in a side alley. But it radiated Jewish warmth which in my eyes, and in the view of many others, was worth more than external splendor.

The faces and clothing of the audience indicated that most of the people were the cream of Moscow's Jewish population. There were not a few high-ranking army officers with numerous decorations. The small number of young people stood out. In the corridor during the intermissions my ears rarely caught conversations in Yiddish. However, I sensed the festive atmosphere and the exaltation stemming from the spectators' satisfaction at the very fact of being among their own. This feeling was strengthened when I saw crowds of people around a book stall in the corridor excitedly turning the pages of works printed in square Jewish characters reading from right to left.

To this day, my heart beats faster when I recall the bookseller in the stall who was unable to conceal his glee when I asked him if he had something other than Shalom Aleichem and the Soviet Jewish writers. He replied that what I saw "was all." But he inquired in wonder where the Jew interested in Mendeli Mokher Sefarim and Peretz came from (I had not dared ask about Bialik). Talking to me, the bookseller introduced pithy expressions in Lithuanian Yiddish into his speech.

I sensed something: Jews came to this theater not only because of the quality and artistic standard of the performances but chiefly for motives like those which brought Soviet Jews to the synagogue — to come among their own people, live a little Jewishness, afford release to a Jewish mood. I could also discern this in the features of the woman with me, a young Jewish engineer from Moscow, a member of the Komsomol, although this was her very first visit to a Jewish theater.

It was doubtful whether the performance which I saw would under ordinary circumstances have been able to satisfy a longing for Jewish experiences. The play's name was *Noisy Forests*, and it was concerned with the deeds of Soviet partisans fighting against Nazi troops. Nearly all the partisans, the leading actors, were Russians speaking Yiddish on a Jewish stage; the commander of the partisan unit was also a Russian whose name was Batya — an attractive, heroic figure. However, the Politruk — the unit's political commissar — went by the name of David Kemakh (the Hebrew word for "flour") which was the only indication that he was Jewish. The play did, however, have one character, Leibovich, who was Jewish from top to toe. The part of Leibovich was played by Benjamin Zuskin, one of the theater's best actors, who took over Mikhoels' place of art director after the latter's murder.

How did Leibovich-Zuskin first appear on stage? His appearance, like his whole character, was shrouded in terror and mystery. Leibovich was seen slowly crawling up out of a pit in which — as the story indicated — the members of his community including his family had been shot and buried alive. He was wrapped in a torn prayer shawl stained with blood. His face and all his movements and gestures evoked horror and chills. His image was not of this world. His appearance perplexed the first partisans who chanced across his path. And it was they he was really seeking — this became clear later on as the plot unraveled — in order to join them. But they could elicit no information from him. Who was he? What was he? Where had he come from and where was he going? In half-words and with strange motions he mumbled vague phrases, nebulous sentences. People he came in contact with did not know whether they were looking at a man or a ghost . . . until he was brought to the tent of the company commander, Batya, who with his human warmth dispelled some of the thick atmosphere of terror hovering over the stage. In the course of a conversation with the commander which gradually built up the dramatic tension on the stage and in the audience, hints as to the man's identity emerged.

"Who are you?" the commander asked.

"I am," the figure mutters enigmatically, "one of those about whom it is said that if the *pitcher* falls on a stone, the *pitcher* is shattered; but if the stone falls on the *pitcher,* then, too, the *pitcher* is shattered."

When those words were being said, the entire audience rose to its feet and cheered Leibovich-Zuskin for many minutes. And it was impossible not to feel that despite the perfect acting of the artist, the stormy ovation was not only a demonstration of appreciation for his talent but, primarily, a demonstration of identification with the searing expression which the artist gave to the fate of a wounded, bleeding people.

Certainly none of the people present at the Jewish State Theater that evening — neither actors nor spectators — imagined that they were witnessing one of its last performances and that Zuskin's cry of agony for his people was his swan song.[1]

The Great Days of 1948

The pitcher was shattered to bits. . . .

But the wounded, bleeding people was tossed about on a wave

---

[1] Benjamin Zuskin was one of the Jewish writers and artists in the Soviet Union who was executed on August 12, 1952.

of hope and solace which reached as far as the vast expanses of Russia and Moscow.

To this very day, I feel greatly privileged to have witnessed the reactions of Russian Jewry to the news of the establishment of the State of Israel. In homes and on the street, in streetcars and subway trains, in restaurants and barbershops, as soon as they learned that you were a Jew from abroad, they heaped questions upon you, "Perhaps you have news from *there?* When will Golda[1] come? What do you think, does all this talk of emigration to Israel also mean *us?*" Those meetings convinced me that years of Communist education and propaganda coupled with isolation and various restrictions on a national life did not succeed in expunging memories of the past, a bond with Jews in other parts of the world, and a longing for Palestine from the hearts of Russia's Jews. Whatever had been throbbing in the recesses of the spirit for many years broke through the shell of external adaptation during World War II, and with greater intensity during the Israel War of Independence and the restoration of the State of Israel.

I happened to be in Moscow several days after Mrs. Golda Meir (Meirson) arrived there. The lady engineer from the Komsomol who had attended the performance at the Jewish State Theater with me told me what occurred — the packed synagogue and the crowded streets adjacent to it; the throngs streaming to hear and express a greeting to the State of Israel and its leaders. Hearts pounded. An entire Jewish community was borne aloft on waves of joy and pride.

They were delighted with the exploits of Jewish diplomats who, according to a rumor, had been praised by top Russian leaders, and gloried in the military victories which had secured the existence of the new state.

I also knew of many Russians who first turned to the news of Israel's War of Liberation on picking up a newspaper. They were

[1] Golda Meir, Israel's first ambassador to the USSR, and later minister for foreign affairs.

more familiar with the battles and fronts in Israel than with details of insurrections and wars of liberation in any other part of the world. You could clearly sense the respect and admiration of the Russians for the Jews of Israel in their grim fight against the Arab armies and the British.

Generally, the Jewish struggle for political independence and our War of Liberation produced even in Russia respect for the Jew, and the restoration of Israel also straightened the back of the Russian Jew. I remember the barbed anti-Semitic saying, "The Jews also took a city — Tashkent." This expression was chiefly heard in the wake of announcements about conquests and victories of the Soviet army — and the venomous insinuation was obvious: these are fighting and spilling their blood while those are managing far behind the lines. But in 1948 I was told of an illuminating incident in which the name Tashkent was again mentioned. In a White Russian city, a brawl broke out in a saloon, and one of the Russians made a nasty remark about Jews. Several Jews got up and beat the living daylights out of him. A Russian citizen looking on from the sidelines observed, "The Jews are not at all fighting in Tashkent style; apparently this is *po Izrailski* [that is, Israeli style]."

I, too, was overwhelmed by the exuberance of being alive at Israel's rebirth. Once I even tried translating back into Hebrew Ben-Gurion's speech at the establishment of the State of Israel, which appeared in a Yiddish newspaper. I began to "restore" the Yiddish translation back to the original Hebrew, that is, try to guess how Ben-Gurion said the words in Hebrew — an exciting exercise after many years of not using the language. I kept this translation of mine (my translation into the original) for a number of months in the hope that I would sometime have the opportunity of comparing it to the real original text and seeing to what extent my conjectures had hit the mark. However, before crossing the border into Poland I was afraid that because of this sheet of paper I would get into trouble and I destroyed it. I remembered nearly all of my translation by heart and when I reached Poland, I compared it with the authentic text from memory — and they were not far apart. After many years, when I went to visit Ben-Gurion at Sedei Boker, this story gave the Old Man pleasure.

At the same time I was troubled by the question of what would become of me personally. My trips to Moscow had not resulted in any material prospects. I would be feverish with anticipation until once more doubts would begin creeping into my heart. Meanwhile I was still in Luniniec corresponding with my friends in Israel. Together with an attempt to bribe the censor a little, my letters reflected my sincere feelings. In a note to Moshe Kol which was also intended for other friends of mine, I wrote:

Dear Uncle, I have written you often and it may be that my letters did not reach you. It is not quiet in your country. I share your experiences as a relative, as a Jew, and as a human being whom Russia has taught sympathy for every struggle for freedom and democracy. I have received several parcels but I do not need any material assistance. I miss Mariana all the time. I have lived so many years alone and it seems to me that I can never love another woman. She is so deeply engraved in my memory that neither time nor distance have been able to make me forget her.

Meanwhile . . .

In spirit I was not living in Russia. I lived in my letters and fragmentary news of Israel. Still, a man is tied to the place in which he happens to be domiciled. I tried to make a living for myself and keep my wits about me.

One day in Luniniec I witnessed an incident which I could only have imagined in my wildest fancy. A criminal judge was invited to a certain house for a drink. The matter was quite simple. Several friends of the family had been arrested for an offense designated as "economic." They had already been in prison for several months and their trial was coming up shortly. The host was consulting the judge who would try the case, what could be done. (I was thinking that if it had been a "political" offense, it would all have been over from the very outset and nothing would have been of any use.) A friendly conversation was going on about various topics. Jokes were told and loud laughter filled the room. And between drinks, the price of acquittal was broached. The judge named a sum, "Two thousand rubles." His host made a counterproposal, "One thousand." To this, the judge replied with touching sincerity, "I really cannot. You must understand, two counts." In the course of the conversation he even pointed out that he had named a fair price, the absolute minimum, which did not exceed his expenses by much, for out of this sum, he had to give something to the jury, the prosecutor, the defense attorney, and the secretary.

Interesting surroundings, but my mind was far away. Running out of patience, I went to Moscow a few more times. The officials at the Polish consulate hinted that they were hopeful of a positive settlement of my case. Encouraged, I enjoyed the sights of the city, its spaciousness and tumult. Although I was not a "welcome guest" in Moscow with my ex-convict's papers, I managed to do considerable sight-seeing, careful not to get in touch with anybody. I visited Lenin's tomb, the opera, and famous art galleries.

In the famous Tretyakov Gallery, the paintings of the classic Russian painters who with their brush immortalized the sorrow of life and the cry of distress of the unfortunate spoke to my heart. There were wonderful canvases there of landscapes and chapters in Russian history. Now, they float up in my memory. But at the time my heart trembled at the sight of a picture like *Funeral Procession* by V. G. Pyerov. I still have a postal card reproduction of it which I purchased during my visit to the gallery. The picture shows a wretched sleigh on which there are three miserable figures embracing a coffin; besides them, only a dog accompanies the deceased on his last journey. Or the picture of Ilya Rappin, *They Did Not Wait*. He shows a member of the family returning home (from Siberia?) unexpectedly — and the moment of confusion and surprise. Or the picture I told about in another chapter: prisoners in a prison car feeding pigeons with their poor man's loaf — *Life Goes On Everywhere*.

I also went to the Museum of Contemporary Soviet Art. One painting hanging there was called *Grain*. Shortly afterward I read violent attacks on the picture and its master, Gerasimov, in the

Soviet press because it shows a field of grain which seems to have grown by itself and there is no allusion to the Soviet man, the lover of toil, who was responsible for its growth. This was one of the attacks of the Zhdanov period in Soviet culture when they ceaselessly berated works which lacked an idea.

I also have a vivid recollection of another museum, the Museum of the Revolution, which had one room devoted to gifts sent to Stalin by all classes of people from all over the world. This was simply idolatry perpetuated in all kinds of arts and crafts.

While in Moscow, I liked to ride for hours in the subway and get off at stations built like palaces. What treasures! What splendor! What garish ostentation!

A Brief Arrest in Moscow

Apparently my prison career would not have been complete without my being arrested in Moscow. There is a Polish Jewish joke which says that if you ask someone in Warsaw for a street, he will answer, "There are so many people all around and you have to pick on me to ask?" An experience of this sort happened to me in Moscow. I was walking in the street once when suddenly it began to pour. I found shelter on the sidewalk under a new building going up. While waiting, I watched the broad street, the noisy traffic, and the policeman directing it. Perhaps I did look at the policeman too much from a distance. However, until the rain stopped I had nothing else to do. Suddenly I saw the policeman stop waving his hand at the cars passing to and fro and point to me. I did not move. I could not imagine that he meant me. He repeated the gesture in my direction making it abundantly clear that he wanted me to go over to him. Really, such throngs of people rushing in all directions in bustling Moscow, and he only has to notice me.

I went over to him. The policeman, in the course of partially directing traffic, quietly conversed with me. What was I doing there near the building?

"Nothing. I was trying to keep out of the rain."

Where was I from?

I told him where I came from and already began to see a gloomy future in store for me.

Why?

"To take care of some matters."

Did I have papers?

"Yes." Dark clouds began gathering above my head. I produced my ex-convict's identity card. He already knew all about me. So be it; I could not wipe out my past just as a man cannot flee from his shadow. But this involved an actual offense. What right did I have to be in Moscow? He also asked where I was working and where was my work-release paper or a pass indicating that I was on an errand. I resolved to tell him the whole truth directly. "I am a Polish national and I . . ." But the policeman interrupted, "Where does it say that you're a Polish national? You have a Soviet identity card in your hand."

"Yes," I replied, "but I am a former Polish subject and I came to Moscow in connection with my *official* [I emphasized the word] endeavors to return to Poland. I came to check with the Polish consulate where I am registered and where I am to receive a reply to my application." All the while I was thinking, does this traffic cop actually know that there are friendly — even more than friendly — relations between his country and Poland? He is simply satisfied with having caught a "suspicious foreigner." His next question was when did I arrive in Moscow and where was I staying? This was already my third day in town and I was staying with friends of mine, but I told him that I had spent two nights in the railroad station. I had no baggage and knew no one in Moscow. I was on my way to the station to board a train back to Luniniec.

Well, I no longer had any need to hurry. Someone else was already concerned with the disposition of my time. The policeman made a sign to a colleague of his. The other man replaced him at the traffic post and my officer ordered me to come with him. He took me to the sidewalk and made a telephone call. A little while later three MGB men in uniform and one in civilian clothes arrived. I noticed a large police car parked at the curb. The policemen took me into the entrance of a building, shut the door, and allowed no one to pass through for fifteen minutes. They searched my pockets thoroughly, frisked me to make sure I had no weapons to put up a fight with, took all my papers, and escorted me to the spacious automobile. We were off.

Moscow, great and mighty Moscow, what revolutionary vigilance!

My whole world collapsed. In my imagination I was already seeing myself, this time because of pure blind chance, being sent to a place from which I would apparently never return. This was the end of my life on the threshold of what had seemed to be the realization of a dream. Once more I saw myself in my fancy in investigation chambers, in prison vans, in various kinds of cells, behind bars and barbed wire. Again I recalled my conversation with the head of the investigation department in the Alma-Ata prison. This had been a monologue without sequel. He knew what he was talking about. Here I was again a prisoner. I would be moved from prison to camp and from camp to prison. And when does this happen to me? Exactly now when other shores are already in sight. Why is all this happening? Go try proving something to them. Try arguing with them. "If we have the man, we'll always find a count."

We were approaching a massive structure. I was taken inside. Everything was done properly. They filled out questionnaires and protocols. I was again searched, this time more carefully. They already took my belt away. All my metal buttons and accessories were cut off. They pulled the laces out of my shoes. My personal possessions — my watch, pen, and wallet — were taken from me. They counted my money, listed the amount, and I signed a slip. It was all quite familiar. Everything was carried out with the strictest propriety.

They brought me something to eat. Then they put me into some sort of cell. In a little while I was already seated in front of an interrogator. He wrote pages on pages. Once more I had to tell my biography from the time I came into the world until that very day. They wanted to know all about my arrests and what I had been doing from my release until I was picked up by the police in a Moscow street. I unfolded the story of my Polish citizenship, my efforts through *official* (again I emphasized the word) channels, and my waiting for a reply. I was repeatedly asked the same question, whom did I have in Poland? My reply was, "I do not know, but I think some of my relatives may still be alive and I am attached to Polish culture."

There was a recess and another cross-examination. And another recess. And another session with the investigator. It lasted from afternoon to evening and still went on during the night. My certainty of a new future in store for me behind bars and barbed wire was growing. I said to myself, you beaten dog.

But before morning a *miracle* happened.

Apparently the Moscow inquisitors had checked my story and it had been confirmed by my registration at the Polish consulate. I learned a little about this investigation from a telephone call the interrogator made in my presence. It may be assumed that the MGB had decided there was nothing illegal about my making an effort to return to Poland. However it may be, it seemed like a miracle to me. "You'll be out of here right away," the interrogator said to me, "and sign here that you'll leave Moscow within twenty-four hours." At first I did not believe him. I thought he was maltreating me. I tried with all my strength to appear quiet and not leap at the news but look as if I were sure that this would happen. I signed. Within a quarter of an hour I received my belt, money, watch, and the rest of my belongings. They gave me a release paper and I walked out.

Where should I go? I decided not to go to the house of my friends with whom I had stayed. Perhaps they had set me free on purpose in order to see where I would go. I wandered around for a while. I cautiously tried to find out whether or not I was being shadowed. There was no sign of that.

The city was beginning to wake up. I boarded a streetcar and rode a reasonable distance away from MGB headquarters. In a bakery I bought something to eat and took another streetcar, changing my seat frequently to make sure I was not being followed. I was thinking about my friends who must be worried. I had to see them, but I would wait a while longer. I had better go to the railroad station first to find out when my train was leaving and buy a ticket. Hadn't I signed that I would be out of Moscow within twenty-four hours?

The depot was noisy and crowded. People waited in lines for days in order to purchase tickets. I took up a place in my line. I stood there for hours and the line did not budge. The area adjacent to the window was like a delta into which rivers and brooks poured from all sides. There were special lines for military personnel, war casualties, and people on official errands. The war casualties, especially, were capricious, nervous, and demanding. How could anyone object to the right of cripples to be first in line? In addition to the lines of the privileged, husky aggressive characters of all kinds went straight to the window as if they had been endowed from birth with the right to be first everywhere. The people standing in line exchanged whispers, protested, and made remarks about "pull" and corruption. However, the protests did not advance the line a single step forward.

After standing in line for several hours, I got a bright idea. I had to leave Moscow. I would go to the station manager and tell him that I was ordered to leave town in twenty-four hours. But to reach him it was also necessary to stand in a long line. The only way was to use your elbows and shove. I pretended I was someone who belonged there and confidently walked straight into the manager's office. I spoke either to him or his assistant. I explained the situation, that I had signed at the MGB, and could not get to the ticket window. He wanted me to bring him a note from the MGB; otherwise he could not help me. He needed cover for doing me the favor of singling me out from the other persons waiting in line.

I do not know what insane notion moved me to request the help of the MGB interrogator for whom I had signed the pledge to leave Moscow. I came to the building and asked for permission to enter. It was not as easy as the previous day when I was respectfully escorted inside. I had to register at the information desk. I told them, "I have something urgent for . . . [I don't remember the investigator's name]." They contacted him by telephone and took me to him.

"What's the matter?" he inquired.

I told him what I wanted. He laughed out loud. He could issue no such requests. Anyway, it had nothing to do with him. They had no connections with the railroad officials or the police (my cross-examination at Alma-Ata came to mind again and I recalled how Pichugin had been profoundly offended to the depths of his secret-agent's soul by any allusion to a similarity between the NKVD and the police). My interrogator of the day before was feeling generous and did not stop laughing. For me it was important that the man who had made me sign a pledge to be out of Moscow within twenty-four hours now asked with a naughty wink, "What are you in such a hurry for? Are you sick of Moscow? Go when you feel like it."

I left him and returned to the railway station. Somehow I managed to purchase a ticket for Luniniec. I also went back to see my friends and told them about my additional adventure. We parted excitedly wishing each other well. I sensed their fears for me, and a hint of envy.

A Night of Good Tidings and Days of Horror

The great day came. To be more exact, it happened at night. Almost all the great events of my life during the last ten years occurred at night. This one was to be a night of good tidings. However, until I was sure that this was the good news I had been hoping for, another dose of nervousness and fear had been presented to me.

At night, a policeman knocked at the door of Babushka's house and asked for me. I became frightened. What happened now, where did they want me at night? "The MGB wants to see you," the policeman said.

"Now?"

"Yes, now."

Dear Babushka gave me half a loaf of bread to be ready for any eventuality and I also took along a towel and change of underwear. Again I was going into the unknown. I recalled Moscow. Perhaps they had been trailing me since my release? Maybe they had gone into my case more thoroughly and had nevertheless decided to arrest me. There was a pounding in my temples. I was once more a bundle of nerves.

I was taken to MGB headquarters. The official whom I had to see was still busy. I had to wait outside in the corridor. The policeman who had brought me there went away, leaving me alone. So here I was sitting unguarded. I really had no place to run to, but how could I be left alone like this? It was not common. And they had not searched me. Only a single policeman had escorted me and there had been no tension between us. What did all this mean? Was it prison or no prison?

I was taken into the commandant's office. It began right away with a questionnaire and protocols. He asked for personal information and biographical details which he recorded. What's this? Again? Again? Until when?

After that, the officer acidly wanted to know, "So you've made up your mind to go to Poland?"

I was beginning to understand. I was again under arrest; this time because of *Poland*. They would prove that I was a Soviet national. It was becoming a dangerous game. I was a native of Pinsk which was now a Soviet city. What was I shooting my mouth off for and trying to have it both ways?

"What do you mean 'I made up my mind?' It's true that I want to go back to Poland. That's why I submitted an application and am waiting here."

He interrupted angrily, "I know the whole story." His tone increased my apprehension. This was the end, the end to all endings, the last stop.

"Why do you want to go to Poland?" He made a grimace as if to emphasize his contempt for me.

In the twinkling of eye, I blurted out my familiar refrain, perhaps I would find relatives, Polish culture, and so on.

"But you are attracted to Poland because you think it is the country you knew before the war. You forget that this is an entirely different Poland."

"That's exactly it." I grasped at his words. "I'm ready to go back there. I would not go back to the old Poland."

"I understand," he said ironically, stressing the disbelief in what I had told him. "Well, if that's the case, go to Poland."

I could not refrain myself, "What are you making fun of me for, comrade commandant?" *Comrade*, I said to him, because I was not brought here as a prisoner but was asked to come. To myself I was thinking, one more day and I'll have to address him as *citizen commandant*.

"No, seriously, you may go to Poland."

"I don't understand."

"Very simple. The Soviet government grants you permission to return to Poland."

"I don't understand how I can go back."

At this point, the commandant leafed through a file until he came to a sheet of paper from which he read pleasantly in an official tone, "To Commandant ———: Inform Citizen Yegoshua (Yehoshua) Globerman, domiciled in Luniniec, ——— Street, that in accordance with his application dated ——— and by decision of the Council of Ministers, he has been granted permission to return to Poland."

I nearly went out of my mind. I did not believe him. I was still sure he was making fun of me. However, he asked me to sign that I heard him read the letter to me.

I asked him again, "But how shall I travel? What documents will I have? Will you give me a copy of this letter?"

No, he would not give me anything. He was only required to read me the letter and add that I was to go to Brest-Litovsk, near the Polish-Soviet border. There was a transit station for repatriates there to which I was to go. They would have all the instructions concerning my case. They would receive me. "Have a nice trip," he terminated the interview.

I returned home. It was nearly dawn. There was no thinking about sleep. All sorts of thoughts were passing through my head and I was swinging between a great hope and the shadow of a doubt. I made an effort to control myself. First of all I had to go to my employer and request a release from my job. For, meanwhile, I had to observe all the laws and regulations in order not to be charged with leaving my work without permission.

I explained the matter to the manager but he failed to grasp what I was telling him. He would not release me; the whole story did not interest him. Poland, the MGB — what he wanted was a paper, official notification. Otherwise, if I left work without permission, he would hold me responsible.

I rushed back to the MGB, to the official who had told me the news and ordered me to go to Brest-Litovsk, and frankly explained the situation to him. They would not release me from my job and I did not want any trouble or complications. I asked him for a paper to show my employer.

He refused to budge from his position. "I am not allowed to give you any paper. I was only ordered to notify you and that is what I did. I have no authority for anything else."

But I would not give up. "You cannot leave me suspended in such a vacuum. I am appealing neither to your authority nor your duty but to human logic."

The word human apparently had some effect. He spoke gently, "I'd like to help you; but try to understand, I cannot."

I regarded him with amazement. I could not think of anything to say and was afraid that some rash sidestep might damage my great chance. Still attempting to speak for myself, I argued, "Under the circumstances, I cannot carry out your order to go to Brest-Litovsk. I am subject to work discipline."

Suddenly, he lifted the telephone receiver and was soon talking to my plant manager, "Lisakovich, release this guy. Make a final account of what you owe him and let him go. He's going to Poland."

His conversation filled me with a nearly unshakable hope that it was really going to be that way. I did not know what he was being told at the other end of the line. However, I had the impression that Lisakovich was arguing that he also needed a cover-up for a written authorization. The MGB man told him, "I can't give you any paper. But listen to my advice. If you don't want any trouble, let this fellow go right away. The decision comes from Moscow. I have a letter from the Council of Ministers. He has permission to go to Poland."

Lisakovich gave me the work release. I settled my accounts, received everything that was coming to me, and the next day I was already in Brest-Litovsk.

I presented myself to the guardhouse of the repatriates' border station and told the man on duty my name. I explained that I had been sent there. The sentry asked, "Where is your pass?"

"The commandant in Luniniec told me that I did not need any pass. He read me the letter and told me that you already had my name."

The sentry looked through a sheaf of papers and notes. I was not there. He was "very sorry."

"Maybe the matter can be clarified at headquarters?"

"Go right ahead, not here, but at MGB headquarters in town."

I went to the MGB and inquired whom to ask about repatriation. They began checking. I waited a long time and was already feeling sorry that I had come here. They finally ushered me into the office of some official. This must have been the department for foreigners. I repeated my story: the commandant in Luniniec had sent me to the repatriation station here and had told me that I did not need any documents; however, they would have nothing to do with me without papers.

He replied authoritatively in all seriousness, "Tell your commandant in Luniniec that he is a fool. How do you send a man anywhere without papers?"

I returned to the commandant in Luniniec. I had no intention of telling him that his colleague in Brest-Litovsk had instructed me to say that he was a fool. However, I did inform him that they would not let me into the repatriation station without a pass. He was a little put out at my pestering him.

"I cannnot help you. With you I'm finished."

The same day, I took a train to Moscow. I would attempt to straighten the matter out at the highest level. At the Polish consulate I was told that they had received no notification or copies of letters about me from anyone. However, to all indications, my return to Poland had been approved. Apparently there had been a technical error. Perhaps the communication to Luniniec had not yet reached Brest-Litovsk. "No need to be concerned," they told me.

I returned to Brest-Litovsk and rented a room for a week. Every day I went to the guardhouse of the repatriation station to see whether or not my name had already come. At the end of the week a list with my name on it arrived. I was permitted to enter the repatriation camp.

The Last Heel of Bread

I spent about ten days in the Brest-Litovsk repatriation camp. They were days full of anticipation. Every time a shipment went out and I was not on it, it was like a blow on the head.

One day I received a surprise. Suddenly I saw before me Noah Eisenberg, one of the four who had shared my dossier at Alma-Ata. I felt as if he had dropped from the sky. I had not had any word of him for years. He had just been brought here. By brought I mean under armed guard, like a prisoner. He was not released but informed that he was being sent to Poland. In this camp, he was already considered a repatriate.

Noah's arrival in Brest-Litovsk is a story of its own. His journey there took five months. He had come from Kalima, from the Far East, from the camps on islands which a sentimental prisoners' ditty calls "the place where gold is extracted." The time was spent in traveling from one transit camp to another on all types of conveyances under armed guard in the company of criminals. For weeks on end he ate only "dry food."

Noah, who had been sentenced to eight years, had been together with me at Aktyubinsk. From there he was shipped to Chelyabinsk. A newcomer, he was at first lost in the new camp. He worked very hard and suffered a great deal. However, the laws of mobility also operated in Chelyabinsk, and in time he had it easier. Put in charge of one of the camp's warehouses, he made contacts and no longer went hungry. But mobility also works in the opposite direction, downward. Someone had it in for him or simply wanted to take over his job and told the authorities that he was planning to escape. He had never even dreamed of such a notion. However, the slander was enough to have him sent off to the escape-proof Far East as an "especially dangerous element."

In the Kalima camps Noah's torment reached unprecedented extremes. One day he was told to get himself and his things ready for a trip to the "continent." That was how he happened to be on the Soviet-Polish border together with me. Was he really going to be released? Just now he was hungry. Whenever I meet him now in Israel he likes to remember the bread heel I gave him in the Brest-Litovsk camp.

It was the very last heel.

One Year in Poland

On September 10, 1948, my repatriation train crossed the Soviet-Polish frontier. In the city of Biala Podlaska I received a temporary Polish document. Then I continued on to Warsaw.

For a long time after my release from the Russian camp, and later on in Poland, I was pursued by a sort of a nightmare. Whenever I came across an ordinary policeman directing traffic or just sauntering along, I felt that he was watching me, following me. Still, little by little my sense of proportion returned.

I had no relatives at all in Poland. Friends of mine gave me the care I would have received from my own family. When I reached Poland, I thought my clothes were the height of elegance. I had a kind of Stalin, Bolshevik tunic which buttoned up to the neck, riding breeches, and boots of calf's leather with folds like an accordion. The tunic and pants were of real wool. I had to get rid of these right away; my friends took me to a tailor to make me look human.

Several days later I had the thrilling experience of meeting the first Israeli consul in Poland, Israel Carmel. In another few days I attended a meeting of the representatives of all Zionist parties and institutions to discuss a reception for the first Israeli minister, Israel Barzilai (later, Israel minister of health). On the day of his arrival I was one of a throng of Jews waiting to welcome the representative of an independent Jewish state. I could not help thinking, what would have happened here in Warsaw if a Jewish minister had arrived when Poland had its three million Jews?

During my first days in Poland I wrote my first Hebrew letters in nine years. Although I had not intended to engage in any organizational activities in Poland, which I regarded simply as a way station, I did do a little Zionist work. This was the period when Zionism among the survivors of Polish Jewry was on its last legs. I did as much as I could.

Meanwhile, my skies were becoming cloudy again. I encountered considerable difficulty in obtaining an exit permit to leave Poland. The authorities gave me the runaround for months. I was quite certain the O.B., the secret police of Communist Poland employing Stalinist NKVD methods, was involved. Because of delays I spent a full year in Poland. It was a period of apprehension and nervousness. Once more people tried to intervene in my behalf to secure my departure from Poland. I shall not go into detail. Suffice it to say that there were days when I was desperate. When I saw no official prospects for leaving for Palestine, I began thinking about other ways and old methods being applied to new situations.

I wrote to friends of mine in Israel, "I'm not feeling so well. It seems that they have tried to cure me for years but I have not yet fully recovered. I have a feeling that my attacks are coming back.[1] I'm trying to take care of my heart as much as possible. I'm thinking of paying Sara Glozman[2] a visit."

[1] I meant police surveillance and arrest.
[2] Author of a book describing Jewish boys leaving the Soviet Union illegally in order to reach Palestine.

However, I did not have to engage in any unlawful acts to leave Poland. On September 10, 1949, exactly one year after my arrival in the country, I left Warsaw for Israel. This happened a short time after I had directed a summer camp for ha-Noar ha-Tsiyoni, the Zionist youth organization in which I had always been active. Zionist organizations in Poland were already doomed to dissolution. This was one of the last camps. After the Zionist flag had been lowered, each of the camp dwellers wrote his name on it. In this twilight atmosphere, the last ha-Noar ha-Tsiyoni flag in Poland was then given to me to take to Israel for safekeeping.

Early in October, 1949, the ship *Negba* brought me to Israel.

Kisses for Izinka

During my stay in Poland I carried on a ramified correspondence with friends and relatives scattered throughout the world. To a certain extent, carefully so as not to harm anybody, I also corresponded with friends in the USSR.

Three letters I received from the Soviet Union during this period were quite precious to me. They are from the girl engineer in Moscow and her parents. The three of them knew that I was planning to go to Israel from Poland. In order to avoid involvements with the security police, they called Israel "Izinka."

On November 5, 1948, the father wrote that he hoped that Izinka would recover from his illness and be able to get back on his feet again. "I strongly urge you to write me in detail about Izinka's health," he closed the letter.

His wife wrote, "Believe me that Izinka is very dear to all of us."

And their daughter, the member of the Komsomol, penned the following words at the end of her letter: "When you see Izinka, please give him a warm, loving kiss for me. O, how much I wish him happiness."

My dear, I have given your passionate, tender kisses to Izinka and on the file I keep in my heart I have engraved the words, "These kisses, too, hold forever."

P. S.

At about the same time when I was being brought to the Aktyu-binsk camp from the Alma-Ata prison, a sixteen-year-old girl was being squeezed in a crowd of Jews in a train station in occupied Poland thousands of miles from there. The Jews had been brought there from the ghetto by the Germans. According to the technical language which the Nazis had adapted to such matters, the "final action" had begun. The human cargo, which included her mother, father, and sister, was jammed into freight cars. The train was going to Auschwitz.

The girl with a "fine appearance," as persons having faces which did not look Jewish were described in those days, invented some tricks and managed to steal away from the shipment. She had then already had behind her several years of underground activity against the occupation authorities as the member of a group of the ha-Noar ha-Tsiyoni movement. Many months of horror and struggle were before her.

Her path led to the Aryan side, to "green" borders. She exchanged numerous hiding places and forged identities. On a number of occasions she found herself trapped in the claws of death, but she succeeded in circumventing fate. Until one day she was caught together with several others in Nazi-occupied Hungary. She was imprisoned, tortured, and waited for her sentence. But the Soviet armies arrived before the sentence. On the liberation of Hungary, Russian soldiers also freed the imprisoned girl.

Deena is the girl's name. While I was struggling for a crumb of bread and a spoonful of soup behind barbed wire in the Soviet Union, she was granted freedom by Soviet fighting men.

Deena became my wife. We first met in Poland at the end of 1948. It was a meeting of worlds, of destinies. I heard almost nothing of her life during the war from her own lips but reconstructed it a little for myself from fragmentary stories from friends of hers. They, too, were reticent. It was possible to sense how difficult it was for them even to dip into the memories of the streams of blood.

In time I became aware of a distinction — in my opinion, typical and instructive — between the oral and written reminiscences of the survivors of the Nazi hell and the tales of former Soviet camp inmates. The latter, even when relating horror stories, always injected an amusing comical tone into their accounts. The terrors seemed to be brushed aside, obliterated, and were replaced by the piquant aspect of their experiences. People recall what they went through in the Soviet world of prisoners with a faint smile, and their memories from there may serve as the subject of conversations at social parties. You will not encounter even one of these marks in the memory world of survivors of the Nazi atrocities: not even the trace of a pause in the blackness of their nightmares, not even a single incipient smile. A heavy burden of memory rests on both, yet how mighty the small difference is!

But let us return to the personal plane. Between Deena and me a mute agreement was concluded not to allow the past to dominate us. We certainly could not free ourselves of memories, but life commanded us to erect a barrier against their pursuit. A certain amount of forgetfulness is necessary for the survival of the remnants of families.

As for myself, I may be allowed to say that professionally I have been devoting myself to the present. Almost from my first days in Israel I have been working on newspapers. I breathe the passing hour. I live in a country which is a mine of problems. You are subject to the flow and pressure of events. That is how I left the past.

However, it seems that the past has not left me. Sometimes it simply encircled me with a cordon of living images within touching distance of my hand. Mixed together as if they were a physical entity I would see the interrogators and jailers, the masses of prisoners, the various kinds of minor officials, the men who distributed bread rations and soup, the bullies and the wretches, the criminal aristocracy of the camps — and in addition, human pearls in the filth. Strange as it sounds, I would sometimes detect a sort of longing in myself for that world.

The experiences and memories were stored up within me, and the images often seemed to entreat me to be recorded. But I continued to put them off. Either I hesitated to publicize my personal experiences or I was defending myself with the excuse, the past won't run away. However, when one day the undeniable report reached me that my dear friend David Pomerantz (of whom I wrote in two chapters of this work) had perished in a prison camp in the Arctic, I felt an overwhelming impulse to do something in order to comply with the order to hold forever with respect to the whole world in which I had lived for nine years. So I took a short vacation from the present and returned with all my soul to the past.

Meanwhile our children grew up in Israel. Here and there they picked up something of what their father and mother had gone through before they had come into the world. When they were still very small, we would sometimes be rendered helpless by their questioning: what had we done or what had we stolen for the police to take us to prison? Years passed and they understood more. The more they mature, the more they understand.

Perhaps these pages will add to their knowledge of a world in which flowers and iron bars still come together.